Ethics

For Vivien (1956–1997)
and the children,
Anna, Claire, Julia, Alex, and Simon

Ethics
An Introduction to Moral Philosophy

Noel Stewart

polity

First published in 2009 by Polity Press

Polity Press
65 Bridge Street
Cambridge CB2 1UR, UK

Polity Press
350 Main Street
Malden, MA 02148, USA

ISBN-13: 978-0-7456-4067-9
ISBN-13: 978-0-7456-4068-6(pb)

A catalogue record for this book is available from the British Library.

Typeset in 11/13 pt Adobe Garamond
by Servis Filmsetting Ltd, Stockport, Cheshire
Printed and bound in Great Britain by MPG Books Ltd, Bodmin, Cornwall.

The publisher has used its best endeavours to ensure that the URLs for external
websites referred to in this book are correct and active at the time of going to press.
However, the publisher has no responsibility for the websites and can make no
guarantee that a site will remain live or that the content is or will remain appropriate.

Every effort has been made to trace all copyright holders, but if any have been
inadvertently overlooked the publisher will be pleased to include any necessary
credits in any subsequent reprint or edition.

For further information on Polity, visit our website: www.polity.co.uk

Contents

Contents

Preface

This is the part where I tell you about the background, benefits, and content of the book you're about to read. First, the background: the book was inspired by two things – death and failure. Not a happy start you may think. You may even be tempted to dismiss it because you may think that anything having its source in such awful things must itself be awful. But that would be a mistake. In fact, this type of mistake is so common it even has its very own label – the genetic fallacy. It's the mistake of thinking that a thing must share in all the properties of its cause. Aristotle knew over two thousand years ago of this error and illustrated it with the absurd thought that 'He who drives fat oxen must himself be fat'. So, just because the drivers of the book were awful doesn't mean the book is too. Let me explain why it's not.

It started life as a promise I made to my wife, who was dying of cancer, that whatever happened I would write something, get it published, and dedicate it to her. That was over ten years ago, and this book, as you can see from the dedication, is the fulfilment of that promise.

Turning now to failure: for a number of years past an uncomfortably large number of my students were failing their philosophy exams. Naturally, like any good teacher, I thought at first it was all their fault, but on reflection it seemed that part of the trouble was that there was no introductory book on moral philosophy that provided my students with what they needed. Despite their other merits, these books were too short, too long, or too complicated. So I started writing my own handouts, and these grew and grew until they formed the book you're now reading, which has expanded beyond A-level ethics to include amongst its readers undergraduates and the general public. The point is that the real source of the book is not the dark clouds of death and failure, but ultimately the determined, hopeful and, in the end, joyful attempt to overcome them. To me it's the silver lining that makes the dark clouds bearable and beatable by providing an ever so small crumb of immortality for its dedicatee, and future success for students and others who read the book. But these aren't its only benefits.

Have you ever witnessed the deeply distressing sight of a really sleek, powerful sports car being 'driven' by some incompetent tootling along at a mere 30 mph, and thought, 'That car is wasted on him'? 'He's driving at 30 when he should be doing 130. The car expects it, wants it, is built for it.' The human brain is nature's Ferrari, but most of us most of the time are driving at 30 mph, wasting our potential. Thinking is what we do best, but still not nearly well enough. No other life-form on the planet or, as far as we know, in the universe can touch us in this respect. We've got it in spades, and even the best of the rest is a poor second best. In evolutionary terms, we're top of the range. Yet we dawdle through life using only a fraction of our thinking power.

Philosophy can change all that. Philosophy is thinking in the fast lane. No, it's more than that. Philosophy is thinking that breaks the sound barrier. This book is an introduction to one area of philosophy and thus delivers a course not just in ethics, but in thinking better, and, if it has done its job properly, by the end of the book you'll be driving your Ferrari twice as fast as you did at the start.

Now for the content. A brief introduction is followed by a conversation on moral relativism – the belief that moral judgements simply reflect either cultural bias or personal taste. I try to show that this popular viewpoint leads to absurdity and therefore should be rejected. Then comes the first main section on *normative ethics*, covering the theories of utilitarianism, Kant, divine command theory, and virtue ethics, in which I argue for virtue ethics as the best theory. The second main section, on *practical ethics*, deals with the application of these theories to the controversial topics of euthanasia, abortion, animal rights, and the environment. The final section, on *metaethics*, takes a step back from discussing practical moral theories and their advice, and asks instead what we mean when we use moral language and in what sense, if any, moral values actually exist. After considering all the rival theories in this area, including transcendentalism, naturalism, non-naturalism, emotivism, and prescriptivism, using a historical approach, a form of naturalism linked with virtue ethics is briefly and tentatively defended as the best of the bunch.

A final word about the book before we get started. This *is* an *introduction*, so what I say is far from the final word on any of the topics. The arguments and conversations could have been continued almost indefinitely but had to be curtailed at some point, otherwise the book would have gone on forever. Other books continue these arguments in more detail and in more depth than an introduction allows, and the recommended reading at the end of each chapter, along with the bibliography, refer you to some of these.

The book is intended to improve the readers' knowledge of moral philosophy as well as their ability to think clearly, accurately, and critically about these matters, but it's also intended to be an enjoyable read, so I hope you enjoy the reading as much as I enjoyed the writing. But now to business . . .

Acknowledgements

First and foremost I'd like to say a big thank you to beautiful Beverley, whose wonderful encouragement and support was vital each step of the way in helping this book see the light of day. Thanks also to Barry Kelly of Thomas Rotherham College who, and this is no exaggeration, taught me more about teaching A-level philosophy in one day than I'd learnt in the previous five years. My appreciation also goes to dashing Dick Smith, principal of Wyke Sixth Form College in Hull, who helped rescue me from the doldrums of academia. I owe my good friend and colleague Belinda Hakes, Head of English at Wyke, a deep debt of gratitude for her enthusiastic support and confidence in the book right from the start. The anonymous reviewers – you know who you are – were a great help to me in correcting errors and restructuring the book for the better. Their many fine suggestions I have tried to implement. Any mistakes that remain are, of course, entirely *their* responsibility. I'm only responsible for the good bits. I must also mention Caroline Richmond who, as copy editor, gave the text a first-class valeting. As a result it now reads as good as a new car interior smells. I'd like to say thank you to my students, who helped decide the front cover and reacted positively to readings from earlier drafts. I'd be remiss if I didn't acknowledge the valued support of my friends and neighbours Cath and Andy, Brian and Margaret, Alison and Jason, Sean, Mick Mead, and others too many to name.

Finally, I must mention the wonderful Andrea Drugan at Polity, whose keen eye was the first to see this book as the work of genius that it is, and who had faith in her judgement and in me. My heartfelt thanks to her for making the whole thing possible.

Introduction

'Most people would sooner die than think; in fact, they do so.'
Bertrand Russell.

My dad used to say, 'As one door closes another one shuts.' I suppose this wryly cynical remark could form a brief commentary on the way the world tends to work. Every dead-end job, every dead-end relationship, and every friend that's ever let you down are all so many doors slammed in your face, and then finally you die – the one door that slams shut forever.

Time to lighten up, perhaps, for I believe moral philosophy can help us overcome all this. No, it won't make you immortal, but it can lend life purpose and make it better. A well-reasoned moral argument can push against these slammed doors and help open them. It was moral argument which eventually opened the door to freedom for millions of slaves worldwide and is opening doors that lock people into racism and sexism. These were and are terrible social ills, but they were propagated by minds locked in a mental prison of their own – a prison of unquestioned assumptions concerning right and wrong. This is the mind of the fanatic, the bigot, the fundamentalist, the smugly complacent 'thinker' who thinks they don't have to think any more because they just 'know' they're right. This probably describes most of us most of the time. Not you and me of course, hmm? Except, that's what they *all* say. Part of being smug and complacent is that you don't think you're smug and complacent. It's the insidiousness of being in a mental prison of fixed ideas and not realizing you're a prisoner. The very prison hides it from you. The ideas are so familiar, and it feels so comfortable, you couldn't possibly be in jail.

Back in Belfast they have a saying that nicely captures this kind of bigoted, narrow-minded certainty of thinking you're always right. For anyone like this they say, 'His head's full of wee doors and they're all shut.' I prescribe a good dose of moral philosophy to open these doors and let the fresh breeze of unfamiliar thoughts blow some of the smugness away, to free the mind for other possibilities. Nietzsche (German philosopher, 1844–1900), a dangerous thinker if ever there was one, once wrote: 'A very popular error: having the courage of one's convictions; rather, it's a matter of having the courage for an *attack* on one's convictions!!!' (*The Gay Science*, sect. 296, n.20; p. 238). Since we're talking of mental prisons, the word 'conviction' is apt. The question you must ask yourself is, 'Do I have the courage for an attack on my convictions?' My intention is that this book will provide the means for such an attack, if you dare, and so perhaps I should add a non-government health warning that this book can seriously damage your prejudices.

Before moving on to the moral theories covered in part I it's essential to examine moral relativism, a view widely held in liberal Western democracies where everyone can have their say about what's right and wrong and, what is more, thinks their say just as valid as anybody else's simply because they say it. Two versions of this are particularly influential and, when challenged, give rise to automatic responses such as, 'Who are you to tell me what to do?' 'That's just your opinion.' 'It's all relative anyway.' The first version of moral relativism relies on the factual findings of anthropologists concerning the wide differences in moral beliefs and customs between cultures in all ages. They argue that this supposed *factual* cultural relativism, that cultures *happen* to disagree over a range of moral issues, supports *moral* cultural relativism, the view that there *cannot possibly* be an objective transcultural set of moral truths; that is, that right and wrong *really* are and *ought* to be relative to each culture, ethnic group, or society. There's no such thing as an objective right and wrong beyond this, and when we say, 'x is right', all we mean is that 'x is right in our culture'. The second version of moral relativism is called *subjectivism*, which cites common experience of widespread moral differences between individuals as evidence for the view that right and wrong are relative to each *individual* person. There's no such thing as right and wrong beyond this, and when we say, 'x is right', all we mean is, 'I like x'.

In the following conversation these two common convictions concerning morality will be aired, attacked, and finally rejected as untenable. If you find it challenging and uncomfortable, so much the better; that's what moral philosophy is supposed to do.

A philosophical conversation about right and wrong

The characters:
O'Reilly: a moral relativist (the cultural sort)
Anna: a moral relativist (the subjectivist sort)
Simon: an ordinary citizen
Bev: a professor of Philosophy

The setting: They're all good friends and can talk freely. They're down at the pub, and after a few drinks the conversation turns to morality . . .

Simon: You know what? The other day I started to read a book about 9/11, and it turns out the author was trying to argue that the terrorists were right to destroy the Twin Towers. I put it down in disgust. I mean, how twisted can you get?

O'Reilly: I'm not so sure. What if it was right from the terrorists' point of view?

Simon: But how can it possibly be right to kill thousands of innocent people? If anything's wrong, surely that is.

O'Reilly: But didn't America and Britain do just this in the Second World War by bombing German cities, with the USA adding to these atrocities by dropping atom bombs on Hiroshima and Nagasaki? Are you saying they were wrong to do this?

Simon: But they were fighting cruel fascist dictatorships bent on world domination. These were evil enemies of liberty, so it had to be done to win the war and save allied lives.

O'Reilly: Ah, so you're saying if the cause is important enough and good enough, then even hundreds of thousands of innocent lives may be sacrificed to that end. But if that's so, then from Al-Qaeda's point of view their cause is also good enough to justify killing thousands of innocents, and if they're part of the Axis of Evil aren't you the Great Satan?

Simon: But they're just thugs and murderers! We weren't at war with them so they don't have a cause.

O'Reilly: That's just your culture talking. It decides what's right and wrong, so they're only thugs and murderers relative to American moral opinion. They're not *really* thugs and murderers. If you adopt their culture's point of view, which is just as valid as yours, they turn out to be heroes and martyrs, and Americans are the thugs.

Simon: But what about my point about not being at war with them?

O'Reilly: Yes, I was coming to that. If they *think* they were right, and their culture backs them, then they *were* right, because in their culture you may not need a war to be able to justify actions such as 9/11. American culture may think you need to be at war to have a chance of justifying such an action, but that's just its opinion, one that doesn't cut any ice in a different culture such as militant Islam. All they're doing is supporting their allies in Iran, Iraq, Afghanistan, and Palestine. All for one and one for all.

Bev: That's all very well as long as it's a nice slogan like that, but listen, O'Reilly, if you're going to say that something's right simply because a culture says so, then you're going to have to agree that, if there was a culture where 'All for torturing one and one for the slave of all' was the accepted norm, then this would be right for them. Surely you don't want to say this?

O'Reilly: Well, I wouldn't *like* what they were doing, and I'd have to let them know that I and my culture morally disapproved of theirs, but in the end I'd have to accept that this sort of thing was their own business not ours. When in Rome you don't have to *do* what the Romans do, and you don't have to *like* it, but you should *tolerate* it; and when *not* in Rome you should definitely tolerate it.

Bev: Oh really, O'Reilly! So, not a word of protest from you if you live next door to a culture that thinks it's fun to lynch blacks, stub out cigarettes on babies, treat women as drudges, and indulge in a spot of Jew-gassing. You can't protest because you haven't got a leg to stand on, having amputated both with your cultural relativism. You say you don't like what they're doing, but what's that to them? If we're talking morality your personal likes and dislikes are not to the point. And *why* would you have to let them know that your culture disagrees with theirs? Again, this is irrelevant because, to them, it will simply register as a curiosity about what your culture happens to think. It will have no bearing on what they think is right, since what is right is what they think is right for them. Even if you up the stakes and start calling what they do 'wrong' this won't wash with them, because it's only wrong from *your* point of view, not theirs.

O'Reilly: Well at least my stance is better than what you've got planned. You'd presumably go wading in there with your army and put an end to their culture by imposing your own values on them. But who do you think you are, trampling on other people's values and way of life? You're assuming you know better than them what's right and wrong, but you don't. No one does, because, there's no objective right and wrong beyond the cultural one. Each culture decides this for itself.

Bev: In that case you've just given me the green light to go wading in with my army if my culture says this is the right thing to do in the circumstances. *They* would think this was wrong but they'd be wrong according to *us*, so these two wrongs would make us right in our eyes, which are the only eyes that matter.

O'Reilly: But shouldn't you tolerate other cultures' moral values despite disagreeing with them, since there's no universal moral truth? Your moral 'truth' stops at your borders, and to impose it on others is a morally illegitimate move to defend an ultimate truth that doesn't exist.

Bev: First of all, although you say our moral 'truth' stops at our borders, it doesn't necessarily follow from your position that our borders have to remain where they are. Your cultural relativism would allow us to *extend* them if *we* think this is right. Secondly, your relativism is in no position to insist on universal toleration and thereby deny cultures the right to invade, dominate, and enslave other cultures if they so wish, because according to you there can be no universal moral values such as toleration or human rights. These can only obtain *within* cultures that espouse them, and, as it happens, my hypothetical culture doesn't. So we'd be okay to invade because we value intolerance and power, and that's why cultural relativism is wrong – because it leads to this.

O'Reilly: Okay. Granted that at international level my theory won't be of much help in the clash *between* cultures, at least *within* each culture morality is stable and guaranteed because the culture itself defines what's right and wrong for all its people. Surely this is a good thing.

Bev: So you must think that Jesus, Gandhi, Dr. Martin Luther King, Nelson Mandela, William Wilberforce, and Oscar Schindler were all vicious and acted wrongly.

O'Reilly: Of course not! What on earth gave you that idea?

Bev: Your theory did. You see, if cultures determine what's right and wrong, anyone who opposes that culture by criticizing it and trying to change it – any moral reformer, in other words – is *bound* to be wicked because the culture, according to your theory, has got to be right by *definition*.

That means that when Jesus opposed the dominant Jewish culture of his day, and Gandhi protested against British colonialism in India, and Martin Luther King led the civil rights movement against a dominant racist culture, and Nelson Mandela fought against the dominant apartheid culture of South Africa, and Wilberforce against slavery, and Schindler against the dominant genocidal culture of the Nazis, that all these great human beings, according to your theory of cultural relativism, were not only wrong, but *necessarily* wrong. In fact, they were literally talking rubbish because, if 'right' is *defined* in terms of the dominant cultural norms, then to claim that these are wrong is to contradict yourself. This is ridiculous, and since cultural relativism leads to this, it must be ridiculous too.

O'Reilly: Not really. These reformers made their culture better, so what they stood for *became* right. They were vindicated in the end by succeeding in changing cultural values to their way of thinking.

Bev: I'm glad you said that, because if that's your best defence I can now demonstrate how truly moronic your theory is.

O'Reilly: Okay. Let's have it.

Bev: Well, first of all, you say these reformers made their culture better, but that can't make any sense at all according to your theory – 'better' in relation to what? The culture that was right by *definition* in the first place? But this is impossible. The new, so-called improved culture is no more right than the old one; it's just *different*, that's all. It might *think* it's better, but that's only from its point of view, and the old culture will think the new one worse from *its equally valid* point of view, so it's still all square. And, of course, there can't be a standard for judging these matters which is independent of all cultures, because cultural relativism doesn't allow this possibility. So that means no culture is morally better than another.

Your problem is that you're appealing to moral *progress* to justify these reformers, but your theory can't allow for *real* moral progress at all, only changes in moral viewpoint, neither better nor worse than the ones that came before. So a free democratic society is *really* no better than a slave state; it's just different.

Secondly, the problem still stands that cultural relativism entails that all reformers are necessarily wrong at the time they were a lone voice. But surely it makes more sense to say they were *right all along*, but society just couldn't see it.

Thirdly, you make being right a matter of culturally successful influence, for if the reformers only *became* right by winning the culture over to their point of view, then that means any obnoxious views could be made morally right if backed by enough force, money, and slick propaganda to persuade the majority of your opinion. The Nazis did it. They were reformers in their own unique way. Do you want to say they were right simply because they succeeded in dominating German culture for a while? Surely not. But cultural relativism implies this, and that's another reason why it's a dead duck.

Anna: I agree, but my theory of subjectivism can get round these problems because, according to it, right and wrong is just a matter of individual personal opinion. When I say 'x is right', all I mean is that 'I like x' or 'I prefer x', and 'x is wrong' is simply the opposite. So what's right for me may be wrong for you and vice versa. There's no objective right and wrong so nobody has the right to impose their moral opinions on others. This leads to a tolerant society and a code of 'live and let live'. So subjectivism is able to say that the reformers were right all along because, even in a minority of one, what's right is right for you as long as it's what you like. And being morally right is not a matter of successful cultural influence because all it takes to be morally right is to have your own opinion of what's right.

Bev: Let me get this straight. When I say, 'x is morally wrong', it's not *really objectively* wrong? Is that what you mean?

Anna: That's right. It's just your opinion. Look at all the wars that have been started because of some moral dispute where both sides just 'knew' they were right. But who's to say what's *really* right or wrong? It's all a subjective matter of taste and personal preference; your opinion is no better than anyone else's because there's no objective truth here, just private feelings and attitudes.

Bev: No, there's more to morality than that.

Anna: What makes you think that?

Bev: Well, for a start, if you're right about what I mean, it messes up your whole theory.

Anna: How come?

Bev: Because when I say, 'x is wrong', if all I'm saying is 'I dislike x', far from its just being my opinion that I dislike x, an opinion which is no better than anyone else's, I turn out instead to be infallible and the world's greatest expert on the subject!

Anna: Yeah, right.

Bev: No, it's true, because your theory's interpretation has me merely commenting on my state of mind, that's all, and how can I possibly get that wrong? Look, it's as if you asked me to think of a number between one and ten; I say that I've picked eight, and then you tell me that that's just my opinion. That's crazy!

Anna: Ah, I see what you're getting at. But my position is still safe because that would mean *everyone* is only talking about their very own state of mind; when they say things like 'Abortion is wrong' and 'Kindness is good', all they're saying is that they don't like abortion but do like kindness. So they'd all be as expert about their own states of mind as you are about yours, which means your opinion is *still* no better than theirs.

Bev: You're just digging a deeper hole for yourself. What this amounts to is that nobody could ever get a moral judgement wrong no matter what outrage they claimed was right. So if Saddam Hussein says that gassing the Kurds was right, he's correct, and you'd have to agree with him because you know he was in favour of it, and he definitely knows he was in favour of it, and under your subjectivist interpretation all he's doing is *saying* he was in favour of it. How could he possibly get this wrong when all he's doing, according to you, is describing the contents of his own brains?

Anna: Yes, but I'd still be right in saying Saddam was wrong to gas the Kurds, because all I'm saying is that I'm not in favour of gassing Kurds.

Bev: True, but then you wouldn't be disagreeing with him, or contradicting him. In fact, nobody would ever contradict anybody else, because each would just be commenting on their own private thoughts. It would be like Saddam saying his favourite colour was blue, and you saying yours was not blue. *Both* would be true. But this makes moral disagreements *impossible*. When people disagree over things such as racism, they take themselves to be *clashing* with their opponents; that one or other is right, but *not both*. But according to your theory of subjectivism, nearly everyone totally misunderstands moral language. Billions don't understand what they're saying. Don't you think they're more likely to be right than you?

Anna: Okay, you've got the statistics on your side, but I could still be right. Time and again majorities have been wrong; most people used to believe in witches but there weren't any really. Perhaps moral language has bewitched people, and my theory will break the spell.

Bev: I suppose that's a possibility, but there are two more arguments which will show that that slim chance isn't even worth considering.

Anna: Shoot.

Bev: Firstly, your theory makes all moral claims completely arbitrary. You turn them all into mere opinions about people's own states of mind concerning things such as theft, murder, and so on, and this leaves no room for any reasons that could justify these opinions. That's what makes them arbitrary. For example, surely the *reason* I disapprove of murder is *because* it *is* wrong. This *justifies* my disapproval. But if we take your analysis, all this says is that 'the reason I disapprove of murder is because I disapprove of it', which gets us nowhere. If your theory of subjectivism is to be believed, Martin Luther King was no more justified in being against racism than the Ku Klux Klan are in being for it; and Lincoln was no more justified in being against slavery than the plantation owners of the Confederacy were justified in being for it.

Secondly, morality is not just about stating justified opinions, but about making things better and acting well. It's about *doing* as well as *saying*. For example, making a moral judgement that courage is good is not just a passive statement about my positive state of mind towards courage, but a way of getting people to *act* more courageously, thus encouraging courage. But, according to subjectivism, it would be as if I was merely making a personal comment about my preference, with no implication as to what needs *doing*.

It's like being in a restaurant and the waiter asks me what I'd like. I tell him, 'The tomato soup looks good', and he, interpreting this as a purely psychological comment about my personal taste in soup, goes back to the kitchen and gets me nothing; as if, like one going to confession, my sole purpose in entering the restaurant was to unburden my soul and inform the waiter that I like tomato soup. The whole thing ends with me soupless and him well informed; yet this is what your theory reduces morality to. Everyone ends up knowing what everyone else thinks, but goes on in exactly the same way as before – torturers torturing, protestors protesting – but all to no effect, because the protestors will have as little influence on torturers as I have on the waiter.

I hope this rather lively conversation has highlighted some of the challenges in moral thinking. Many of these issues will be revisited in more systematic detail in the final section, on metaethics. Meanwhile, it's time to examine four of the most influential normative ethical theories, each of them, rightly or wrongly, arguing that it's the only objectively true account of morality. Though I've given what I consider to be a fair appraisal of each theory, it seems to me that virtue ethics is the most adequate of the four, as will be clear from the overall tenor of the discussion. I may be wrong about this, but I don't think so, on balance. You'll have to think this through for yourself and make up your own mind.

A good way of engaging with the book is to try and overturn its arguments and, by thinking critically and philosophically, carve out your own perspective on moral philosophy. That way, you're not just *reading* philosophy, you're *doing* philosophy.

Part I
Normative Ethics

Introduction

The theories in this area of ethics are called 'normative' because they attempt to set down rules, or *norms*, for our moral behaviour in everyday life. It's similar to the way the Highway Code sets out norms for how people ought to drive, and just as it's wrong to endanger lives by ignoring the rules and driving badly, so these theories would call your action wrong if it flouted their rules for good behaviour, and right if it obeyed them.

This *seems* pretty straightforward; all you have to do to find out the difference between right and wrong is look up the rule laid down by the normative theory. But things aren't what they seem. The problem is that there are *three* main types of normative theory, each trying to sell its own brand of morality, which is often incompatible with the others. The moral 'customer' is stuck in the middle, not knowing which of the rival rules is *the* right one – that's if there is a right one. Imagine trying to learn how to drive if there were three rival Highway Codes to choose from. Well, normative ethics is in a similar state of disarray, and in the following chapters we'll examine the carnage and try to extract a workable ethical theory from the ones on offer. But, for now, a very brief outline of the theories will suffice.

Three types of normative theory

Each theory listed below is a major player in contemporary moral, religious, and political debate and, as such, is worth careful study.

1 **Utilitarianism**
2 **Deontological theories**
3 **Virtue ethics**

For every action there are *three* components:

1) the consequences
2) the action itself (including the motive)
3) the agent or doer.

These help to distinguish the three types of theory.

- *Utilitarianism* concerns itself with the *consequences*.
- *Deontological* theories, which include the theory of Immanuel Kant and divine command theory, concern themselves with the *action/motive*.
- *Virtue ethics* concerns itself with the *agent/doer*.

Each of the next three chapters will be devoted to one of the above theories, explaining it, and discussing the arguments for and against.

1   Utilitarianism

General features

Utilitarianism gets its name from the word 'utility', which means happiness rather than usefulness. Broadly speaking, utilitarianism has three basic features.

1 It is *consequentialist*: this means that it's the *results* or *consequences* of the action that count in deciding whether it's right.
2 It holds that *happiness/utility is good in itself*: this means that happiness is worth pursuing and increasing *for its own sake*. Another way of putting this is to say that happiness is *intrinsically*, or *inherently*, good. Everything else is good merely insofar as it is a means to the production of happiness, which is the ultimate goal. So things such as money, power, friendship, and so on are only *instrumental* goods because they are ways and means, i.e. instruments, for achieving happiness.
3 *The principle of utility (greatest happiness principle)* is the most fundamental moral principle according to utilitarianism, and by applying it to your actions you can find out whether they are right or wrong.

> **The principle of utility:** You should always try to bring about '***the greatest happiness of the greatest number***'.

So when you have a choice of things to do, you work out which action will produce the most happiness compared with unhappiness or pain, and that's the one you ought to do. If you don't, you've done the wrong thing.

Advantages of utilitarianism

A first advantage of utilitarianism is that it promotes *what everybody wants*, i.e. happiness, so this seems a good thing and is strongly in its favour. Secondly, it's a relatively *simple*, straightforward theory, because there's only *one* rule to worry about, i.e. the principle of utility, so people should find it easy to operate without worrying about possible clashes between principles. Thirdly, it's *democratic*, as everyone gets counted equally in the calculation of happy and painful consequences. According to utilitarianism, each counts for one and nobody for more than one. Fourthly, unlike its rivals, it strives to be *scientific* because it tries to settle moral problems by observing, predicting, and calculating the empirical/psychological data of happy consequences. People prefer a 'no nonsense', down-to-earth theory that promises tangible, measurable results so that they know where they stand. Lastly, being a *secular* theory, it sidesteps the problems of relying on God for moral guidance – problems such as how to prove God exists, or which religion is true.

Classical utilitarianism

'Classical utilitarianism' denotes the kind of utilitarian thinking that was going on in the late eighteenth and the whole of the nineteenth century. This was during the early years of the theory, when it was bright, brash, and abrasive – it can still be (see chapter 6) – and burst upon a morally moribund English social scene like a breath of fresh air, bringing in its wake calls for prison reform, votes for women, improvements in education and public health and hygiene – all in the name of the greatest happiness principle. The originator of this movement, and the man who has by far the strongest claim to be the inventor of utilitarianism, is one Jeremy Bentham.

Bentham (1748–1832) was born in London, educated at Oxford, and qualified as a lawyer. He had a very practical mind: he had the idea for central heating, the sleeping bag, the Panama Canal, and even the portable house – Bentham, father of the caravan. His 'Panopticon', an innovative circular design for a prison, allowed one warden, sitting at the centre, full views of all the cells simultaneously – surely the precursor of CCTV. It's no surprise, then, that Bentham was the founder of the most practical moral theory of them all, utilitarianism. He saw it as an antidote to the misery-inducing injustices of English law to which he'd had a ringside seat as a trained lawyer. Thus he became leader of a reforming group called 'the Philosophical Radicals', who were influential in educational, prison, and legal reforms, amongst others. He was a close friend of James Mill, John Stuart Mill's father; they were even next-door neighbours for a time. True to his utilitarian beliefs, Bentham found a way, albeit a creepy one, of making people happy even after his death. His wish was for his embalmed body (called an 'auto-icon') to be left to University College London, which he helped to found, and there he sits to this day, dressed in a suit of his own clothes, on display in a glass cabinet. His wish has been a spectacular utilitarian success, bringing amusement to thousands. Indeed, Bentham's post-mortem career has been, if anything, even more eventful than his pre-mortem one. It's reported that from time to time he attends official university dinners (his head falling into a bowl of soup on one occasion). He has also travelled extensively, having at one time accompanied a group of students to a beer festival in Germany (his head at another time being found in a left luggage locker at Aberdeen railway station in Scotland; it is now kept under lock and key in a safe, while a wax spare sits on his shoulders in the glass box).

Key ethical work: *An Introduction to the Principles of Morals and Legislation* (1789)

Bentham's utilitarian theory

Being utilitarian, Bentham's theory was, of course, consequentialist, adhered to the principle of utility, and held that happiness was the only thing of intrinsic value, but the theory has six basic features in addition to all of this. First of all, it's *hedonistic*, which means that happiness is the *same* as pleasure and is the **only good thing in itself.** All else is merely instrumentally good as a means to getting pleasure. Hedonism therefore implies that nothing apart from pleasure is worth having for its own sake, for example, knowledge, beauty, truth, and so on. These are only instrumentally good insofar as they lead to pleasurable states of mind. Pleasure is therefore always good, and happiness consists of having pleasurable experiences. Secondly, it's based on a theory of human motivation called *psychological egoism.* This holds that everyone always acts for the sake of their own pleasure and never just for anyone else's benefit. In other words, it's psychologically impossible for anyone to be truly altruistic by putting other people's interests before their own. Thirdly, it's a form of *act* utilitarianism. This means that Bentham applies the principle of utility *directly* to people's *acts* to test whether they are morally good. You test your proposed action by calculating its predicted consequences in terms of pleasurable or painful outcomes for all concerned. The fourth feature is that it employs the *hedonic calculus*, a method invented by Bentham for measuring the amount of people's pleasure. It has seven categories:

1 *Intensity.* To apply this feature it may help to imagine a scale of intensity running from +10 maximum (say, an orgasm) through zero (say, looking distractedly out of a window) to −10 (say, someone taking a power drill to your knee-caps). A nice cup of tea might score +1, for example.

2 *Duration:* From a few seconds (say, being tickled) to years at a time (say, pleasure from the knowledge you're rich).
3 *Certainty:* For example, whether to buy a tasty take-away meal (pretty certain pleasure), or whether to put the money on a 100/1 outsider in the Derby (very uncertain).
4 *Nearness in time:* Spend the money now, or save for retirement?
5 *Fecundity:* Pleasures that bring further pleasures, e.g. the pleasure of the taste of a few lagers leading to the further pleasure of easy laughter.
6 *Purity* (the flip side of fecund): Some pleasures bring pain, e.g. binge drinking, leading to vomiting, hangover, injuries from fights or falling over, and possible arrest. These would be impure.
7 *Extent:* Number of people/animals affected by the action.

The fifth feature is that *quantity* of pleasure is *all that matters*. The main thing is to produce as much of the stuff as you can for as many as possible; that's what morality is all about. Lastly, there are *four* sanctions to encourage us to think of other people's happiness and not just our own. Sanctions are punishments or threats used to keep people in line. These are:

i) *Physical* sanction: *Nature* will get you, e.g. if you're greedy this will naturally tend to overeating and health problems.
ii) *Political* sanction: The Law will get you and you'll go to jail.
iii) *Popular* sanction: *People* will get you, e.g. if you're nasty you'll lose your friends; nobody will talk to you.
iv) *Religious* sanction: God will get you, i.e. you'll go to hell because, like the Mounties, He always gets His man.

Criticisms of Bentham's utilitarianism

It seems that each of the six features of Bentham's theory has significant problems. We'll deal with each of these in turn.

1 Problems with hedonism

The case of the happy torturer

This example questions the hedonistic idea that pleasure is *always* good. Imagine two torturers, one happy and one not. The happy one gets a real kick out of his job. He can't wait to get in to work each morning to start zapping his 'clients' with some serious voltage. Another favourite is the blow-torch. Talk about job satisfaction! The unhappy one hates his job. He's only doing it because the state has threatened his family if he doesn't. He can't sleep at night. He's getting counselling, is on nerve tablets, winces every time his victims scream in pain, and agonizes about it to his girl-friend.

Which scene is better? If you're a hedonist you'd have to say the one with the happy torturer, because at least there's some pleasure there – in fact, quite a lot – and this is good, because pleasure is always a good thing no matter how it's achieved. But this seems a crazy moral judgement. Surely the very opposite is true. The very fact that this torturer gets pleasure from such horrific acts makes it even worse, not better. Doesn't his pleasure compound the evil rather than compensate for it? The unhappy torturer is the better man because his own mental anguish somehow partly atones for the pain he inflicts. If so, this means that pleasure is *not always* good, because in *this case* it is bad, and that makes hedonism false, which makes Bentham's theory false.

The experience machine

This example is derived from Robert Nozick's book *Anarchy, State and Utopia* (pp. 42–5). Ask yourself this: if you could plug yourself into a machine that would give you all the pleasurable experiences you could desire, but which was totally fake (although you wouldn't know this once plugged in), would you really want to spend the rest of your life being deceived about the worth of your pretend 'achievements'? It seems most people would rather *earn* their pleasures in the *real* world, even if it means having *fewer* of them. This indicates that things such as *truth, honesty,* and *real achievement* are valued as *intrinsically* good *in addition to* pleasure, so it can't be the only thing good in itself. This is borne out by other examples of people sacrificing their pleasure in the name of *art, God, moral duty, their country.*

If Bentham were to reply that they're not *really* sacrificing their pleasure for these things, because they're still doing what they *want* to do and so get some pleasure out of it, this assumes that psychological egoism is true. So to refute his reply we need to refute psychological egoism, which takes us on to the next feature of Bentham's theory.

2 Problems with psychological egoism

Psychological egoism holds that people can only ever act for their *own* plea-sure. Fundamentally, this is their only motive for doing anything. Everyone looks after number one, and *can't do otherwise.*

But is this true? It seems not, for the following reasons:

1 It couldn't possibly be checked or verified because it's a wildly general claim about *all* the motives of *all* the people who have ever lived and who ever *will* live. There is no way we could ask them all what their intentions were when they acted, so psychological egoism is simply a wild guess.
2 There is ample evidence against psychological egoism in the form of people putting the happiness of others *before* their own, for example: the soldier dying for his comrades, a mother saving her child from a burning house and dying herself in the process, and someone giving money to charity with no hope of compensation. The point is that it only takes *one* exception to disprove a universal claim. '*All* swans are white' is disproved by finding *one* non-white swan. So, '*All* people seek only their own pleasure' is disproved by finding *one* person who doesn't, and we have *lots* of these cases, not just one. So psychological egoism *must* be false.

A psychological egoist might reply as follows: 'These aren't really counter-examples to psychological egoism, because the *very fact* that all these people *wanted* to help others instead of themselves *proves* that they did it out of a *self-interested* motive to get pleasure in that way. Since they only did what they *wanted* to, they acted for their *own* pleasure and not *really* for others. This is simply selfish pleasure-seeking disguised as altruism.' This reply looks as if it wins the day by getting rid of all the awkward counter-evidence, but it does this by illegitimately redefining words to suit itself. In so doing, psychological egoism dies as an interesting, but false, empirical theory of human motivation, and becomes instead a trivial, private word-game that tells us nothing about the real world of human psychology.

A couple of examples should help clarify the flaw in this kind of verbal trickery. The first is taken from *Thinking about Thinking*, by Antony Flew (pp. 47–8).

The 'no-true-Scotsman move'

Angus McSporran reads in a tabloid paper that an Englishman has been found guilty of rape. Outraged, he declares, 'No Scotsman would ever do such a thing.' Next week he reads that Andy McPorridge, born and raised in Glasgow, was convicted of rape. This counter-evidence appears to refute Angus's theory, but Angus has a reply. He now insists, 'No *true* Scotsman would have done that, and since Andy McPorridge did do that, he *can't* have been a *true* Scotsman.' So Angus can still hold on to his pet theory. Let's examine what has gone wrong with Angus's reasoning.

What he has done is to defend his theory by redefining 'Scotsman' to suit himself. He departs from the ordinary meaning of the word (person born in

Scotland, etc.) and adds on to the normal meaning (person born in Scotland *who would never rape a woman.*) This is what a *true* Scotsman is. But now his theory is no longer a *factual* statement about *real* Scotsmen in the *ordinary* sense of the word, a statement that may be tested against the evidence, but merely about Angus's *private, arbitrary,* and *peculiar* use of the word 'Scotsman'. He ends up merely playing with words. His theory becomes true *by definition* and thereby ceases to be a theory. It self-destructs.

Another example would be to suppose I say, 'All bananas are perfectly yellow.' This seems to be a theory about ordinary bananas, but it could easily be challenged by citing some counter-examples. What about bananas that are green because they haven't ripened yet? No problem: these aren't *real* bananas, they're only potential bananas since they haven't matured yet. But what about the ones that have gone black because they are over-ripe? No problem: these *used to be* bananas but are so no longer since they've gone black. But what about the mature bananas that are bruised or spotty and so have black patches? Surely these disprove my theory. Again, no problem: the very fact that they have bruises or spots proves that they are not *true* bananas, for only *true* bananas are perfectly yellow. My 'victory' is hollow because all I do is keep shifting the goalposts by redefining 'bananas' to suit myself. I'm just playing my own private 'banana' word-game and end up saying nothing about bananas in the *normal* sense of the word.

Hopefully, it should now be clear that psychological egoism has made exactly the same mistake as the 'theories' above. It starts out using 'want' and 'desire' in their normal sense, e.g. 'Everyone only wants their own happiness all the time.' But faced with counter-examples (people dying for others) where other people's happiness is desired instead of your own, psychological egoism redefines 'want' so as to make this impossible. None of these examples of altruism is allowed to count as wanting other people's happiness because, by the mere *wanting* of it, it becomes selfish. 'Selfishness' and 'wanting' have now been arbitrarily redefined so as to mean the *same* thing in order to save the theory from being disproved; but this is not what 'selfishness' *normally* means.

- If I *want* to be happy at *your* expense, this is selfish.
- But if I *want* you to be happy at *my* expense, this is altruistic, *not* selfish.
- So *wanting something* and *being selfish* are **not the same thing**.

We can all agree that most people most of the time are pretty selfish, and sometimes pretend to be altruistic when they in fact have ulterior selfish motives, but there are nevertheless many clear cases of altruism where it is highly implausible to suggest that the person concerned was *really* out for their own benefit. So psychological egoism is false. If it tries to get round these counter-examples by redefining words to suit itself, it becomes utterly trivial and says nothing. So psychological egoism is either false or trivial. Either way, we can reject it.

3 Problems with act utilitarianism

- There's *no time to calculate* consequences in *emergencies*.

Imagine Bentham as the Good utilitarian Samaritan coming across a victim of a mugging lying by the roadside. With hedonic calculus at the ready, he'd have to ask a host of questions in order to assign a numerical value to each of its seven categories for measuring pleasure and pain, questions such as:

- 'On a scale of one to ten could you tell me how much it hurts?' (to gauge intensity)
- 'How long do you think you'll be pain-free after I help you?' (to gauge duration)
- 'What's the likelihood of my help easing his pain?' (to gauge certainty)
- 'Should I help you right now, or call an ambulance? How long will that take?' (to gauge nearness in time)
- 'Tell me, are you a miserable person? Because if you're leading a totally miserable life, any pleasure you get from my helping you will only lead to more misery the longer you survive.' (to gauge purity)
- 'Are you a masochist? And do you lead a happy life? Please estimate this on a scale of one to ten.' (to gauge fecundity)
- 'Are you a serial killer, rapist, paedophile? Do you have many friends, and do they like you, or are you a loner? How many will be made happy or unhappy by my help?' (to gauge extent)

Only now can our 'Samaritan' get down to some number crunching to see if the total balance of pleasure and pain results in more pleasure than pain. Needless to say, by this time the victim is probably dead.

- It *condones outrageously unjust actions*.

For example, framing and executing an innocent person in order to avoid a race riot in which many would be killed; or killing a rich old miser to give his money to charity, thus saving hundreds of lives. The hedonic calculus would approve these acts, yet our sense of justice would unreservedly condemn them as cold-blooded murder. A moral theory that condones this sort of thing is courting serious trouble.

- It's *too demanding*.

The case of the cinema and the tramp

Imagine you're an act utilitarian on your way to the cinema with £10 to spend on your ticket, some sweets, and ice cream, but you pass a hungry tramp who begs you for some money for a hot meal. What should you do? Well, after a quick bit of maths on your hedonic calculus you realize that more overall happiness would be achieved if you gave the £10 to the tramp than if you spent it on yourself at the cinema. He clearly needs it more than you. So the right thing to do is to hand over all your money to him. This example can be generalized to cover *all spending* on any 'luxury' beyond the bare necessities of life, for since there is *always* someone worse off than you, it is immoral to spend any money on, for instance, the cinema, Christmas presents, holidays, CDs, and so on. It ought to be given to some charity or other because this would produce more overall happiness than spending it on yourself. A theory that demands this level of commitment is useless because impractical; most people would regard these moral demands as unreasonable and unworkable. Who's going to sacrifice their whole lifestyle for total strangers?

• It turns *trivial non-moral* decisions into *acts of conscience*.

The case of the meal and the menu

If I pick a meal from a menu which turns out to be less pleasurable than some alternative, then according to act utilitarianism I have done a *morally* wrong thing because *each act* is tested by the *principle of utility*, and this *act* fails the test. This seems absurd. Surely I've just made a mistake, or been unlucky; it's surely not a *moral* matter.

4   Problems with the hedonic calculus

Pleasure seems incalculable, yet Bentham treats us as if our pleasures can be counted like beans in a can. Instead, it seems that pleasure/happiness, like love, cannot be quantified in the way Bentham's hedonic calculus requires. For example, to be told that you are loved to the tune of 83.6 per cent of affection is as ridiculous as calculating that you ought to keep your promise rather than break it because, according to the hedonic calculus, the former nets 43 units of pleasure overall whereas the latter nets minus 21 units of pain. Even comparing relatively straightforward pleasures on a quantitative basis seems impossible – for instance, the intensity of a cold drink on a hot day compared with the duration of a beautiful sunset. Besides, some *pains* are *pleasurable*, and vice versa. How are these measured (for instance, squeezing a blackhead, or worrying a loose tooth with your tongue)? It seems these things resist the blandishments of the hedonic statistician.

5 *Is* Quantity *of pleasure the* only *thing that counts?*

For Bentham, it doesn't really matter whether you get pleasure from, on the one hand, boozing, stuffing yourself with food, and lolling about all day watching rubbish TV or, on the other hand, writing poetry, learning an instrument, and studying history, as long as you get the greatest *quantity* of pleasure from it. This left him open to the stinging jibe that utilitarianism was a philosophy fit only for swine. No need for humans to have aspirations for higher things; as long as you get your nose in the pleasure trough of animal sensations that's fine and is morally good. This criticism hits home because most of us feel humans have a higher side to them than the merely animal instincts, things such as rationality, science, artistry – desires to know and understand and create. These are worth pursuing *even if they give us **less** pleasurable sensations.* So *quantity alone* does *not* capture what we value in life.

6 *Problems with the four Sanctions*

These sanctions don't really *justify* utilitarianism but act merely as a piece of motivating arm-twisting. You don't *prove* your theory by leaning on people via various threats, which is what these sanctions are, but by rationally defending it with *argument*. Putting a gun to my head may be very *effective* in making me *say* '2 + 2 = 5', but it is powerless to *make it true*. Similarly, threatening people with the law, God, and the rest, unless they act for the general happiness, may be very *effective* in *making* them so act, but it is powerless to *prove* that they *truly ought* so to act. Besides, they're not even effective as *threats* if you're an atheist, a loner, and a smart criminal on a good diet.

With his innovative theory Bentham was breaking new ground, being the first to attempt a systematic defence of utilitarianism, so no wonder every aspect of his theory comes under attack. Any new idea will be at its most vulnerable when it's young and taking its first steps. The question is whether it should be abandoned or improved. John Stuart Mill, brought up on Bentham's theory, was aware of its flaws but opted for improvement. We'll see below what changes he made and whether they fare any better.

Mill's utilitarianism

John Stuart Mill (1806–1873) never attended school or university, being educated entirely by his father, whose stated aim was to turn him into 'a mere calculating machine'. As a result he was something of a prodigy, learning Greek when he was three, Latin, arithmetic, and history from the age of seven onwards, and of course, utilitarianism. Bentham, no doubt, helped oversee all this. But all this extraordinary educational and paternal pressure took its toll, and at twenty Mill had a nervous breakdown, realizing that even if universal happiness were achieved it wouldn't make him happy. However, he came through this with the help of poetry, and in 1830 met the love of his life, Harriet Taylor. Unfortunately, she was already married, but that didn't stop Mill, whose 'close personal friendship' with her shocked Victorian society – not to mention her husband. But once he was out of the way – he died in 1851 – they married in 1852. Mill was a member of parliament from 1865 to 1868, and famously advocated votes for women, though they didn't get it until 1918, and even then they had to be over the age of thirty. He was way ahead of his time in this respect. Mill's influence was a powerhouse behind the spread of utilitarianism and the freedom of the individual, making him probably *the* greatest English philosopher of the nineteenth century.

Key ethical work: *Utilitarianism* (1863)

Because of the heavy criticism directed at Bentham's utilitarianism, Mill wanted to improve on it by making a number of modifications which would side-step those problems. He made *four major changes*.

1 He added *quality* to quantity of pleasure by distinguishing between *higher and lower* pleasures. He did this to combat the '*pig philosophy*' criticism levelled at Bentham.
2 He switched from Bentham's *act* utilitarianism, according to which each act is tested separately against the principle of utility, to *rule* utilitarianism, whereby it's the *rules* or *policies* that govern *types* of action, which the principle of utility tests. This was to combat accusations that utilitarianism *condoned injustice*. (Now and then Mill still talks like an act utilitarian, causing some debate as to his real position; however, I think the *rule* interpretation of his writings is stronger, so for the purposes of exposition I'll assume this is the correct line.)
3 He dropped the *hedonic calculus*. This was to avoid criticisms that it was *unworkable*.

4 Unlike Bentham, he tried to *prove* the *principle of utility*. Whereas Bentham merely took it to be obvious, Mill wanted to *demonstrate its truth* for all to see.

Each of these changes will be explained and critically assessed.

1   *Mill's distinction between* higher *and* lower *pleasures*

Explanation

Mill introduced a distinction between higher and lower pleasures based on *qualitative* differences. The higher quality pleasures are intellectual, such as the joys of poetry, the arts, philosophy, music, and so on. The lower pleasures, such as eating, drinking, and sex, stem from our bodily, animal natures. Whereas Bentham didn't care how you got your pleasure as long as you got lots of it (quantity only), famously saying that pushpin (a children's game) was as good as poetry if you enjoyed it as much, Mill did care about this. For Mill, the higher quality of a pleasure, such as going to the opera, more than compensated for the lesser quantity you obtained compared with getting drunk instead. He contended that it was better to be an unhappy intellectual than a happy idiot, and in this way tried to place utilitarianism on the side of human dignity instead of regarding people as little more than pleasure-seeking pigs.

Critical assessment

Mill faces three major problems regarding his distinction between higher and lower pleasures.

- It *abandons hedonism*.
- It makes pleasure *even harder to calculate*.
- It makes it *impossible to decide* between higher and lower pleasures.

We'll consider these problems in turn.

a) Abandons hedonism – This is a problem for Mill because he wants to maintain Bentham's hedonistic view of happiness, namely that happiness and pleasure are the same thing, and that this is the only thing good in itself. But if only pleasure counts, how is it possible to prefer something which gives you *less* pleasure over something which gives you more? Higher pleasures give you less, so it seems the only way you can justify these is to invoke *values other than pleasure* that compensate for the lesser pleasure – for example, values such as the greater artistry and profundity to be found in Shakespearean tragedy. But if hedonism says pleasure is the *only* standard for judging actions, then Mill is *inconsistent* in trying to stick to hedonism while at the same time using standards *other* than pleasure to justify the higher pleasures. It's as if someone were to say that the *amount of heat* they throw out is the *only* way to judge between fires, and then goes on to say that they prefer a coal fire to an electric fire even though the coal fire generates *less* heat. It seems the only way they could do this is to justify it on the basis of something *other* than heat, e.g. pretty flame, cheaper price, and so on. But then the heat standard (*heatonism*) is inconsistently ditched for alternative values to do with beauty or economy rather than heat. Since no correct theory can be inconsistent, and Mill is inconsistent here, it follows that his theory of higher and lower pleasures, combined with hedonism, is wrong.

b) Even harder to calculate – It was hard enough, if not impossible, to calculate pleasures quantitatively when we had only *one* scale, i.e. the hedonic calculus, but it becomes out of the question when we try to use *two or more* scales to compare *qualitative* with *quantitative* pleasures. This would be like using a weather vane to weigh out ingredients for a cake, or a tailor using a barometer to fit a customer for a suit. These things are *incommensurable*, i.e. they cannot be compared because they don't talk the same language. The aesthetic beauty of a flame cannot be costed against the amount of heat, and the profundity of a Shakespearean tragedy cannot be costed against the amount of pleasure you get from eating a pizza instead.

c) Impossible to decide which are higher pleasures – It's useless to distinguish between higher and lower pleasures if we can't tell, or can't agree, which is which. Chaos would soon ensue, so we need a decision procedure for judging this. Mill offered the following test or criterion of what should count as a higher pleasure. If the *majority of experts* who have *extensive experience* in competing pleasures *prefer* one pleasure over another, even though it gives *less* pleasure, then this is a *higher quality* pleasure. So, basically, what Mill offers us is a 'team' of people with 'superior' tastes who will tell us what we ought to like, based on their 'authority'. Their only qualifications are that they have indulged thoroughly in the pleasures of the flesh, and of the arts and sciences, and prefer the latter. This is unsatisfactory in a number of ways.

- *Firstly*, can anyone really *fully* experience both types of pleasure in all their variety? You would have to be superhuman to be able to indulge yourself in all the pleasures of food, drink, sex, drugs, and rock and roll, and also to spend time at the opera, art galleries, cinema, and the lab, do philosophy, read poetry, and then make a balanced judgement.
- *Secondly*, since no one is infallible, they might make a mistake in their judgement and so not be a true guide anyway.
- *Thirdly*, how are we to recognize these people? Must they publish all the pleasures in which they have indulged? Who is going to do this, and how would we check on this anyway?

- *Fourthly*, Mill himself admits that sometimes the so-called experts revert to piggy pleasures on account of things such as weakness of will, boredom, and mid-life crises. However, this is a fatal admission because it, in effect, abandons his very own test of higher pleasures. If the 'experts' themselves change their minds about which pleasures to prefer, then they also don't know what is best and can't be relied on for their 'superior' judgement. So Mill's test collapses.

We now move on to explain and criticize Mill's next modification of Bentham, from act to *rule* utilitarianism.

2 Mill's rule *utilitarianism*

Explanation

Mill replaced Bentham's act utilitarianism with an early form of rule utilitarianism mainly because act utilitarianism led to the *condoning of morally outrageous actions* on the basis of their good consequences. But there were also problems with *finding the time to calculate* the pleasurable consequences of each and every act. The difference between act and rule utilitarianism is that, in act utilitarianism, the principle of utility is brought to bear *directly* on *every act*, judging it right or wrong according to the balance of utility over pain that results from *it*, whereas, in rule utilitarianism, the principle of utility is brought to bear on the *code of rules* by which society abides, and only *indirectly* on the actions that are in *accordance with those rules*. Rule utilitarianism can be defined as holding that: '**An act is right if and only if it is in line with the *code or set of rules* whose *widespread acceptance* would result in at least as much utility as any alternative code.**'

So you should only do actions that *conform to the rules* because the *rules* satisfy the principle of utility. Examples of good rules that tend to promote the happiness of society are things such as:

- *tell the truth*
- *don't steal*
- *don't murder*
- *keep your promises*
- *help others*
- *don't torture*
- *don't punish the innocent.*

This improves on act utilitarianism in the following two ways:

1 If an action obeys the rules, you know to do it *automatically* because the rules have already passed the principle of utility test, so you don't have to spend time calculating the consequences.

2 It prevents the unjust and outrageous actions that act utilitarianism advocates, because these involve breaking good social rules, such as *Don't murder*, that have already been passed by the principle of utility and therefore should be obeyed on utilitarian grounds. Breaking them for extra short-term utility is bad because, longer term, these exceptions undermine the rules and the social fabric, which unsettles people; they will lose confidence in the law and morality, and we will all be on the slippery slope that leads to anarchy and the jungle. In other words, the longer-term utility of keeping the rules is better than the short-term utility of breaking them, so we should keep them.

Critical assessment

Rule utilitarianism does have some advantages. Not having to calculate the outcome of each and every action is an improvement because, among other things, in emergencies you can get on and help the injured party without losing precious moments in time-consuming fruitless hedonic calculations, knowing that your actions conform to the tried and tested rule 'Help others in need', which has *already passed* the principle of utility test. It also better fits our basic moral feelings, namely our sense of justice. For example, any code of social rules containing the rule 'Innocent people may be framed and executed when it suits' is very likely to bring widespread misery in the long term due to the debilitating fear of being next no matter how law-abiding you are. This far outweighs any short-term benefits injustice might bring through avoiding the odd riot.

But there are *four problems* it has difficulty overcoming.

a) The problem of *relativism* – What can the rule utilitarian say about different codes of rules in different countries, especially if some of these codes are obnoxious? If the Nazi code makes most Germans happy at the expense of a small minority of Jews, then this satisfies the principle of utility, so the rule utilitarian can't criticize them. Moral values become *relative* to the society and set of rules you happen to be under, so they're unable to condemn vicious regimes. But a happy, slave-owning society is not made good just because they're happy. However, rule utilitarians can say nothing against such a society, because the slave-owning rule is morally good according to the principle of utility as applied to *that* society. Any moral theory that can't find the resources to condemn the Nazis is unacceptable.

b) The problem of *rule worship* – If this criticism is correct, it is devastating to rule utilitarianism, because it would mean rule utilitarians *giving up* their utilitarianism altogether and replacing it with a non-utilitarian habit of following the rules simply because they are the agreed rules, rather than because obedience to them leads to the greatest happiness of all. The idea is this: if an *exception* to one of the rules, e.g. *Don't steal*, were known to produce a lot more pleasure than pain for more people – say £2,000 stolen from a rich person and given to Oxfam – then *to insist on keeping the rule simply because it's the rule, in preference to producing a definite surplus in utility by breaking it*, is to deny one's own utilitarian values and to start worshipping the rules instead of the principle of utility.

The rule utilitarian does a lot of wriggling here, but in the end can't seem to get off the hook. Imagine the following conversation between an act utilitarian and a rule utilitarian concerning the rule '*Never jump a red light*'. This rule is widely accepted and is normally very good for promoting utility by preventing crashes, injury, and traffic chaos. However:

Act U: 'It would be okay to jump a red light in the early hours of the morning when no other traffic is about and you were a bit late for a train. You'd be happier getting the train, and so would the people you've arranged to meet.'

Rule U: 'No. This is wrong because it undermines a good rule.'

Act U: 'In what way?'

Rule U: 'It sets a bad example to others, who will then copy you.'

Act U: 'But no one else sees me, so it's not a bad example, and I won't tell.'

Rule U: 'But *you* know about it, so it will undermine your future obedience to the rule by starting a bad habit.'

Act U: 'No, because I'm not tempted to go through red lights in heavy traffic just because I did it when no traffic was around.'

Rule U: 'But you will lose utility through feeling guilty and having sleepless nights because you did the wrong thing.'

Act U: 'No I won't. I'm an act utilitarian, so my conscience is clear.'

Rule U: 'The police might have got you on CCTV, so results will still be bad.'

Act U: 'They didn't. I knew there was no CCTV in the area.'

Rule U: 'But you can't trust your personal judgement in disobeying the rules; it's biased.'

Act U: 'No more so than the rules themselves; these were made by people too, and I can be as objective as them.'

It seems the rule utilitarian has run out of things to say. If the act utilitarian wins this argument then the rule utilitarian should allow this exception in the interests of utility. If he does not, he thereby rejects utilitarianism in favour of rule worship. The rule utilitarian is in a dilemma here because if he does allow the exception, he falls into another trap; he falls back into the act utilitarian camp.

c) The problem that *rule utilitarianism collapses into act utilitarianism* – The only way to avoid the 'rule worship' objection is for the rule utilitarian to concede the act utilitarian's exception, but this is jumping from the fridge into the freezer, for once on this road there is no stopping until you end up agreeing to *all* the act utilitarian's exceptions, which, in effect, means *saying the same thing as the act utilitarian* only in a more complicated way, using top-heavy rules loaded with exceptions. For example:

Rule U: A good rule is, *'Never tell lies'*. We'll call this **Rule 1.**
Act U: Exception: what about lying to be polite?
Rule U: Okay. We'll modify **Rule 1** to read, *'Never lie unless for politeness'*. We'll call this **Rule 1a.**
Act U: Exception: what about lying to mislead a mugger?
Rule U: Okay. We'll modify **Rule 1a** to read, *'Never lie unless for politeness, or to mislead a mugger'*. We'll call this **Rule 1a/b.**
Act U: Exception: what about lying to help a friend in trouble?
Rule U: Okay. We'll modify **Rule 1a/b** to read, *'Never lie unless for politeness, or to mislead a mugger or to help a friend in trouble'*.

And so it goes on, and rule utilitarianism ends up with an enormously complicated set of rules, Rule 1a/b/c/d. . ./n, allowing for all the act utilitarian exceptions, until there is *no difference at all* between the two. In which case you might as well test *each act* via the principle of utility as test a *highly complex set of rules* that boils down to the *same thing*. But this is to give up rule utilitarianism to become an act utilitarian.

d) The problem that *rule utilitarianism permits injustice* – To see this, have a look at the following example:

Assume we have two completely independent communities, each with a total population of 110. Each community has two classes of people, class A with ten individuals, and class B with 100. Assume also, that we can measure happiness in units ranging from 1 (poor and minimally happy) to 10 (extremely well off and happy) In the first community, under Rule Code 'Alpha', the minority class A are the poorest and have only 1 happiness unit each, making a total of 10 units. But the majority class B are extremely well off and have 10 units of happiness each, making a total of 1,000 units. The *grand total* for the whole of this first community is therefore **1,010** units.

Things are very different in the second community, for here, under Rule Code 'Beta', the minority class A have 8 units each, making a total of 80 units of happiness. But the majority class B are only slightly better off, with 9 units each, making a total of 900 units. So the *grand total* for the whole of this second community is **980** units. The problem for rule utilitarianism is that it would judge the first community, with Rule Code 'Alpha', to be the morally better community, because it produces the greatest amount of total happiness, outperforming the Rule Code 'Beta' community by 1010 to 980 units. But this seems highly unfair and unjust, because the goods in the Rule Code 'Alpha' community are not equitably distributed. The discrepancies between rich and poor are enormous and unwarranted. Most of us would morally approve of Code 'Beta' rather than Code 'Alpha' despite its having *less* overall utility, simply because the minority under Code 'Beta' is not unfairly discriminated against. It gets its fair share of the cake. Rule utilitarianism is therefore at fault for approving this sort of injustice.

3 Mill's rejection of the hedonic calculus

Explanation
Mill's first two changes to Bentham's version of utilitarianism led naturally to his rejecting the hedonic calculus because:

a) rule utilitarianism avoids the need to calculate the consequences of every action, so the hedonic calculus becomes redundant
b) introducing differences in *quality* between higher and lower pleasures makes them virtually impossible to calculate and compare with each other so there was no point trying.

Critical assessment
A plus point is that the hedonic calculus was unworkable anyway, so getting rid of it was no great loss. However, there's a drawback because this undermines utilitarianism's scientific aspirations. One of its selling points was its supposed down-to-earth approach to morality. But what becomes of this if happiness is no longer measurable? A knock-on effect is that Mill must place more reliance on people's subjective feelings regarding the likely outcomes of their actions. But this makes doing the right thing a lot more miss than hit, which is not good news for a normative theory whose job is to tell you how to hit and not miss.

4 Mill's 'proof' of the principle of utility

Explanation
The final difference between Bentham and Mill is that Mill thought he could prove that the principle of utility was true, whereas Bentham thought it was

mere common sense, and anyone who couldn't see this could be knocked into shape with the four sanctions. While not rejecting the sanctions, as being effective against most thugs, Mill wants to bolster them with not just mere common-sense intuition, but a rational argument which might persuade all reasonable non-thugs to become utilitarians. It's a bit difficult to follow, so here's a step-by-step reconstruction of Mill's argument (see chapter 4 of Mill's *Utilitarianism*):

> Premise 1: Each person desires his/her own happiness.
> Premise 2: If seeing something means it's *visible*, and hearing something means it's *audible*, then desiring something means it's *desirable*.
> Premise 3: Therefore each person's happiness is desirable.
> Premise 4: Whatever is *desirable is good*, so each person's happiness is good.
> Premise 5: But since the general happiness (i.e. the happiness of every-one) is made up of (is composed of) the individual happiness of each of its members, *the general happiness itself must be desirable because the bits that make it up are desirable.*
> Premise 6: So the general happiness is good because it's desirable.
> Premise 7: Everyone ought to promote what is good.
> Premise 8: So everyone ought to act so as to promote the general happiness.
> Premise 9: The principle of utility says that everyone ought to promote the general happiness (i.e. the greatest happiness of the greatest number).
> Conclusion: Therefore, everyone ought to obey the principle of utility.

Critical assessment

Mill's 'proof' does not work because of *two logical errors* made in the course of his argument. These are:

a) the fallacy of *equivocation*
b) the fallacy of *composition*.

a) The fallacy of *equivocation* – 'Equivocation' means using the same word in two different senses. Any argument that equivocates on any of its words is invalid, i.e. its conclusion will not follow from its premises. For example:

> Premise 1: Pigs can be kept in a *pen*.
> Premise 2: I have a *pen* in my pocket.
> Conclusion: Therefore, pigs can be kept in the *pen* in my pocket.

As you can see, equivocation on the word 'pen' makes this argument ludi-crous and invalid. Likewise, Mill's argument is invalid because it equivocates on the word 'desirable'. This isn't as easy to spot as the 'pen' example, but it's there all the same.

The problem is that, although 'visible' and 'audible' mean '*capable* of being seen, or heard', the word 'desirable' not only means '*capable* of being desired' but also has the *extra* meaning of '*ought* to be desired', and it's this extra meaning that Mill needs to make his argument work. The trouble is, the *fact* that people *actually do* desire something (that it's *capable* of being desired) does not prove that they *ought* to desire it, i.e. that it is a *good* thing that they desire it. This kind of equivocation is also known as *the naturalistic fallacy* because it illegitimately jumps from *natural facts* to *moral values*. For example, the *fact* that someone happens to desire to torture children (i.e. it's desirable in the sense that they are *capable* of desiring this) does not mean that this is desirable in the *moral* sense of its being what they *ought* to desire, or what it is *good* to desire. Mill makes this mistake in the move from premise 2 to premise 4. In premise 2 'desirable' is used in its *factual* sense of being *capable* of being desired, but in premise 4 it is used in the *evaluative* sense of *ought* to be desired, or *good* to be desired.

Another example of this sort of logical error might help to make things a little clearer. The word 'kissable' is very like 'desirable' in this respect, so here is the same fallacy of equivocation in action in the following argument:

> Premise 1: If something *can* be seen, this means it's visible, so if something *can* be kissed, this means it's *kissable*.
> Premise 2: The thin, wrinkled lips of this ugly, toothless old hag *can* easily be kissed (because I'm sitting next to her).
> Conclusion: Therefore, she must have very *kissable* lips.

'Kissable' has two different meanings:

1 *can* be kissed
2 *good* to kiss.

From the *fact* that someone's lips *can* be kissed, it doesn't follow that they are *good* to kiss. Such a move is invalid because equivocal. Mill's 'proof' collapses because of this mistake alone, but we can see how he commits yet another logical error in the next section.

b) The fallacy of *composition* – The fallacy of *composition* is the mistake of arguing from the fact that, if all the *parts* that make up or *compose* a thing have a certain property, then the thing itself (as a *whole*) must have this very same property, since it's composed of nothing but parts that have it.

Here are a few examples of this fallacy in action:

1 Just because *each part* of a jigsaw fits in to other parts does not entitle one to conclude that the *whole* jigsaw must fit in somewhere.
2 Just because *each* footballer on a team is good does not mean the team as a *whole* is good. Individually they may be brilliant, but as a team they may not gel well.
3 Just because *each part* of a machine weighs less than a pound does not mean the machine as a *whole* must weigh less than a pound.

Now to apply this to Mill's 'proof'. Just because each *part* (individual) of society finds it good to desire his or her own happiness, this does not mean that *society* as a *whole*, i.e. the total number of individuals that *compose* it, must find it good to desire the happiness of society itself. Mill makes this invalid move from premise 3 to premise 5 (see p. 31). If it won't work for jigsaws it won't work for societal 'jigsaws'.

So Mill's 'proof' fails twice over, which means it's not a proof at all.

The various problems with Mill's position led to the abandonment of hedonism and the search for a more viable formulation of utilitarianism, resulting in *preference* utilitarianism, one of the most popular versions of the theory today.

Preference utilitarianism

The most influential preference utilitarian around today is the Australian philosopher Peter Singer (b 1946), currently professor of bioethics at Princeton University. In this form of utilitarianism you act so as to satisfy the greatest number of *preferences* of the greatest number of people. Instead of calculating *amounts* of happiness and pain that may result from your action, instead of trying to distinguish between higher and lower pleasures, both seemingly impossible tasks, all you have to do is find out what most people would *prefer* to happen and then do it. *Happiness* is still the name of the game, but now it consists in satisfying people's preferences, whether these are for pleasure or *other* values, such as knowledge, beauty, and freedom, which side-steps the awkward hedonistic insistence that people only prefer pleasure.

Let's think critically about preference utilitarianism, beginning with its advantages:

1 It gets round the problem of calculating pleasure/happiness. It's far easier to count hands or simply ask people what they'd prefer and note their replies.

2 Since the best judge of what will make me happy is *me*, and likewise for everyone else, preference utilitarianism is more likely to get things right than its rivals in the utilitarian camp who try to make judgements *on behalf* of others rather than listening to *them*.

3 It encourages people to speak up for themselves and to make known what they want/prefer. By so doing it acknowledges the value of letting people choose for themselves. Thus it is very *democratic*.

However, preference utilitarianism also comes with its own problems:

1 You don't always know what people affected by your actions would prefer, because most of the time it's not feasible to ask them or take a vote. So to some extent you're acting in the dark.

2 It's unclear whether you should take account of what they *actually* prefer or what they *would* prefer if they knew all the facts, e.g. people may have risky preferences for fatty foods, binge drinking, smoking, and unprotected sex. If you meet their *actual* preferences, i.e. give them what they want, this will lead to long-term unhappiness, and in trying to do good you'll end up doing bad.

3 On the other hand, if you give them what they *ought* to prefer if they were wiser, then
   i) you make them *unhappy* **now**
   ii) you *patronize* them by making their choices for them because 'you know best'. This undermines advantage 2 above because you no longer respect their autonomy.

4 Many people aren't in a position to express a preference, e.g. babies and people on life-support machines; what do you do then?

5 What if most people in your society *prefer* exploiting blacks and/or women? Preference utilitarianism would seem to pander to them.

We've seen that no version of utilitarianism is satisfactory in delivering a viable principle of morality, which both squares with our basic intuitions and helps us live well. Perhaps, then, it's time to turn to deontological moral theories, and see if they can do any better.

2   Deontological Theories

Deontological theories can be described as duty-based; 'deon' comes from the Greek word for 'duty'. They concentrate on the *nature of the action itself* as well as its *motive* in order to determine whether it is right or wrong. Unlike the situation with utilitarianism, **consequences don't count** in deciding how to act morally; it's the *rules* that tell you what motive to act from and what action you ought to do, i.e. what your moral *duty* is.

In this section we'll cover two deontological theories, namely:

- the moral theory of Immanuel Kant
- divine command theory.

Kant's moral theory

Immanuel Kant (1724–1804) was born in Konigsberg in East Prussia (now Kaliningrad in Russia). He never married, and all his life never ventured more than 40 or so miles out of town. He was the son of pious, hard-working parents – his father was a saddler. Kant was an academic all his life, getting various tutoring jobs on graduating, and eventually winding up at the age of forty-five as professor of logic and metaphysics at Konigsberg University. His rigid daily routine has become legendary. It's been said that his daily walks were so precisely timed that the housewives of Konigsberg could set their clocks according to when Kant passed their windows. If he passed at 2 p.m. and your clock said 1 minute past, your clock must be wrong, not Kant. No disruption to this orderliness could be tolerated. For example, Kant always ate breakfast alone, but one day, when an unexpected caller came in, he couldn't manage to finish his tea and toast while the man was there, and had to ask him to leave until he'd done. This rigidity in his behaviour reflects the inflexibility of Kant's categorical imperative and his treacle prose style. However, if you only knew Kant as a walker and a writer you'd get a misleading picture, for by all accounts he was a witty conversationalist and a brilliant lecturer, and threw great parties. And what he lacked in physical adventurousness he more than made up for when it came to the academic kind. In philosophy in general, not just in ethics, he was revolutionary, and is commonly regarded as one of the all time greats.

Key ethical work: *Groundwork for the Metaphysics of Morals* (1783)

Kant's moral theory is by far the most *philosophically* influential theory of the two, so it will receive most space here. It is about as un-utilitarian as you can get.

The categorical imperative

The categorical imperative is Kant's fundamental principle of morality. It acts as the criterion or standard for judging which actions are right and which are wrong. It does the same job for him as the principle of utility does for the utilitarians, but does it very differently, for instead of testing an action by looking at its consequences, it looks at its rationality, its consistency.

The categorical imperative distinguishes between right and wrong actions by **universalizing** the action's **maxim** and seeing if this can be done *consistently*, i.e. without self-contradiction (maxims are the everyday reasons or principles that lie behind our actions and motivate them, e.g. 'when in danger, run'; 'finders keepers'; 'never give a sucker an even break').

If the maxim can be universalized without self-contradiction, then the maxim and its action pass the categorical imperative test and it is therefore morally right. This means that it's *morally permissible* for *everyone* at *all times, no exceptions allowed*. If it can't be universalized then it's wrong, and *all are duty-bound never to do it, not even if the consequences look good*.

A more concrete image may help us to understand the job the categorical imperative has to do. Let's look at this from a maxim's point of view. Imagine a nightclub called 'The Cats & Imps'. This is a moral club and it's the hottest spot in town. Lots of our maxims want to get in there and be seen as moral because, once in, they beat all other non-moral maxims (the ones stuck outside). What this means is that moral maxims, on account of their higher status, override or trump all non-moral maxims when they clash with them. However, there's just one problem. You have to get past the bouncer on the door. He's the **categorical imperative**, and he'll put just one question to each of the throng of maxims pushing to get in, namely, '*Are you universalizable?*' If they can prove they are, then they're in and can become moral duties. But if they fail the test, then they get thrown out as immoral and must not be acted upon.

So, how do you go about universalizing a maxim? Well, all you have to do is ask yourself, 'What if *everybody* did that?' In other words, you have to imagine if it's possible for people *universally* to do what you're proposing to do. If it turns out to be impossible, then this tells you that the action is wrong, and if it is possible, then it's right. Kant's thought is that, if it's right for you, then it must be right for anybody else, and if it's wrong for you, it's wrong for everyone.

The categorical imperative is a *universalizability* test; actions that pass the test become moral laws, and those that fail are morally taboo. No one is allowed to make an exception of themselves or give themselves preferential treatment. This is why it is called '*categorical*', because there are no 'ifs' or 'buts', and no get-out clauses from your moral duty. You *must* do the right thing; it is *imperative*, that is, commanded by the moral law.

Kant uses two main formulations of the *one* categorical imperative:

1 the *formula of universal law*, which states,
 '**Act only on those maxims which you can will to be universal laws.**'
2 the *formula of ends*, which states,
 '**Always treat other persons as ends in themselves and never only as means.**'

Let's look at an example of the categorical imperative in action. Kant himself gives the following illustration:

Suppose I want to borrow some money and I know that I can't pay it back, but I also know that the only way to get it is to promise falsely to pay it back. Ought I to do this? Is it right? Well, we have to use the categorical imperative to test the maxim that lies behind the proposed action. The maxim would be something like: '*Whenever I need money I'll borrow it on the basis of a false promise to pay it back, even though I never will.*' To apply the categorical imperative test you have to universalize this maxim by asking yourself the following question: '**Can I *consistently* will that *everyone* borrow money on false promises when they need it?**' Kant argues that this maxim fails the test because it can't be universalized without self-contradiction, which makes it not only **immoral**, but also **irrational**, ever to do it. It is self-contradictory because false promises must presuppose a context of general or *universal* reliance on true promises in order to work at all, i.e. in order to succeed at deceiving. But imagining or willing a world where *everyone* borrowed money on false promises would pull the rug out from under your own feet for, in a world like this, no one would believe you when you promised to pay the money back, and therefore wouldn't lend it to you in the first place. So it is irrational because, in making the false promise, you *want* to be believed (that's the whole point), but in applying the universalizability test, you *will a world* where *you won't be believed*, and it is *self-contradictory* to will incompatible things at the same time. *In effect, you end up wanting your promise* **both to succeed and to fail**, *and that can't happen because, like a square circle, it's* **logically impossible.**

The categorical imperative imposes various kinds of moral duties on us. Kant distinguishes between:

1 **perfect and imperfect duties**
2 **duties to self and duties to others.**

When combined, these generate *four* kinds of duties:

i)   perfect duties to self
ii)   perfect duties to others
iii) imperfect duties to self
iv)   imperfect duties to others.

The difference between self and others being obvious, we'll examine more closely the perfect/imperfect duty distinction.

The difference between perfect and imperfect duties is that perfect duties allow no leeway at all as to whether or not they should be done on any particular occasion. They are *absolute and without exception at all times*. Disobeying them leads to a contradiction in **conception/nature**, that is to say, a strict logical impossibility (akin to the impossibility of having a married bachelor). It is this that justifies their stringency. Imperfect duties, on the other hand, do give you some room for manoeuvre in choosing how and when to obey them. But if you disobey them once too often, this will result in a contradiction in **will**, i.e. not an absolute conceptual or theoretical contradiction, but the slightly softer *practical* contradiction in terms of denying yourself what you might need as a *human being*, rather than as *abstract logical mind*.

Kant gives four examples, one for each of the four types of duty, illustrating how the two kinds of contradiction (in *conception/nature*, and in *will*) generate perfect and imperfect duties.

1 *Perfect duty to self*
   Kant's example: **Never commit suicide.**
2 *Perfect duty to others*
   Kant's example: **Always tell the truth.**
3 *Imperfect duty to self*
   Kant's example: **Always improve your talents.**
4 *Imperfect duty to others*
   Kant's example: **Always help others in need.**

Let's consider each of these examples.

1 – 'Never commit suicide' is a perfect duty to our*selves* because this would involve reason killing itself: a rational being, reasoning that its reasoning must stop. The self-love that is supposed to promote the continuance of rational life is being used for its exact opposite, and it's impossible to imagine a world in which this can happen. It's important to understand that Kant is *not* arguing that you shouldn't commit suicide because of the terrible *unhappy consequences* if everybody did this. He is saying that it is strictly irrational, a contradiction in conception, it being impossible to imagine reason using reasons to not reason any more. Therefore, it is *everyone's* moral duty to *themselves* **never** to commit suicide, with *no exceptions*, no matter how terrible your life is.

2 – 'Always tell the truth' is a perfect duty to *others* because every lie necessarily presupposes a social context of general truth-telling. It's the soil lies need in which to flourish, in order to succeed in deceiving. Universalizing your maxim to lie, so that everyone would do this, completely pulls the rug out from under your own lie because it would take away the only conditions in which your lie would work. The lie **logically requires** truth-telling in general in the same way that counterfeiters require genuine currency in order to copy it. But *universalization* removes the logical underpinning and so the lie is self-defeating. Rationally speaking, it self-destructs. Therefore, **no one should ever lie no matter what**: it's irrational and immoral.

3 – 'Always improve your talents' is an imperfect duty because, although it is not a contradiction in conception/nature – the reason being that it's easy consistently to imagine a world where everybody lets their talents rot, being too busy sunbathing, sleeping, getting drunk, being couch potatoes, and so on. This is a *logical* possibility because universalizing your maxim not to bother improving yourself (let my talents rot) is not explicitly self-contradictory. Letting your talents rot does not require that others do not let theirs rot. The whole world could decide to go to seed, chill out, and switch off. But, according to Kant, it does generate a contradiction in **will** because, despite the fact that **reason** allows a world of talentless good-for-nothings, our **human nature** with all its needs can't allow it. Why can't it allow a universal neglect of people's talents? Because each of us wills/needs a whole host of things for survival, safety, comfort, and our well-being in general, and these needs can only be supplied by other people who have improved their talents in various ways – e.g. doctors, plumbers, electricians, farmers, teachers, lawyers, pilots, musicians, playwrights, architects, etc. Kant argues that, although a world without any of these is certainly a theoretical possibility – i.e. it is not a self-contradictory concept like a square circle – no rational *being* could possibly **will** for this to happen in the light of its effects on them as a **person** who **needs** these things.

Someone who knows they need x but deliberately denies themselves x is irrational in this sense. So improving one's talents is an imperfect duty to oneself, and this permits us some room to 'manage' this duty.

For example, although we are under a moral obligation to improve our talents, we can pick and choose which ones to cultivate, for how long, and to what degree. Let's say my talents are in music, cooking, football, and maths; I can't have an obligation *always* to be improving *all* of them *all* the time – I'd have a heart attack or a nervous breakdown. So I can either try to improve them all gradually, allocating various times of day to them, or I can concentrate on one or two and let the others wither. But as long as I'm doing *something (enough)* towards self-improvement, then I have obeyed this moral imperative. **Only people who do nothing, or not nearly enough, to improve themselves are being immoral.**

4 – 'Always help others in need' is an imperfect duty to others for the same reason 'improve your talents' was an imperfect duty to yourself. It's perfectly possible for a world to exist in which no one helped anyone else; it's easily imaginable, so it's not a contradiction in conception/nature. Granted it's not a pretty sight and would cause great unhappiness, but this is not Kant's point; this is not what would make it immoral.

However, yet again, **willing** such a world (by universalizing our maxim not to help others) would be a contradiction in **will**, given our *human nature*, because we know that there will be times when we are in trouble and need help. Human beings are liable to fall ill, have accidents, and go through hard times, but it surely **can't be rational** that, despite knowing we are likely to need help, we nevertheless **will** a world where our needs will not be met because nobody will help anyone else, including us. So while it is a duty, an imperfect duty, to help others in need, this can't be performed *all* the time towards *all* people in need with *all* our resources. This would be *physically impossible*, and therefore couldn't count as an absolute duty, for it's irrational to be given obligations which are impossible to perform through no fault of your own. 'Ought' implies 'can'. This means we have a certain amount of leeway to choose who to help and how much help to give, and as long as we do *something (enough)* towards helping others we will have fulfilled this duty – e.g. we could give to charity, but which charities and how much to give is left up to us. We could instead do voluntary work or raise funds for cancer research, and so on. There are lots of ways to help others. Only someone who does nothing, or not nearly enough, is disobeying this type of categorical imperative, i.e. is disobeying this imperfect duty. They are being irrational because they are willing a world in which future needs of theirs will not be met, where there will be situations when **they want help but don't want it**, as a result of their *universalized maxim* that no one should help anyone else, *including themselves*.

Morality and rationality

The source of the categorical imperative is in **objective reason**, which demands consistency, universality, and necessity. For example, in the same way that *everyone* **must** believe that 2 + 2 = 4, so *everyone* **must** (ought) *always* to keep their promises. For Kant, moral rules, i.e. those maxims and actions that pass the categorical imperative test, are unbreakable. They are as objectively rational, and as universally necessary, as geometry and arithmetic. Breaking a promise is as self-contradictory as saying that sometimes 2 + 2 = 5, or that triangles sometimes have four sides.

Morality and autonomy (freedom)

It is important to recognize that the moral authority of the categorical imperative does not come from God, or from the law of the land, or from social custom, or from parliament, nor is it written into the nature of the world like the law of gravity; rather it issues from **our very own reason**. This is what Kant means by autonomy. True freedom means not lawlessness but giving oneself one's own moral laws and abiding by them. Rejecting the moral law, far from being the gateway to freedom, is instead the road to a kind of bondage of the will to laws given by another, which Kant calls heteronomy. Giving in to an immoral desire or instinct is to lose one's proper freedom and dignity, and to become a slave to the craving. In contrast to this, we **freely** impose the moral law on ourselves yet at the same time see its *necessity*. No one forces us. The categorical imperative is like maths. Maths is true, not because the teacher says so, or the law, or God, but because **reason** says so. Triangles have just **got** to have three sides; 2 + 5 has just **got** to equal 7; **we** just see it **can't** be any other way. Likewise, we freely impose rational moral duties such as truth-telling and promise-keeping on ourselves. Morality can't be any other way.

Categorical imperatives versus hypothetical imperatives

Hypothetical imperatives are maxims that express desires/wants/needs in terms of a means–end relationship. For example, 'If you want x, then do y.' The bit after the 'if' is the hypothetical part relating to a want; the 'do' is the imperative bit, and 'y' is the means to 'x' (the end in view). Here are a few examples with x and y filled in with some content.

- If you want a pizza, then try Luigi's.
- If you need a wash, then use the shower.
- If you'd like some sweets, then just ask.

These are hypothetical because they *depend* on your *wanting* the end. Hypothetical imperatives can be side-stepped if you change your mind about what you want, so they last only as long as your desire or need. Their sheer contingency and variable nature means that these can *never* be moral imperatives. They can't be categorical, universal, and necessary, because people's desires are different and constantly change, so what is appropriate for one person (because they happen to like pizza) is not appropriate for others. Kant argues that you can't base ethics on hypothetical imperatives because, if you did, people could always get out of doing their moral duty by simply changing their mind. Take, for example: 'If you want a good reputation, then tell the truth.' This hypothetical imperative is no good as a moral principle. What would you say to someone who replies that they don't have to tell the truth because they don't care about their reputation, or that they've found a way of lying and still maintaining a good reputation? They can wriggle out of their duty to tell the truth in this case because it is **conditional** on their **desiring** a good reputation, and once they cease to desire the end, i.e. the reputation, then they no longer need to desire the means, i.e. the truth.

Because the categorical imperative embodies our *moral duty*, whereas hypothetical imperatives express our *desires* and how to achieve them, any clash between the two is a case of *duty* versus *desire*. Kant knows that self-interested desires often tempt us to neglect our moral duty. What we **want** to do is often at odds with what we know we **ought** to do, but **duty should always triumph over desire, because the categorical imperative is a stronger principle than any hypothetical imperative**, being universal and necessary rather than piecemeal and contingent. Iron moral law is more authoritative than wishy-washy hypothetical imperatives that come and go with our changing states of mind. It *should* always triumph, but very often it doesn't. My desire for the money may be stronger than my strength of will to do my duty and keep my promise to repay it, and I end up doing wrong by falsely promising to pay it back.

The good will

According to Kant, the *only thing good in itself* is the *good will*. All other things, if they are good, are only *instrumentally* good and may turn out to be *bad* in some circumstances, e.g. happiness, money, talents, beauty, intelligence. These can all be used for bad purposes: happy torturers are worse than miserable ones, intelligence in a criminal makes him even more dangerous, and so on. So, what's so good about the good will? The reason is that the good will is *always* good *no matter what*, because it *only ever acts from* **one motive** and this is **RESPECT FOR DUTY**. It does the right thing simply because it is right, full stop. *Duty for duty's sake.*

This is the *only* motive that has *moral* worth.

For one's truth-telling to count as *moral* one must not only tell the truth, but also do so because telling the truth is the *right thing* to do. You do it because it is your moral duty, and not for any ulterior motive or hidden agendas. Another way of describing a person with a good will is to say that they are *conscientious*, or that they *act on principle*. However, it *is* possible to act *according to* or *in line with* the categorical imperative and yet *not* have moral worth because your motive is not right.

Take, for example, Kant's illustration of two shopkeepers, both honest as the day is long. Each welcomes customers; everything is properly priced; neither of them sells bruised fruit or mouldy cabbages or fiddles people's change. Yet one is honest because it's *good for business*, or because he *loves* his customers, or simply because he *enjoys* it. However, *none* of these are *moral* motives because none need involve being honest because it is *right*. This shopkeeper is acting *in accordance with* the categorical imperative – which, after all, requires us to be dutifully honest, and he is honest – but he is not acting morally or dutifully in the strict Kantian sense since he's not being honest *because of* the categorical imperative.

The other shopkeeper may feel none of these emotions – no love, no joy, no sympathy – yet he is the *truly moral* shopkeeper so long as his motive is to be honest because that is his *moral duty*. The big difference is in the *motive*. To all outward appearances both shopkeepers are the same, but nevertheless there is a real moral difference between them, which would become visible if things changed and honesty was no longer so good for business. The formerly 'honest' shopkeeper would become dishonest because his reason or motive for being honest has disappeared. That's why 'Honesty is the best policy' is not a Kantian sentiment; it harbours a hypothetical imperative of self-interest. The truly honest shopkeeper, on the other hand, will continue to be honest despite its being bad for business. Why? Because he has a *good will*. His honesty wasn't inspired by profit margin in the first place, but by *moral duty*, and this will never change. Up to this point we've been looking at the way the categorical imperative works in terms of its *first formulation of universal law*, but Kant employs a second formulation of the *very same* moral principle.

The second formulation of the categorical imperative

'Always treat other persons as ends in themselves and never only as means.'

The reason Kant bothers with this second formulation is that it empha-sizes the fact that *respect* for the categorical imperative or moral law or duty (these all come down to the same thing in the end) extends naturally to having *respect* for the *originators or source* of that moral law, ie. *rational* beings – *people*, in other words. The second formulation brings this out very clearly. Since one should do one's duty for its own sake and not for some further end in view – some hidden purpose which you *use* morality to get to – so you ought *never* to *use* people merely for your own purposes. That's why they are *ends in themselves*, not *means* or *instruments* or *tools* to be manipulated by others, because this reduces them to the status of a *thing*. So Kant is strong on human *rights*, human *dignity*, and *justice*, since all *equally* are *rational agents* and deserve on this basis to be treated with *respect*. So, for Kant, sacrificing human beings for the sake of an increase, even a significant increase, in the general happiness is completely out of the question, because it is *expressly* forbidden by the categorical imperative and its *second* formula-tion, the *formula of ends*. This would also rule out things such as slavery, exploitation, rape, lying, bullying, killing people who get in your way, killing the innocent, torture, or any abuse of human rights for the sake of a happier society.

As long as you treat people as ends in themselves, i.e. with respect and dig-nity, it's also okay to treat them as means to your own ends, provided they freely consent to this. For example, when you go to a restaurant you treat the waiter as a means for getting your meal, but as he *voluntarily* does this, because of a *contract* he has *freely* entered into with the owner of the restaurant to be paid for his work as a waiter, what you do *respects* his *freedom* or *auton-omy* as a *rational agent*, and does not involve using him as a mere instrument.

Comparing Kantian ethics with rule utilitarianism

One difference is that, although both theories use rules or principles to deter-mine what is moral, they differ in how these rules are *justified*. As far as rule utilitarianism is concerned, the rules are justified by their *consequences*. The rule is only moral because obeying it brings happier results, and disobeying it brings painful results overall and in the long term. But the rules or maxims that obey the categorical imperative don't depend on consequences at all. Instead, they're justified by their *consistency*, i.e. by their *rationality*. To dis-obey is to *contradict yourself*. Even if obeying a categorical imperative leads to a lot of general unhappiness, it still must be obeyed because reason and the moral law demands it – no exceptions.

Secondly, under rule utilitarianism there'd be no point obeying a rule if you were the only one doing so, because it's the effect of the rule-as-widely-accepted-in-society that is tested against the principle of utility. In contrast to this, any maxim that satisfies the categorical imperative test, thereby becoming a moral rule, must be obeyed, even if you're the only one in the whole world who pays it any mind. If it's rational it's right, even if no one else can see it.

Thirdly, the moral rules in rule utilitarianism depend for their validity on the contingent desires and needs generated by the vagaries of human psychology. If human nature or cultural opinions changed, then the rules would have to change to fit in with our new desires. Kant will have none of this. The demands of the categorical imperative and the rules that satisfy it can as little change as those of geometry and mathematics. These are not subject to human desires, or changing cultural fashion, for they are based on objective reason; that's why Kant says they are a priori, i.e. prior to or independent of changeable, contingent experience. That's what makes the moral rules absolutely necessary, brooking no exceptions.

Fourthly, speaking of exceptions, rule utilitarians sometimes mention a get-out clause attached to their rules. You don't have to obey them if, on any occasion, obeying them leads to a personal or social disaster, whereas Kant insists that you tell the truth even if it kills you.

Assessing Kant's theory

Kant has always had a strong following because of the advantages his theory brings. For example, it explains and justifies many of our ordinary moral thought processes, such as our tendency, when confronted by wrongdoing, to challenge the culprit by asking, 'What if *everybody* did that?' This common response is captured admirably by the universalizability test. Kant's doctrine of the good will also explains our intuitive belief that, when it comes to evaluating an action's moral worth, 'It's the *thought* that counts.' And our *experience* of the tug of war between *duty* and *desire* is accounted for by the clash between categorical and hypothetical imperatives.

In addition, Kant is strong on human *rights* and human *dignity*. He refuses point blank to sacrifice the rights of any individual for the sake of the happiness of society. Kant's uncompromising attitude to *justice* strikes a chord deep within us because, for him, justice is not negotiable, and he won't bend the rules of fair play to get a happy result. Again, Kant's *egalitarianism* shines through in his insistence that *all* are *equal* before the moral law, which does not depend on God but on universal *reason*, making morality *objective* and *not open to relativism*. If Kant succeeds, then we can *prove* which actions are right and which wrong.

The categorical imperative works very well against many examples of free-loading behaviour in which individuals exploit the honesty of others, e.g. queue-jumping, cheating, tax fiddles, not paying bus fares, and so on. For example, say your maxim is: 'When there's a queue I'll try to jump it so I don't have to wait my turn.' If you test this rule by universalizing it, you will find that, since everybody would be doing it, there would be no queues in existence to jump. If queue-jumping is right for you, it must be right for everybody, and therefore doable by everybody, and since this is not doable by everybody, it can't be right for everybody, and therefore not right for you in the first place. And, finally, the categorical imperative also picks out some universally recognized moral duties such as truth-telling, promise-keeping, respect for others, not stealing, not killing the innocent, and so on.

Let's now turn to the ways in which Kant's theory can be criticized.

1 – *Good maxims* can fail the test and become immoral, for example:

- 'Give more than average to charity.'
- 'Always let others go out of the door first.'
- 'Love your enemies.'
- 'Come first in exams.'

None of these are universalizable, and so are condemned as immoral, yet they all seem admirable. Not everyone can come first in exams at the same time; if everyone loved their enemies there'd be no enemies to love; if everyone tries to let others out of the door first no one would ever leave a room; and it would be impossible for everyone to give *more* than average to charity, because the average has *by definition* people *below* it as well as above.

2 – *Clashes between duties* can't be resolved by the categorical imperative – e.g. promising not to tell your friend's secret, and then being asked about it on oath to tell the truth in a court of law. It's impossible to fulfil both duties, and the categorical imperative can't tell you what to do because it's telling you to do *both*. This is irrational, because no one can have a duty to do the impossible. What's happened here is that two maxims, truth-telling and promise-keeping, having been okayed by the bouncer (the categorical imperative), have got into 'The Cats & Imps' moral nightclub, and are having a fight at the bar. Kant's problem is that he doesn't have a bouncer on the inside, because he thinks any maxim that gets past the categorical imperative on the door must be rationally consistent with all other maxims that get through, and therefore can't contradict (fight with) each other. The fact that they can

shows that the categorical imperative is insufficient to do all the moral work on its own. Kant needs a back-up principle, but he doesn't have one.

3 – *Hyper-specific maxims* can get past the categorical imperative. How about this for a maxim? 'When you've got fair hair, your name is Alex, your birthday is 23/12/91, and you own two love birds . . . (ad infinitum), it's okay to break your promises.' These maxims can be made so specific that they could only apply to one unique individual, so when they're universalized they'll always pass the categorical imperative test because they'll *still only apply to you*. But this makes a mockery of morality.

I think Kant can get round this objection by insisting that maxims should only contain considerations which are motivationally relevant. Including utterly irrelevant stuff such as hair colour as part of your *reason* for breaking promises exploits a loophole in Kant's *presentation* of his theory because he didn't think to exclude these things. But this loophole can easily be closed by explicitly confining the content of maxims to one's *willed intentions*. Past facts such as hair colour and date of birth are neither subject to one's *will* nor relevant to one's *intentions*.

4 – *Fanatical maxims* are universalizable precisely because of the fanatic's consistency, so they are also approved by the categorical imperative. A consistent and fanatical Nazi could have as his maxim 'To Kill every Jew I meet', and could *consistently* will this as a universal law. Firstly, it's not a contradiction in conception, because such a world is easily imaginable. Secondly, in the fanatic's case, it's not even a contradiction in will because, even if it transpired that the Nazi himself was a Jew, being a fanatic, he could consistently will that he should die like all the other Jews. But, since most of us think that genocide is badly wrong, the categorical imperative must be an inadequate test of morality for allowing it.

5 – *Trivial etiquette maxims* form a kind of categorical imperative and so may be seen as moral duties, which is ridiculous. 'Always wear a black tie to official dinners' is a universalizable maxim, yet it's hardly a *moral* duty.

6 – The categorical imperative is *too rigid and strict*. Kant allows no exceptions whatsoever, and even if a would-be murderer asks you where his intended victim is hiding, Kant says it's your moral duty to tell him the truth because no one must ever lie under any circumstances, even to save a life. Since *you're* not the one doing the murder it's not *your* fault since you did the *right* thing. So that's okay then. *No one agrees with Kant here.*

Yet it seems that, with a simple modification, Kant's *theory* has the resources to meet this objection, for why can't one's maxim be 'Always tell the truth *except* when doing so helps murderers kill'? This is easily universalizable, but Kant *himself* couldn't stomach even this exception to the absolutely rigid rule *never* to lie. His *theory* can bend a little, but *Kant* couldn't.

7 – Seemingly *good moral motives* become *morally irrelevant* in Kant's theory because the *only moral motive* is **duty for duty's sake** or, in other words, **respect** for the categorical imperative. But this means that, if someone acts simply out of natural *sympathy* for others, or from *love*, or from *pity*, or just because they *enjoy* being generous, their actions have *no moral worth* because they weren't done simply out of duty. Ask yourself this: which do you find more praiseworthy, the person who has no pity for starving children, but who nevertheless grudgingly gives money to Oxfam because it's their moral duty, or the person who, from a spontaneous feeling of sympathy, gladly gives money to Oxfam without even thinking of things such as duty? If you prefer the second person, then you'll see the force of this criticism.

8 – Non-rational people are *denied respect and human rights*. It follows from the second formulation of the categorical imperative that *we are not morally obliged to treat these unfortunate people* (e.g. Alzheimer's sufferers and brain-damaged children) *with dignity and respect, as ends in themselves having basic human rights*, because these rights are based on the *subject's rational acceptance of the moral law*. Non-rational people such as these don't even know what day it is, never mind have moral awareness. But this goes clean against our basic moral intuitions about how to treat children and the mentally deficient.

These problems are sufficiently severe to warrant abandoning Kant's theory as *he* states it. Let's see whether the remaining deontological theory centring on God's will fares any better.

Divine command theory

According to divine command theory the difference between right and wrong depends on *God's will*, i.e. on what *God commands* should be done and forbids us to do. Morality doesn't depend on the consequences of our actions but on the *rules* God gives us for living good lives. These do not depend on our reason, or on intuition, but on God. So if you want to find out what your moral duty is, you have to find out what God's will is, and then obey it.

- 'x is right' means 'x is commanded by God'.
- 'y is wrong' means 'we are commanded by God *not* to do y'.

This is a deontological theory because *consequences don't count*. Only *actions* and *motives*, which figure in God's will for us, enshrined in sets of *rules*, need to be considered.

The most famous set of rules is the Ten Commandments, which contains such exhortations as: Don't steal; Don't kill; Respect your parents (see Exodus 20 for the rest).

Other rules are derived from the teachings of Jesus, e.g. Love your enemies; Forgive those who harm you; Help people in need.

Jesus was born around 6–4 BC and died around AD 28–30. He was the founder of one of the world's great religions, and is seen by Christians as no less than God incarnate and as Saviour of the world through his crucifixion, dying for the sins of mankind and thereby blazing a trail to heaven for all who have faith in him. According to this picture he was sent by God the Father, born of Mary and the Holy Spirit – the third person of the Trinity – and was himself the Son of God – the second person of the Trinity. He lived a sinless life, performed miracles, preached a message of universal love and forgiveness, died, rose again from the dead after three days, ascended to heaven forty days later, and is still there, waiting to return at the end of time. Many of his sayings, such as 'Love your neighbour as yourself', are seen as God's commands to us and thus help form the content of divine command theory.

However, by treating the gospels as *purely historical* sources, the following tentative sketch of a more secular Jesus emerges. Jesus of Nazareth was born naturally, to Mary and Joseph out of wedlock. His parents had other children after him. His father was a carpenter and Jesus grew up learning the trade. We know little about him until the last year or two of his life, when he downed tools and went on the road preaching a politically risky message of universal love. He taught that you didn't have to go through official channels involving the Jewish priesthood to get forgiveness from God. Instead you could ask God direct. This represented a serious threat to the livelihood and power base of the authorities responsible for the Temple sacrifices and interpreting religious law, because his teaching made them irrelevant. He also had the people on his side, being a charismatic preacher, and he reputedly possessed healing powers for which he made no charge. He was poor and his message was for the poor. Theirs was the kingdom of heaven. They who had nothing could have it all, and they had only to ask. As always, religion mixed with politics, and what was seen as a threat to the Temple hierarchy in Jerusalem was also seen as a threat to Roman law and order, since the Romans ruled Palestine through the local dignitaries at the Temple – the sadducees (priests), and the pharisees (lawyers) – the very people Jesus was undermining. They plotted to eliminate him, and got their chance when Jesus made a bad political mistake by causing a one-man riot in the Temple precinct – the very heart of government – at the most volatile and politically sensitive time of year, the Jewish Passover festival. Jerusalem was at its most dangerous, awash with Jewish pilgrims no doubt nursing anti-Roman hatred. Although Jesus was not interested in provoking a violent insurrection, the revolutionary potential of his actions and message was not lost on the Roman prefect Pontius Pilate and his puppet government of Temple priests. They moved quickly. Within a week of Jesus's Temple disturbance he had been betrayed, arrested, tried, and executed.

Assessment of divine command theory

Again, we'll consider the strengths of this theory first. If God's existence can be established, then:

1 This would be the most solid basis you could have for morality, for it would be as real as the universe since both came from God, and He's as real as you can get.
2 Ethical rules would apply to everyone at all times because God never changes His mind. We hanker after an absolute moral standard, and divine command theory gives us this.
3 You can *prove* what's right and wrong if you know God's will. Again, this is highly desirable when dealing with people such as Stalin.
4 No one gets away with doing wrong because God sees everything. If you include the after-life, this grants us a world of perfect justice.
5 We have a very strong motive to do good because of *inevitable* punishment for evil and *eternal bliss* for doing good. Heaven and, especially, hell concentrate the mind wonderfully.

Again, there are problems to be taken into account:

1 *God's existence is uncertain.* So this puts divine command theory in doubt, since it rests on God's will.
2 *Even if God exists, we still can't tell what his will is* because we can't tell which religion is true. God is supposed to reveal his commands in sacred scriptures, but if we can't tell whether the Bible or the Qur'an is the correct scripture, then how can we be expected to be moral when we don't know the moral rules?
3 Even if we were lucky enough to hit on the right religion and the right holy book, there are many different interpretations of what it says. So, if *people can't agree about the meaning of the moral rules* in say, the Bible, we are no further on in our quest for the foundation of morality. Divine command

theory will be problematic as a guide to morality if we're kept in the dark about what these commands are.

The fourth problem, *the Euthyphro dilemma*, requires a closer look. This is probably the most serious objection the divine command theory has to face. It gets its name from the title of a dialogue written by Plato, an ancient Greek philosopher who lived in the fourth century BC. Plato was the first to discover this problem. A dilemma is where you are faced with only two choices, each of which is out of the question, yet you have to choose one.

The Euthyphro dilemma goes as follows:

- 'Does God command things because they are good?' *or,*
- 'Are they good because God commands them?'

This may seem an insignificant difference, but it is of the greatest importance, generating the following four problems:

i)   the *U-turn problem*
ii) the *silly morals problem*
iii) the *horrible morals problem*
iv) the *trivial tautology problem.*

i) The *U-turn problem* arises if the divine command theorist chooses the first horn of the dilemma, for if God commands things **because** *they are good,* then this means they must have **already** been good **prior** to God commanding them, and therefore their goodness would have a *source* **independent of** *God's will.* So the divine command theorist can't choose this option, for it means doing a *U-turn* by *giving up his theory* and admitting that morality doesn't depend on God's will after all. That means the divine command theorist must choose the other option, i.e. that things/actions are *good* **simply because** *God commands* them. But now the remaining three problems have to be faced.

ii) The *problem of silly morals* stems from the simple observation that, if God can make anything good simply by commanding that it be so, then any whimsical or arbitrary divine decision might be the foundation of ethics. God could command *anything* He wanted to be good and it would be good by *definition.* For example, if God were to command you to sew buttons on your socks, it would be immoral not to do so. And if He forbade you to plant your roses in with your tulips, to do so would be a moral disgrace. This may seem fanciful, yet taking Christianity as representative it would appear God has actually issued similar commands. In Leviticus 19:19, God commands, 'Do not plant two kinds of seed in the same field', and in Deuteronomy 22:12, He says, 'Sew tassels on the four corners of your clothes.' No adequate moral theory can rest on such an absurd foundation. No doubt many Christians will object to such examples as being misconstrued, arguing that these commands were addressed only to the people of Israel a few thousand years ago and should not be interpreted as having any relevance for us today. However, two things may be said in reply. One is that this still does not remove the possibility that God could give us silly commands. The other is that no adequate criterion has yet been offered by Christianity to distinguish accurately between the commands we may ignore and the ones we must obey, which is why some Christians obey the old Jewish food laws and others don't; some are against homosexuality and others aren't; some think contraception is immoral and others don't; and on and on. This brings us back to the old problem of finding out just what God's commands are. It seems, as revelations go, the Bible is not very revealing.

iii) The *problem of horrible morals* follows directly from the silliness problem, for, among the crazy commands that God might give, there could well be some that are horrific. For example, if actions are *made* good because God commands them, then it seems to follow that, if God had commanded 'torturing children for laughs' as a moral duty, this would become a good thing to do. The same goes for rape, genocide, cruelty, ethnic cleansing, racism, sexism, slavery, and so on. Again, referring to the Bible as our source book for divine commands, we can see that God actually does include such things in His repertoire; for example, in 1 Samuel 15:3, God issues the following command to Saul, king of Israel: 'Go and attack the Amalekites and completely destroy everything they have. Don't leave a thing; kill all the men, women, children, and babies; the cattle, sheep, camels, and donkeys.' Not even the donkeys escape this God-inspired genocide. Christian divine command theorists may think the New Testament is free of this kind of thing, but they'd be wrong. Acts 5:1–11 tells the story of how a husband and wife were executed by God for not putting enough money in the collection plate and then lying about it to the church authorities. If we think these sorts of thing can't possibly be good, despite being commanded by God, it looks as if divine command theory must be rejected.

In reply, the divine command theorist might argue that this misrepresents God's nature; that God would never ever will such horrible things because God is by *nature* good. It's true that moral rules depend on God's will for their goodness, but the reason they're good is because they come from the will of a *good God*. So *God commands only the good*. This should reassure us that horrible morals are not a possibility. This defence won't work because it falls victim to the trivial tautology problem.

iv) *The trivial tautology problem* works as follows. According to the divine command theory, 'good' *means* 'is commanded by God'. If this is correct, then the attempt to reassure us that God's commands can never be bad will fail. It will fail because it involves appealing to the following explanation that *'God commands only what is good, because he himself is good.'* But this is completely empty of significant meaning; it is a ***trivial tautology***, like saying, 'This pen belongs to me, because it's mine', or 'Death is bad because it's fatal'. These 'explanations' don't explain. *Why is this?* Because, by substituting 'commanded by God' for 'good' in the italicized passage above, which we are entitled to do since the divine command theory says they *mean the same*, we get the following ***trivial tautology***: *'God commands only what is commanded by God because he himself is commanded by God.'* This explains nothing, and guarantees nothing, because it says nothing. All this amounts to is that 'God tells himself to command whatever he wills', which means it's open season on us, because it's as true of any monster as it is of God.

What with the difficulty of knowing God's will, let alone the problems involved in establishing His goodness and His very existence, it seems we'd be better off with a more down-to-earth theory that depends on human nature rather than that of God, which is what virtue ethics claims to do.

3   Virtue Ethics

Introduction

About fifty years ago there began the first murmurings of dissatisfaction with the theories of **both** the utilitarians and the deontologists. What started as a trickle, with an article by Elizabeth Anscombe (British philosopher, 1919–2001) entitled 'Modern Moral Philosophy' in 1958, has now become a groundswell of books and articles advocating a major alternative to these rule-governed, action-centred systems of ethics. The major alternative was virtue ethics.

But why the dissatisfaction? Well, if you look back at the previous two chapters, you will get some idea of the problems these theories met with. No matter what the rule, be it God's will, the principle of utility, or the categorical imperative, there were circumstances when they advocated downright bad actions, or impossible actions, or no action at all; and then there were the constant disputes *between the theories* as to what the right action was, whether the problem was abortion, or euthanasia, or whatever (see part II for these). It's been pretty much like this for the past 200 years; these three theories monopolized moral thinking. But now there's a new theory to challenge the usual suspects – or, rather, an old theory making a comeback – namely virtue ethics. Aristotle is the ancient but major inspiration behind the recent surge in virtue ethics, which is challenging the supremacy of the three action-centred theories.

So what does virtue ethics have that the others don't? Here's a quick check list.

Virtue ethics	versus	The utilitarians and deontologists
1 Agent centred	v	1 Action centred
2 Being	v	2 Doing
3 Virtues	v	3 Rules
4 Community	v	4 Individual
5 Life as a whole	v	5 Moment to moment
6 Agent benefits	v	6 Agent's benefit irrelevant

The above list of six differences could be summed up in the statement that virtue ethics is *holistic* whereas the other theories are *atomistic*. We'll come back to this below. Although a list of one-word differences is good as an aide memoire, it does not aid understanding, so each of the six will be briefly explained before we take a closer look at Aristotle's theory.

Explanation of differences between virtue ethics and rival theories

1 Agent versus action

Virtue ethics is concerned with the doer, the person or agent behind the actions, not so much with the actions themselves. It's not that virtue theorists don't care what actions are performed; it's that they think getting the **person** right is the *most important* thing, and once you've done this, good actions will follow automatically. Make the apple tree good and you'll get good apples. The other theories focus on actions. Even utilitarianism does this, despite looking particularly at *consequences* of actions because these are its method of judging the morality of the *action*.

2 Being versus doing

This is closely related to the first difference. 'Doing' is the same as 'action', after all, but the difference here is that 'being' refers to the whole *character* of the person or agent *whether or not* they are doing. Virtue ethics considers one's emotions, feelings, attitudes, habits, and lifestyle as morally relevant – in other words, the way you *are* can be good or bad. For example, if, privately, you're eaten up by jealousy, this is morally bad, even if you *never **do** anything about it.*

3 Virtues versus rules

Virtue ethics holds life to be far too complex for rules to be of any use in guiding our actions and lives. Experience of utilitarianism and deontology shows that there are no simple recipes for doing good or living a good life that we can learn off pat, like times tables, in the hope that they'll churn out the right action every time. Instead of rules virtue ethics offers virtues, ideal character traits, that lead to and are part of the good life, but there is no moral algorithm, or set of rules, that you can rote learn in order to acquire the virtues. It takes experience, good role models, mentors, and lots of practice to become a good person.

4 Community versus individual

Virtue ethics sees one's social setting or community as crucial for one's chances of acquiring the virtues, and of displaying them. How you *are* with different people will depend on their *social* relationship to you; different virtues may be appropriate depending on whether you're dealing with friends, family, school-mates, work colleagues, neighbours, and so on. But with utilitarian and deon-tological theories, morality is a matter for the individual and the rules, abstracted from the community. For example, the principle of utility tells you to count *everyone* as a **happiness unit**. The categorical imperative tells you to respect *all equally* as **sources of reason**, and God's will tells you that *all are equally **God's children**. This means that the rules regard *no one* as **special to you** in virtue of their role in your *social* life, so the moral life is more like acting as if one were an individual in a *crowd* rather than in a **community**.

5 Life as a whole versus moment to moment

Each action you perform is a moment in time, a *particular* event in your life. These are like snapshots or stills taken from the whole movie that is your life-time. Utilitarianism and Kant, the main alternatives, focus on getting the actions right and so focus on the *moments* that make up your life rather than the bigger picture. It's rather like someone who keeps looking down at their feet at each step in a long journey instead of looking ahead to where they should be going. In contrast virtue ethics looks down the road to what a human life should be, life as a *whole*; only when you know life's point, its end or purpose (Greek: *telos*), will you be in a position to see how the moments/actions fit in.

Compare how you would do a jigsaw. It's much easier to fit the parts together well once you've seen *the whole picture* than if you concentrate on the parts that make it up without knowing what the final picture (the telos) you're supposed to be constructing looks like.

6 Agent benefits versus agent's benefit irrelevant

Virtue ethics unashamedly promotes the virtues as being of benefit to their owner. Being virtuous is good because it's good for *you*. Unlike Kant's theory, according to virtue ethics, honesty is good because it's *your* best policy. If you want the best life for yourself, a fulfilled, flourishing life full of well-being, then get the virtues, for these are an essential part of such a life.

If you're generous, courageous, loyal, friendly, witty, wise, just, honest, and kind, you won't lack for friends and admirers. These virtues are very attractive qualities. Who wouldn't want to know a person like this, to employ them, promote them, be friends with them, fall in love with them, invite them to parties, trust them, respect them, treat them well? In addition, the virtuous agent will have contentment, self-respect, and integrity knowing that they're true to themselves, plus the bonus of the *pleasure* of exercising the virtues. If you don't *enjoy* being virtuous you're not really virtuous. Contrast this with Kant's theory. If you obey the categorical imperative because you *enjoy* it, this does *not* add to your goodness, but in fact tends to cast *suspicion* on it. Morality, for Kant, is not about the agent's benefit or even about anybody else's benefit, but about doing the right thing simply because it's right. It's about being consistent, obeying reason, doing your duty. Good consequences for all those affected, including the agent, are irrelevant.

And when we look at utilitarianism, although beneficial consequences are relevant, it's not the *agent's* benefit that's of concern but, rather, the benefit of *the majority* of those affected by the action. The agent's happiness counts for no more than anyone else's and will therefore normally be overridden by sheer weight of numbers.

Finally, to summarize the distinction between being *holistic* and being *atomistic*, virtue ethics can be classified as a *holistic* theory of morality because it deals with the **whole character** of the agent in all its complexity, the **whole life** of the agent in all its variety, and the **whole social setting** of the life and character of the agent, in all its intimacy. Both utilitarianism and Kant's moral theory can be seen as *atomistic* because they deal with each *action* as an *atom* of a life, the *individual* as an *atom* of society, and the agent's *motive* – whether it be duty for duty's sake or to produce the greatest happiness of the greatest number – as an *atom* of the agent's character or personality.

The central questions of virtue ethics

Unlike utilitarianism and Kant, whose central question is 'What ought I to *do* in these circumstances?', the central questions of virtue ethics are:

- 'What is the *good life* for *me* as a human *being*?'
- 'What kind of *person* should I want to become?'
- '*How* do I achieve both of these goals?'

The answer to *all three* questions involves **the virtues.** The good life is a virtuous life. You should try to become a virtuous person, and the *how* of achieving these goals is via the virtues. The virtues are the *means* and the *end.* Only when you've got the virtues can you be relied on to do the right thing as the natural outcome of a good character. None of this will be of much help unless we know what the virtues are and how to get them. This is where Aristotle comes in.

Aristotle (384–322 BC) was born in Stagira in the north of Greece. His father was doctor to the king of Macedon, and the young Aristotle was a childhood friend of Philip of Macedon, later to be father of Alexander the Great. At the age of seventeen Aristotle was sent to study at the top school of his day, obviously Plato's Academy in Athens, and he stayed for twenty years, as both student and then teacher. (Imagining these two philosophical giants chatting, it must have been the most amazing 'staff room' ever.) When Plato died in 347 BC there was a vacancy for the top job but, strangely, Aristotle didn't get it. Maybe he flunked the interview. No doubt feeling peeved at being overlooked, he took off for pastures new, eventually winding up back in Macedonia in 343 BC as tutor to the young teenager who was to become Alexander the Great – he who conquered the known world in about ten years flat and then promptly died. (I wonder whether battle tactics featured in Aristotle's lessons.) Anyway, Aristotle was back in Athens in 335 BC and opened his own school, called the Lyceum, to rival Plato's Academy – if you can't join them, beat them. If anyone can claim to be the most influential philosopher ever I suppose it's Aristotle. It's impossible to overestimate this man's breadth and depth of learning and ability. He lectured on and pretty well invented whole disciplines, such as logic, which was hardly improved on until the nineteenth century. In 323 BC the Athenian democratic authorities charged him with impiety – just as they'd done in the case of Socrates, who was executed in 399 BC – but Aristotle left town before things got out of hand, saying he wouldn't let the city sin twice against philosophy. He died a year later of a stomach problem, though it's alleged that he drowned by throwing himself into the sea because he couldn't explain the tides. This is probably a myth: it doesn't sound like something he'd do. Being an advocate of the mean rather than such extreme action, he'd have thrown a bucket of water over himself instead.

Key text: *Nicomachean Ethics*

Aristotle's theory

Aristotle begins his explanation and justification of the virtues and the good life by pointing out that all things in the universe have a purpose. They aim at some end, which is built in to their nature. For example, the purpose of the sun is to give light and heat to the earth; the rain's job is to water the ground so plants can grow. The plants' job is to feed the animals, and the lower animals are food for the higher animals, and so on. This focuses on how different species of things are interrelated in what we now call ecosystems, or what 'the Lion King' calls the circle of life. But, in addition, each species has a telos internal and peculiar to itself. For example, the purpose or goal of an acorn is to grow into an oak tree, of a kitten into a cat, lambs into sheep, bulbs into tulips, tadpoles into frogs, and so on.

But if all things in the universe have a telos, then so must human beings. Aristotle uses a further argument to prove this, namely, *the function argument*, which has three strands. Firstly, people make things to have functions or jobs, e.g. a knife's function is to cut; a wheel's function is to roll. So the cause of these functioning things must also have a function, and that means us.

Secondly, people are part of society and they have functions within it – e.g. plumbers, farmers, bakers – so society itself must have a function, since it's made up of functioning parts – us.

Thirdly, people's bodies are made up of parts that have functions. For example, the function of the eye is to see, and the ear to hear. This must mean that the whole human being must have an overall function, since it's composed of bits that have functions.

Aristotle concludes that there's a meaning, or purpose, to human life, which it is in our nature to aim for. Human nature has a function; it is *for* something. The big question is, 'What?'

An initial and partial answer is that all things, and therefore we too, aim for *the Good*. Our purpose is our essence; it's the realization of our natural potential. The same goes for everything else, only their ends will differ according to their natures. Nothing well made seeks its own destruction, but rather targets its good. What makes a good tiger is not what makes a good apple, but each is good relative to its nature (a stripy, furry apple that bit your head off would be a very bad apple). So, realizing our potential is good for us, given *our* nature. But although a thing's end or telos is good for it, it won't do it any good if it's no good at achieving this. It must 'choose' good or efficient *means* to achieve its *end*. The means are as important as the end, for without them you get nowhere. So we need to find out *two things*: what is our *end*, and *how* (by what *means*) do we achieve it?

You need good, efficient, *excellent* means to achieve an *excellent* end. The Greek word for 'excellence' is *arete*, which is normally translated 'virtue.' This has a broader application than our modern usage. In ancient Greece 'virtue' meant *any* kind of excellence. Sharpness is a virtue in knives because it's part of their purpose to be sharp. Sharpness is one of the characteristics that make a knife good. A virtuous tiger is one that has excellent tiger-qualities, such as speed, cunning, good camouflage, strength, aggression, sharp teeth, and so on. These are what make it a *good* tiger. The virtues needed in a good apple are to be juicy, shiny, round, fresh, and so on. Notice that these qualities, these virtues, don't spring into existence overnight, just as the tiger or apple reaches its maturity, but are instead gradually refined and honed; they're there all along and indeed are part of the means as well as being the end product. So virtues are excellent features, or *character*istics, that make a thing good.

To find out what the **human virtues** are, we need to know two things. Firstly, what is the *good life* for *human* beings? Secondly, what are the most *excellent character* traits for achieving the goal of the *good life*? There are two clues to finding out the answer to the first question. Firstly, find out what is *distinctive* of human nature as opposed to any other kind of thing or animal – something belonging *only* to us. Secondly, ask people what they *ultimately want* from life.

For Aristotle, what is distinctive of human nature is **reason**. He defines human beings as 'rational animals' because reason is the feature that singles us out from the throng of other animals on the planet. Aristotle's answer to the second clue is that what people ultimately want from life is to be **happy**. He argues that what's distinctive about us can't be *nutrition, perception, sociability,* or the having of emotions, because the higher mammals also have these things. No, it must be *reason*; no other animal can even begin to match us in this respect, so *reason* is the crucial element in our telos. The other things are part of it but not the nub. So, the good life is the life lived according to *reason*. Somehow or other the virtues are bound up with this. But where does happiness come in?

Well, although everyone wants to be happy, people have very different ideas about what happiness is. Aristotle considers three main candidates:

- pleasure
- honour or prestige
- virtue.

i) Pleasure is the hedonist concept of happiness, and Aristotle rejects it because, since we share this capacity with animals, it can't be distinctive of us.

ii) Honour or prestige is better than pleasure, but it's still not distinctive enough to be our telos, since animals also have a pecking order. In addition, it is to some extent unsatisfying because it's possible to have honour under false pretences. The only honour that counts is *true* honour, honour that's *deserved*. All the things that are sought for the pleasure and honour they bring must therefore also be rejected as the purpose of life – things such as money, fame, and power. People who live for these ends are misguided; they are not the telos we seek.

iii) The *virtues* are the only things worth pursuing for their own sake, for they constitute the deepest happiness and true honour. True happiness is not the same thing as having pleasurable *states* of mind, but is instead the *process* of *flourishing*, of one's nature flowering. It is the joy of being what you're meant to be, of doing what you're meant to do, and doing it well – of being a good specimen of your species. It is fulfilling your '*destiny*'. The virtuous life is our telos. Aristotle's word for the true happiness of a fulfilled and flourishing life is **eudaimonia**.

Let's take a look at the nuts and bolts of a *normal* human life. It has *physical* needs – food, drink, sex, shelter, security; *social* needs – family, friends, lovers, community; *creative* needs – humour, literature, the arts, music. We have *intellectual* needs, being curious creatures, so we educate ourselves in science, maths, history, philosophy, etc. A normal human life will also involve a career, and possessions. And in *all* of these things we invest our desires, feelings, emotions, and attitudes. We invest our *character*, our *Selves*. But we don't want just normal lives; we want happy, flourishing lives – eudaimonic lives. How do we turn 'alright' into 'good'? 'So-so' into 'happy'? 'Ordinary' into 'extraordinary'? Aristotle's answer is that, since *reason* is our *distinctive* feature, the eudaimonic life will be guided by *it*. This will involve all the facets of our life being pursued in a *reasonable* way, i.e. with **wisdom** or **prudence**, as it's also known.

Human emotional, mental, and interpersonal life is extremely complex and can go disastrously wrong in countless ways, leading to despair and misery – in a word, unhappiness. *Practical reason* or *wisdom* is a major or cardinal virtue which regulates and controls the *proper level* or *proportion* that we should allow each activity, emotion, and desire, so that none of them gets out of hand and enslaves us. ***Too much* or *too little* of anything is bad for you.** This is a truth of **reason**. *So the right amount is somewhere in between the two extremes.* This is Aristotle's famous doctrine of **the mean**, also known as 'the golden mean' or 'the happy medium'. ***This is where the virtues lie – on the mean between the extremes of emotion and character.*** On each extreme lies a vice: if too much, it's a vice of excess; if too little, it's a vice of deficiency. For example:

Vices	Virtues	Vices
Deficiency	Mean	Excess
Cowardice	Courage	Rashness
Boorishness	Wittiness	Buffoonery
Miserliness	Generosity	Prodigality

(See the end of this chapter for a full list of Aristotelian virtues and vices.) It's worth emphasizing that Aristotle offers *no handy rules* for 'magically' revealing the mean in every situation, because *there are none.* Life is far too complicated for such quick fixes.

Virtues are settled dispositions, tendencies, or habits of character that are the most appropriate for achieving eudaimonia *overall* in your life, but they also help you to have the appropriate *feelings* and *attitudes* in any social context, and will lead you to make the right 'call' in any situation that requires *judgement and action.*

This is all very well, but just *how are the virtues acquired?* If there are no rules, how are we to learn these virtues? Aristotle's answer is that we learn them by *practising* them. You become courageous by practising it, trying it out, attempting it on appropriate occasions. The more you do this, the more of a habit it will become, until it is part of your nature or character. You also need good role models, mentors, or coaches who can guide you. It's a bit like learning to ride a bike. There's no formula for this. Nothing short of 'riding' the bike until you *get the hang of it* will do the trick. Compare learning to drive, or learning the violin. Just as you need a competent (virtuous) driving instructor or violinist (virtuoso), so you need the help of a virtuous person who can help you acquire the virtues by showing you how it's done and 'coaching' from the sidelines when you have a go – people such as your parents and teachers, a team captain, a minister, or a friend you admire.

There are four cardinal virtues of ancient Greece. Cardinal virtues are the crucial, central ones, the most important. These are:

- courage
- temperance
- justice
- wisdom.

Modern virtue theorists have added many others, e.g. industriousness, professionalism, and so on (see end of chapter for some plausible suggestions for a list of contemporary virtues).

So what's Aristotle's answer to the moral sceptic who asks: 'Why should I be moral?' He'd say, it's in your interests to be moral because to be moral is to acquire the virtues, which are the high road to a deeply satisfying and worthwhile life, a life of well-being and true happiness – the sort human beings are meant to have. It's true you'll need some luck as well, for example, good health, reasonable physique, supportive family, etc. But assuming you have these, you'll be laughing all the way to eudaimonia.

Assessing virtue ethics

We'll begin with some of the advantages virtue ethics enjoys over the other moral theories. There are cases where utilitarianism and Kant (the main rivals) give the wrong moral judgement but virtue ethics gets it right. Take, for example,

1 The case of the man who likes to urinate on graves

This man enjoys a pint or two down at the pub and takes a short cut home via the cemetery late at night when there's no one else around. Rather than wait until he gets home, he thinks it's a laugh to urinate on the graves instead. What do utilitarianism and Kant say about this? Utilitarianism would have to say that, since no one sees him, and nobody's harmed, least of all the dead, there's more pleasure produced than pain because the man enjoys his fun and relieving himself. So the principle of utility says that the man does the right thing.

Kant would apply the categorical imperative, but what happens when we universalize the man's maxim, which would be something like, 'When I'm in a cemetery at night and nobody else is looking, I'll urinate on the graves'? Well, it's not a contradiction in conception, because a world where everyone acted like this is perfectly imaginable. But it's not a contradiction in will either, because when the man is dead and buried he won't have a will to be able to want people not to urinate on his grave. So the maxim passes the test and becomes morally permissible. But this is ridiculous. Both theories go badly astray here because they ignore the man's *character*. What we want to say, and virtue ethics allows us to say, is that the man's action is wrong because it flows from one or more vicious character flaws, such as callousness or spitefulness.

Then there are cases where Kant and the utilitarians give us the right answer, but for the *wrong* reason, whereas virtue theory gets *both right*. Imagine, for example:

2 The case of visiting your friend in hospital

Both utilitarianism and Kant say it's the right thing to do, and so does virtue ethics, but let's see why. Utilitarianism would say it was right because it increases the overall amount of happiness in the world. This treats your friend as a means to the general happiness. If a complete stranger would have got more happiness from your visit, the principle of utility would have bade you visit him instead. It's of little comfort to your friend to know he comes second to your quest for maximum utility. Similar problems attend the Kantian visitor, who is only there because it's the rational and consistent thing to do in obedience to the categorical imperative. Again, it's cold comfort for your friend to be told that you're visiting him because it's your moral duty.

Of course, the blindingly obvious and natural answer is that you're visiting him because he's your *friend.* Virtue ethics allows us to say this because friendliness is a virtue, and it suffices to justify your visit without needing to appeal to abstract moral *rules.*

3 The case of the loner in mental turmoil

Here is a man who shuns company and is tormented by racist feelings of contempt for blacks, hatred of women, lust for children, and fantasies of lurid murders, yet he never behaves in a racist, sexist, paedophilic, or murderous fashion. Neither utilitarianism nor Kant can form a moral judgement on this man because he has not *done* anything wrong, yet there's something disturbingly inadequate about this lack of response to what is clearly a bad scene. As a specimen of humanity this man is stunted, warped, marginalized. This is emphatically not a picture of human flourishing or eudaimonia and so, virtue ethics pronounces him *vicious* because his *character* is so, never mind whether he has *actually done* anything bad; he *is* bad. Virtue ethics scores over utilitarianism and Kant because, unlike them, it can give a moral verdict in cases such as these which fits in with our basic intuitions.

4 Utilitarianism and Kant underestimate the value of the whole person

Utilitarianism picks on a particular and important feature of people, namely *pleasure,* but focuses on the *feature* rather than the person. The *essence* of morality is to produce the greatest amount of *pleasure/happiness,* and treating people well is a *means* to this end. This is bad because it sidelines people. Kant also ignores the *whole* person in two respects. Firstly, although he says you should respect the individual, this is merely due to your respect in them for *reason.* Secondly, Kant singles out only *one* motive that has moral worth, i.e. respect for duty, and ignores all the rest of a person's emotions, attitudes, and feelings as they affect their actions. Again, this sidelines the value and relevance of the whole person as engaged in moral deliberation.

In contrast to utilitarianism and Kant, virtue ethics takes into account *all* aspects of a person's character in forming a judgement as to their moral worth, which seems much more satisfactory.

5 Utilitarianism and Kant undervalue family and community

This one-sided, narrow-minded attitude to the importance of the individual, as seen in point 4 above, spills over into utilitarianism's and Kant's treatment of particular individuals – family members and friends – who are specially related to us in more or less intimate ways. Virtue ethics can deal with aspects of morality as it relates to these areas better than utilitarianism or Kant because it recognizes that the *extra* commitments we have here are based on unique, special, emotional, biographical, and biological relations rooted in the concrete setting of our community. We have *extra* responsibilities to these people because they are, and *should* be, *more important to us than* those who are strangers. Utilitarianism has trouble here because each counts as one and no one for more than one, so you should toss a coin to decide whether to save your mum or a complete stranger; and if you save your mum because it brings greater happiness, we're back to the problems of point 4. Kant also has trouble here, because the abstract rule of the categorical imperative is incapable of deciding between saving your mum or the complete stranger. Let's consider why.

Taking the formula of universal law first, we can see that both the maxim to save your mum and the maxim to save the stranger are equally universalizable – I can easily imagine a world where everyone decides either way, so there's no contradiction in conception resulting from a decision to save the stranger. This means it's not a perfect duty to save your mum. But is it an imperfect duty? To decide this we must see if it's a contradiction in will. Well, for a start, it seems half the human race (the males) couldn't apply this categorical imperative thought experiment to themselves, because they'd have to say something like: 'I can't will that I should not save my mum because some day I might be a mum and in need of saving, so it would be inconsistent for me not to save my mum now.' This is absurd, since there's no way they'd ever be a *mum*. So for Kant it's not an imperfect duty to save her. (In fact, even if somehow it *were* an imperfect duty, that entails some leeway in obeying it, which leads to the ludicrous conclusion that you can pick and choose the times when you save her and the times when you can't be bothered.)

We fare no better in using the 'formula of ends'. This should come as no surprise, since it's merely a different formulation of the *same principle* and so, logically, should give the same result. The formula of ends bids us 'treat *humanity* never merely as a means but also as an end', because people are *rational* sources of the *moral* law. But the problem here is that the stranger is no less a part of *humanity* than your mum, and is no less *rational*, so there are no grounds for favouring your mum over the stranger. I suppose, yet again, you should toss a coin to decide, for the categorical imperative is no help.

But whether it's your mum or your friend, virtue ethics bases the moral need to save them instead of the stranger, on the concrete historical, biographical, emotional relationship that *you-as-a-social-being* have with these other special people with whom you share memories, warmth, love, laughs, and life.

6 As against Kant, virtue ethics values pleasure in doing good

Kant's a bit of a killjoy; it's duty *versus* pleasure. There's no moral worth in doing your duty because you enjoy it. This is deeply unattractive, because we normally give people *extra* moral credit for *happily* helping others and taking *pleasure* in being kind. Virtue ethics acknowledges this. Aristotle didn't think that a person was truly virtuous if they found the virtues a chore. Taking pleasure in being courageous and wise is a *mark* of true virtue.

7 As against utilitarianism, virtue ethics values personal integrity

Imagine a party of utilitarians in power. What wouldn't they stoop to in order to achieve the greatest happiness of the greatest number? If by lying, cheating, scheming, and double-dealing, or through false promises, hypocrisy, gossip, propaganda, and God knows what else, they were able to succeed in making the majority of voters happy, this would be morally praiseworthy on their principles, especially if they could keep all this secret and hidden from the electorate so as not to set a bad example.

What's clearly lacking here is a bit of moral fibre: virtuous people with enough backbone to be true to themselves; people with *character* who won't be blown about by every wind of change; politicians with integrity, who shun dishonesty, double-dealing, and spin, because these vices are *beneath them.* This means women and men who have too much *self-respect*, too much *pride*, to allow themselves to indulge in the petty, dirty tricks of 'that' sort of politician. The virtues that virtue ethics recommends *guarantee integrity.*

8 Virtue ethics is better on moral education

With utilitarianism and Kant it's basically a matter of the individual and the rules. All you need to do is learn the theory: the principle of utility or the categorical imperative. Learn a few technicalities such as how to calculate amounts of pleasure, or how to universalize maxims, and you're set. Just go out and obey the rules and that's morality. What these theories leave out is all the years of experience growing up and growing old, still learning every day the almost impossible task of adapting the almost infinite complexity of the human personality to the almost infinite diversity of its world. Think of the role your parents, siblings, friends, and fictional heroes play in setting an example, in being role models. Think of all the numerous and varied experiences of life you've already had and how these have moulded your attitudes and character.

If morality is just a matter of learning the rules, how on earth have you managed to be a decent person long before you learned about the principle of utility and the categorical imperative in philosophy? Virtue ethics gives moral education a central place in acquiring the virtues, because it's precisely through one's roots in family and society, and one's continual practising of the virtues with the help and guidance of friends and community over the years, that one is gradually moulded, and moulds oneself, into a good human being. The moral *wisdom* that comes with practice and experience is not the *cleverness* of the person who can learn the rules by rote. That's why there are no moral whiz-kids – because there aren't any pat answers.

9 Utilitarianism and Kant are wrong to think morality can be contained in one rule

Having only one principle of morality distorts and oversimplifies an amazingly complex and puzzling phenomenon. Compare trying to play good chess armed only with the rule 'Always look at the board', or 'Always go for checkmate'. These are patently inadequate.

Increasing the number of rules won't help much, because there'll never be enough to cover every eventuality in life, and so they too will oversimplify moral difficulties and form a straightjacket for our thinking. Rules may be okay for hard knowledge such as maths and geometry, and formulae may be essential for science, but the quagmire of war and the anguish of life and death decisions are not resolved by applying a set of pre-established rules. That sort of approach might work for knitting patterns and flat-packs from MFI, but not for deciding whether to have an abortion.

Virtue ethics, while not rejecting them altogether, displaces rules from their *pivotal* role in the other theories as *constituting* morality, and **replaces** them with the virtues – dispositions of character which, if trained properly, will result in the happy knack of getting it right almost every time. It may help here to compare learning to be good with learning to drive. The Highway Code is like a set of moral rules, but simply learning them won't help you to drive well. You must also *practise* driving. You need an expert instructor to guide you and show you how it's done. The rule that you should stay on your own side of the road, while important, is perfectly useless without the hundreds of minor adjustments to the steering wheel you continuously need to make in order to do this. There can be no rules for this sort of thing. The contention of virtue ethics is that life is so much more complicated than driving that you need years of practice and many virtuous instructors before you will 'pass your virtue test'; rules of thumb are the rules of good practice derived from the naturally virtuous who don't need rules in order to know how to be good.

Arguments against virtue ethics

1 Aristotle's 'function argument' doesn't work

This criticism must be accepted. Aristotle does indeed commit two fallacies in his function argument, namely the fallacy of *composition*, when he argues from the fact that we are composed of *parts* that have functions (the eye to see, the ear to hear, etc.) to the conclusion that we, *as a whole* must have a function. But this is like arguing that, if the human race is composed of *parts* (*individuals*), each of which has a body, then the *human race as a whole* must have a body.

He also commits the *genetic* fallacy by assuming that causes can only work by transferring their properties to their effects – e.g. a thing must already be red (paint, for instance) in order to cause the effect (a wall, for instance) to be red. But there are many exceptions to this which ruin Aristotle's argument. For example, murderers can kill their victims without already having to be dead themselves. Similarly, we can make (*cause* to exist) utensils that have a function, e.g. knives, without having to have a function ourselves. Despite our abilities in this direction, we might be functionless, and not have a telos.

2 Aristotle's teleology made obsolete by evolution and modern science

In modern science things happen (are caused) by being, as it were, pushed from behind by prior events. This is called efficient causation. There is no Mind guiding nature to some purpose or end product. The universe is not *aiming* at a telos. Things just occur in a regular way and we learn to predict and so control them. Evolution tells the same story. Species are not endeavouring to achieve their telos; there is no telos. They evolve by lucky mutations that give them better chances of survival than their rivals. It's simply a matter of brutal statistics; the better-armed gladiators tend to survive longest, that's all. But this means that the foundation of virtue ethics in eudaimonia, as the telos that human nature should be striving for, is a myth that science has exploded, and if the foundation goes, so does virtue ethics.

How would virtue ethics reply to this charge? Modern virtue ethicists can concede that Aristotle was wrong in thinking that each species in nature has a *built-in* aim or telos which is *objectively out there*, like gravity, while arguing that this does not wreck virtue ethics if it can find a *new* foundation compatible with modern science. It looks something like the following.

You can still have eudaimonia despite the mindless grinding of nature's purposeless, causal mechanisms because, although they had no end in view when, for example, they evolved the eye, you'll still tend to do better, flourish more, be happier, with 20/20 vision than being short-sighted, or colour-blind. The point is that the virtues and eudaimonia can be seen as successful survival habits that give you the edge against your competitors in the struggle for life, for a flourishing life, in the midst of a universe that's going nowhere. Just because *it's* got no telos, doesn't mean *you* can't have one.

3 Virtue ethics doesn't give us adequate guidance about what to do

This is a serious criticism because virtue ethics is a normative theory and normative theories are supposed to guide actions – that's their job. So if virtue ethics can't do its job properly, it's in trouble. The criticism goes as follows.

When I ask what I should do, virtue ethics tells me I should be virtuous. This is no help unless I know what the virtues are and which one to apply in my situation. How can I get help with this? I'm told that a virtuous person would be able to advise me, or perhaps act as a role model, and I could observe how they acted in a situation like mine. But *what if I don't know any virtuous people?* And it seems I couldn't get to know them if left to my own devices, because I'd need to be able to identify them as having the virtues. Yet how can I do this if I don't know what the virtues look like in practice? I wouldn't have any criterion for judging who's virtuous and who isn't.

What if virtue ethics tells me to follow the mean, since that's where the virtues lie? Will this guide me? But this just raises more problems, for only a virtuous person can tell me this, and *what if I don't know any virtuous people?* I'm back at square one, eight lines ago.

Again, how would virtue ethicists answer this criticism? Firstly, they might say that the utilitarians and Kant don't do such a good job themselves at giving us clear guidance. Secondly, the criticism is unfair, since it's based on the supposition that the person is *totally clueless* about the virtues. But hardly anyone capable of acting would be in this position, because they'd have been brought up in a family, in a society that would have trained and advised them how to behave wisely and appropriately in various situations. To have such an upbringing and still be clueless verges on the psychopathic, and no theory can deal with this kind of person. So if they have *some* idea of virtue, this gives them at least something to work on. They can ask themselves, in any situation, what would be the courageous thing to do, the compassionate thing, or the generous thing. In fact, this is the very practising of the virtues that virtue ethics recommends as essential for acquiring them. Thirdly, if life is too complicated for easy formulaic answers to moral problems, as virtue ethics insists, the fact that it doesn't try to give simplistic recipes for moral decision-making turns out to be a plus.

4 The virtues may clash, leaving you in a dilemma

What do you do if you are torn between loyalty and honesty? An example is whistle-blowers who leak sensitive documents that are in the public interest, but who also owe allegiance to their employers. Something's got to give, which means that, in order to be virtuous, you also have to be vicious.

5 Virtues may be bad on occasion

For example, a courageous criminal is *worse* than a cowardly one. A witty rogue's misdemeanours may be overlooked because his wit has charmed his victims. Isn't wit acting as a vice here?

6 Is there such a thing as one human nature?

Just look at the endless variety of cultures, religions, customs, traditions, values, art, music, taboos, political arrangements, diet, fashion, and so on. Aristotle must be wrong to hold that there is only one human nature with one telos. Surely eudaimonia comes in all shapes and sizes?

Virtue ethics can mount a reply to this. Firstly, it's worth pointing out that, at the micro level of DNA, we *are one human nature*. Secondly, despite the endless variety outlined above, there are many *constants* in the human condition. For example, *no one* flourishes if they're starving, tortured, imprisoned, abused, humiliated, destitute, disease-ridden, homeless, or made a slave. Dread of these can provide the basis of human solidarity, and the groundwork for a shared conception of the virtues and what it means to flourish as a human being. Thirdly, some human differences aren't due to radically different values or virtues, but to the application of the *same* virtues to *different circumstances*. For example, we put our old folk in homes while the Inuit put theirs on ice flows to die. These differences mask an underlying unity of value, which is that each society is doing the best it can to preserve as many of its citizens as it can without risking the whole community. A harsh climate calls for harsh measures.

7 Virtue may require self-sacrifice; how is this eudaimonic?

Doing the courageous thing can lead to an early death. This doesn't look very fulfilling. Surely an extra thirty years of happy life is worth the price of a cowardly act?

A virtue ethicist may reply that this may not be such a happy life if it's eaten up by feelings of shame and painful memories of what you did. It's arguable that it's better to die heroically, being true to yourself. Besides, the claim is that virtues are *likely* to lead to a long and fulfilling life; no one said anything about a *guarantee*. So the virtues can be recommended as *generally* leading to eudaimonia. But this also depends on luck, and if you're unlucky enough to be caught up in a situation that demands the ultimate courageous sacrifice, don't blame the virtues, blame the universe.

8 Can't some vices make you great?

Literary envy, for example, can goad someone to emulate their rival and, say, write a great novel. And, isn't preferring greatness more noble than the desire for eudaimonia got by middle-of-the-road virtues?

9 The mean is a bore; truth and happiness may lie at the extreme

There seem to be elements in human nature that aren't catered for by Aristotle's mean. His portrayal of the self-satisfied, middle-class Athenian gentleman 'the magnanimous man' leaves most of us cold. There's something wrong with Aristotle's account of the virtues if this is the best a human being can aspire to under their guidance. What about the tortured geniuses who have achieved greatness and given humanity so much, but at the cost of their own eudaimonia?

Van Gogh cut off his ear and later shot himself in the chest, dying by his own hand. Gauguin left his wife and children in destitution to pursue artistic inspiration on a tropical island. George Best, sparkling genius of a footballer, drank himself into an early grave. Mozart died in his thirties and was buried in a pauper's grave. Shelley drowned in his twenties. Bobby Fischer, chess genius and former world champion, was obsessional and paranoid. Alexander the Great died at thirty three, having conquered the world. Greatness is a serious rival to eudaimonia. At least it's not boring.

Summary

None of the normative theories has all the answers, but the challenge of assessing their relative merits is unavoidable if you are to have a rationally defensible ethic, or even a rationally defensible opt-out from ethics. My assessment is that virtue ethics has the edge over the others, despite any drawbacks it may have, so this may be a good point in the book for the reader to take stock, and consider whether or not they agree, and why. The suggested further reading below should help with a more detailed investigation, and the practical ethics section to come should also help decide which of the theories does the best job when it comes to making real-life decisions.

Further Reading (the easier first)

Utilitarianism
Palmer, Michael, *Moral Problems*. 2nd edn, Cambridge: Lutterworth Press, 2005, ch. 3.
Mulgan, Tim, *Understanding Utilitarianism*. Stocksfield, Northumberland: Acumen, 2007.

Kant
Graham, Gordon, *Eight Theories of Ethics*. London: Routledge, 2004, ch. 6.
Driver, Julia, *Ethics: The Fundamentals*. Oxford: Blackwell, 2007, ch. 5.

Divine Command Theory
Gensler, Harry J., *Ethics*. London: Routledge, 1998, ch. 3.

Rachels, James, *The Elements of Moral Philosophy*. 5th edn, rev. Stuart Rachels, Boston and London: McGraw-Hill, 2007.

Virtue Ethics
Bowie, Robert A., *Ethical Studies*. Cheltenham: Nelson Thornes, 2001, ch. 10.
Benn, Piers, *Ethics*. London: UCL Press, 1998, ch. 7.

ARISTOTLE'S VIRTUES

DEFICIENCY VICE	MEAN VIRTUE	EXCESS VICE
Underreaction	Perfect judgement, practical wisdom	Overreaction
Cowardice **Insensibility** Puritanical, can't enjoy yourself, misery-guts, party-pooper	**Courage** **Temperance** Self-control	**Rashness** **Intemperance** Binge-drinking, chain-smoking, drug addiction, glutton, sex maniac
Illiberality miser, mean, tight	**Liberality** generosity	**Prodigality** spendthrift, waster
Pettiness	**Munificence** Big financial projects, throw big parties	**Vulgarity**
Humble-mindedness Doormat	**High-mindedness** Pride	**Vaingloriness** Self-obsessed, vain, narcissistic
Want of ambition Listless	**Right ambition**	**Over-ambition** Hubris
Spiritlessness Wimp	**Good temper**	**Irascibility** Short-tempered, road rage, going berserk
Surliness Unfriendly, impolite, bit of a loner	**Friendliness/Civility**	**Obsequiousness** Toady, sycophantic, fawning, flattering
Ironical Deprecation Economical with the truth	**Sincerity** Honesty	**Boastfulness** Arrogant
Boorishness Glum, dull, boring, bad jokes	**Wittiness**	**Buffoonery** Clownish

ARISTOTLE'S VIRTUES

DEFICIENCY VICE	MEAN VIRTUE	EXCESS VICE
Shamelessness	**Modesty**	**Bashfulness**
Callousness Thoughtless, uncaring, don't give a damn	**Just resentment** Justice, fair-minded	**Spitefulness** Revenge, feuding

CONTEMPORARY VIRTUES

DEFICIENCY VICE	MEAN VIRTUE	EXCESS VICE
Uncaring, insipid	Love, passion	Obsessive, stalker
Betrayal	Loyal	Die-hard
Lazy	Industrious	Workaholic
Lacklustre	Committed	Fanatic
Lack of self-confidence, geek, nerd, panicky	Cool	Cold
Sexless, 'just there'	Sexy	Tarty, pimpy
Graceless, rude, 'rough and ready'	Charming	Smarmy
Ugly	Good-looking	To die for, drop-dead gorgeous
Misanthrope, uncaring, snub people	Interested in others	Voyeur, peeping Tom
Squeamish	Doing what has to be done in tough circumstances	Cruel
Hardhearted, callous	Sympathetic	Bleeding heart
Indecisive	Decisive	Dictatorial, overbearing
Flaky, disorganized, shambles	Organized	Anally retentive
Fickle, brittle	Determined	Ruthless
Bigoted, prejudiced, narrow-minded	Open-minded	Empty-headed
Talentless	Talented	Show off
Stupid, thick	Intelligent	Smartass
Unprofessional, amateurish	Professional	Bureaucratic, officious, rule-bound, jargon-prone

Part II
Practical Ethics

So far we've examined the four normative moral theories at a rather abstract level without getting down to practical cases. But the proof (i.e. test) of the pudding is, as they say, in the eating, and this section of the book is where we'll test our four normative 'puddings' by applying them to the consumer (us) in four problematic, practical areas of life where tough decisions have to be made, namely:

- euthanasia
- abortion
- animal rights
- environmental ethics.

Each theory has already run the gauntlet of theoretical criticism when compared with the others. Now it's time to test them in the messy practicalities of real life.

4   Euthanasia

Background information

'Euthanasia' comes from the Greek 'eu', meaning 'good' or 'easy', and 'thanatos', meaning 'death'. Sometimes the term 'mercy-killing' is used instead of 'euthanasia', but I'll stick to the latter. Cases that might justify euthanasia would be ones that involve severe pain that drugs can't control and ones with a tragic prognosis regarding the patient's quality of life. This normally means the chronically or terminally ill (usually the very young or the very old) but also profoundly damaged humans, e.g. coma cases, PVS patients (PVS = persistent vegetative state), whose conditions are not life-threatening. We also need to distinguish various types of euthanasia, such as:

- **voluntary** euthanasia . . . i.e. the patient requests it
- **non-voluntary** euthanasia . . . the patient is not in a position to decide, e.g. PVS patients
- **involuntary** euthanasia . . . i.e. the patient does **not** want it.

Involuntary euthanasia will be very rare. An example is where two spies, one young, one old, are caught and the old one kills the young one because he knows they'll be tortured and thinks the young one is better off dead, whereas the young one, not realizing this, decides he doesn't want to die. I'll pretty much ignore this third type because, in normal circumstances, almost all moral theories would prohibit it, the patient's choice being of paramount importance.

We can also distinguish two further types of euthanasia, according to whether the *method* is **active** or **passive**. **Active** euthanasia is when something **positive** is done to bring about death, such as lethal injection. The patient is **killed**. **Passive** euthanasia is when something **negative** is done or permitted so as to bring about death, for example withdrawing food, or switching off a life-support machine. Here the patient is **allowed** to die. If you simply keep the patient comfy until they die, e.g. don't withdraw food, but control the pain, then this is **palliative** care, not euthanasia. If a person wants to die, and would do it themselves but can't get the necessary drugs, then if you supply these and the person dies by their **own hand**, it's called **assisted suicide**.

Ignoring involuntary euthanasia, we can combine the distinctions between voluntary, non-voluntary, active, and passive euthanasia to form four main categories of euthanasia, which are important for the remainder of the discussion:

- **active voluntary** euthanasia
- **passive voluntary** euthanasia
- **active non-voluntary** euthanasia
- **passive non-voluntary** euthanasia.

Finally, there remain **two** important *intermediate* but disputed moral principles. I call them 'intermediate' because both seem to operate halfway between the relatively abstract principles associated with the main normative theories (e.g. principle of utility/categorical imperative) and the immediate, hands-on decisions doctors have to make regarding their patients. The two principles are

- the **doctrine of double effect**
- the **acts/omissions distinction**.

Doctrine of double effect (DDE)

The DDE supports the view that it's wrong to kill a patient *intentionally*, but it's okay to help a patient by easing their pain while merely *foreseeing* (but not *intending*), that, as a *side effect* of the treatment, they will die. The treatment and death are the *double effect* of your action, but what makes it okay is that only the treatment was intended. The doctrine of double effect allows you to say that you did not deliberately, intentionally kill someone (for this is wrong), but that you eased their pain, and merely foresaw that they'd die sooner as a result of your action. A quicker death then becomes collateral damage.

An example will help to clarify this. According to the DDE, it is wrong for a doctor to give a patient a lethal injection of potassium chloride, because this is intentionally direct killing – potassium chloride having no therapeutic effects whatsoever. But the DDE approves the intentional giving of a lethal series of morphine injections as long as the intention is to ease the patient's pain, while foreseeing that this will, as a side effect, shorten their life (morphine suppresses breathing).

The DDE is a controversial intermediate moral principle – deontologists favour it as a working principle of ethics, whereas utilitarians and virtue theorists reject it as morally irrelevant. The reason for this is that deontologists think one's intentions are crucial in determining the morality of one's actions, and so see DDE as morally relevant, whereas utilitarianism doesn't rate intention as morally significant, thus ignoring DDE in its decision-making procedure. Virtue theorists, while rating the agent's intention in terms of whether it's virtuous or vicious, see *both* double effects as *character*-driven by, hopefully, *virtuous intention* on the one hand, and *wise foresight* on the other, the latter having the *self-same* impact on eudaimonia as has an *overt* intention to kill. What this boils down to is that, for virtue theorists, DDE is morally insignificant.

Acts/omissions distinction (A&O)

This implies that there's a *significant* moral distinction between *actively bringing* something about and simply *omitting to act* to prevent its happening. According to this distinction, killing is worse than letting die. A plausible example is when we condemn someone *more* for *sending* poisoned food parcels to third world countries, thereby *killing* ten people, but condemn someone *less* for merely *not* giving money to Oxfam, thereby *allowing* ten people to die. As you'll appreciate, the acts/omissions distinction is closely tied to the distinction between active (act of killing) euthanasia and passive (omitting to act/allowing to die) euthanasia, and the dispute about whether there really is a significant moral difference between the two.

For example, according to A&O it's okay to withdraw feeding tubes from a PVS patient because this doesn't kill him – it merely lets him die by omitting to help him live – but it's wrong to give him a lethal injection of potassium chloride because this is an act of killing. A&O is as controversial as DDE, and the split between the moral theories is the same. Deontologists favour A&O precisely because it stresses the wrongness of the *act* of killing, which suits the *action*-focused categorical imperative and an *action*-commanding God. Utilitarianism dismisses the A&O distinction as morally irrelevant because, if consequences are the only thing that count in determining whether an action is right, it doesn't matter whether those consequences are brought about by an act or an omission: the morality of both will be the same. Virtue theorists also disregard A&O because they focus on the character of the agent and eudaimonic outcomes rather than the nature of the act itself. So, for example, it won't make any difference whether a person has beaten up a friend or stood by watching, omitting to help while someone else beats up their friend; that person is equally vicious on each occasion.

The current legal position on euthanasia in the UK is that active euthanasia is illegal in all cases and that passive euthanasia needs to have the permission of the courts, which needs to be applied for in each individual circumstance; there is no general law covering these cases, each being decided on its own merits. Medical ethics permits doctors to prescribe pain-killing drugs for the terminally ill, knowing that in some cases these drugs will hasten death as a *foreseen but unintended* consequence, and uses the doctrine of double effect to justify this. Before moving on to the application and assessment of normative theories regarding euthanasia, it may be helpful to keep some actual cases in mind, along with our intuitive response to how they should have been handled; that way, when we've looked at the advice of each theory, we can test them by comparison with our intuitive responses. The theory that fits them best will most likely be the best theory (this is *not* a tautology).

Two cases of euthanasia

The following cases are adapted from Gail Tulloch's book *Euthanasia: Choice and Death* (pp. 81–2).

The case of Doctor Cox

In 1992, Dr Cox, a hospital doctor, was tried for injecting a double dose of potassium chloride (which has no curative or pain-killing properties) in addition to a dose of heroin into his patient, Mrs Boyes, who had suffered from rheumatoid arthritis for twenty years and, in excruciating pain, was close to death. Her two sons were with her and supported her request for euthanasia. It seems neither they nor Dr Cox had any financial incentive. Dr Cox was charged with attempted murder and found guilty. Nevertheless, he was given a twelve-month suspended sentence and was not struck off the medical register.

The Tony Bland case

The circumstances of the Tony Bland case were tragic. In 1989, the seventeen-year-old football fan went to Hillsborough football stadium for an FA Cup semi-final. Supporters were crowding into the ground as the match started and a fatal crush ensued, when fans were pushed against the security fencing. Ninety-five people died. Tony Bland's lungs were crushed and his brain was deprived of oxygen; only his brain stem survived, and he fell into a persistent vegetative state. Such patients may survive from ten to thirty years. For three and a half years his body was maintained by artificial hydration and nutrition via a nasogastric tube. The part of his brain responsible for consciousness had turned to fluid.

Neither his family nor his doctors could see any benefit in keeping him alive in such a state, so in November 1992 they petitioned the High Court for permission to withdraw hydration and nutrition. The case eventually ended up at the House of Lords on appeal, and their decision was momentous: they ruled that artificial hydration and nutrition constituted medical treatment, and that a doctor had no duty to continue treatment where it would be of no benefit and . . . had not been consented to. On 22 February 1993 antibiotics and feeding were discontinued, and Tony Bland died nine days later.

Now for the application and assessment of the normative moral theories. We'll go through each in turn and see how they would help us make moral decisions in these cases.

Divine command theory

As a deontological theory, divine command theory emphasizes rules for determining one's actions and motives in ethics. Taking Christianity as our representative, there are two rules of particular relevance here, 'Thou shalt not kill' and 'Love your neighbour as yourself'. So what exactly does divine command theory recommend we do?

Well, its general stance is that human beings have a strong right to life, based on the belief that we are made in God's image, meaning more or less that we have an immortal soul, are rational, and have both free will and a moral conscience. The command 'Thou shalt not kill' reflects this attitude to the sacredness or sanctity of life, i.e. the inviolability of a human life.

For all this talk of sacredness, we still have only a *strong* right to life, *not* an *absolute* right, because this right can be overridden in certain circumstances, such as a just war, capital punishment, and self-defence in extremis. These exceptions open the door to the possibility that active euthanasia might also join them as an exception to the command not to kill. However, this door has been firmly shut by the majority of both traditional and liberal Christians on the grounds that all three exceptions involve victims who have either already killed unlawfully (capital punishment), or are out to kill unlawfully (the soldiers on the unjust side in a war, or someone trying to murder you). It's easy to see that a terminally ill patient is not in any way life-threatening to other people, and hence is a complete innocent. 'Thou shalt not kill' is normally interpreted as meaning 'Don't kill the innocent', so it follows from this that *divine command theory imposes an **absolute** ban on **all** forms of **active** euthanasia, no matter how painful the process of dying.*

But what about the other command, to 'Love your neighbour'? Doesn't this give us permission to put people out of their misery? Surely easing someone's pain is a sign of love? Of course, this is generally true, but if it's made into an absolute duty on a par with the duty not to kill the innocent, then the divine command theorist, and God, would be advocating contradictory and impossible things because the two principles could clash in the following way: where the only way to ease someone's pain, thus *obeying the command to love them*, is to kill them painlessly, thus *disobeying the command not to kill them*.

Divine command theorists try to escape this dilemma via two steps:

Step 1 Give priority to the command not to kill.
Step 2 Adopt the doctrine of double effect in these cases.

Taking step 1 resolves the dilemma by making the command not to kill win automatically every time there's a head-on collision between it and the command to love your neighbour. Step 2 makes it morally okay for doctors to prescribe pain-killing but death-hastening drugs, on the grounds that they're intending to ease their patient's pain, not to kill them, although they foresee that these very drugs will speed up their patient's death. Intention is paramount in deontological ethics, and as long as the doctor intends not to kill, but only to help their patient, they can't be held responsible for a foreseen but unintended and unavoidable side effect of the drugs used to alleviate the pain. So we have clear guidance from divine command theory on *active* euthanasia, i.e. *never* do it, even if the patient wants you to.

What about passive euthanasia? This isn't killing, it's merely letting die, and in the Bible there's no explicit command not to let die. So in this area there won't be a clash between the command to love your neighbour and the command not to kill, which seems to imply that the divine command theory would let doctors 'pull the plug' or withdraw food in suitable cases where a painless quicker death is more in the interests of their patient than a slower pointless life. Wouldn't such an act obey the command to love your neighbour? Yes, but divine command theorists worry about this sort of thing being the thin end of the wedge and that, if it becomes widespread and routine amongst doctors and patients, it's likely to have catastrophic side effects on the public's attitude to the sacredness of life. They fear a gradual weakening of our protective concern for human life, such that we start down a slippery slope, practising passive euthanasia on less and less severe cases until we end up doing what the Nazis did and performing not just passive but active euthanasia, and not just in terminal cases, but on the disabled, on political opponents, and on other 'undesirables'.

So divine command theory tends to be against all forms of euthanasia (the cases covered by double effect don't count as euthanasia but as 'treating the patient') and advocates palliative care instead, keeping the patient comfortable and pain-free while 'nature takes its course'. It *doesn't matter what the patient wants* because, if it's *absolutely* wrong to kill the innocent, the innocent's wanting this won't make it right, and if the patient isn't in a position to want anything in particular, i.e. in non-voluntary cases, even *passive* euthanasia is of dubious moral worth, not only because of its supposed tendency to lead to the sin of active euthanasia and the killing of the innocent, but also because it still looks like you're 'playing God', by usurping His right to dispose of life. 'The *Lord* giveth and the *Lord* taketh away', *not* us. The thought is that, since life's a gift from God, God's the one to decide when your time's up, not you or the doctor.

Assessing divine command theory

Firstly, the opposition of divine command theory to all forms of active euthanasia rests on a highly controversial factual basis involving the alleged existence of God, the divine commander, a supposedly authoritative moral text called the Bible, and the questionable assumptions that we have souls and have been specially created by God in his image, not that we have evolved naturally over millions of years as a higher form of animal. Doubting these undermines the sanctity of human life, which divine command theorists support (for example, life can't be a gift from God if there's no God to give it in the first place), thereby undermining the reasonableness of their absolute rejection of active euthanasia.

Secondly, when it comes to resolving the dilemma between implementing the command not to kill and the command to love your neighbour, the divine command theorists can't just **decide off their own bat** to give priority to the command not to kill, because *both* of these commands are in the Bible and, since nowhere in the Bible has God adjudicated on *which* is to have priority in the event of a clash, *both* should be given *equal* authority in the absence of any divine directive to the contrary. But then the once clear guidance we got from God evaporates, because the old dilemma is back concerning which command to follow in terminal cases of extreme pain. Do you kill painlessly out of love, or keep comfortable out of obedience to 'Thou shalt not kill'?

At this point the doctrine of double effect is supposed to ride to the rescue, allowing doctors unintentionally, but foreseeably, to kill off the patient while intentionally merely easing their pain with pain-relieving but death-enhancing drugs – for it's not really killing if you don't intend it but intend instead to ease the pain. The question must now be raised, 'Is the doctrine of double effect valid?'

First of all, it's a disputed principle. The utilitarians reject it because, if the consequences are all that count, and death is the outcome, then it doesn't matter either way whether you intend or merely foresee the death. Secondly, there are a great many examples where the difference between intending and foreseeing, if it exists at all, is so fine that it would be absurd to insist that, if there's an intention to kill, it's murder, but where death is merely foreseen as a side effect of one's action, it's not.

For example, is there any significant difference between pulling the plug in my bath with the intention of emptying it, and intending to pull the plug, foreseeing my bath will empty? And what would you say to the crazy doctor who intentionally kills an innocent visitor to the hospital in order to use their organs as transplants for some patients who would otherwise die, and justifies his action as not being murder because he intended not to kill the person but only to use his organs, and merely foresaw that as a side effect the visitor would die? And would this be an adequate defence for the 9/11 terrorists if Al-Qaeda had claimed, in justification of the atrocity, that the suicide pilots *intended* only to destroy *real estate* and *fuselage*? They didn't *intend* to kill anyone but merely *foresaw* that lives would be lost as a *side effect* of their action, so that means it wasn't murder.

Many think that double effect is a distinction without a difference. If this is correct, then we won't be able to get any coherent guidance from divine command theory concerning active euthanasia. But is it right about passive euthanasia and the slippery slope to the Nazis? The first point to make here is that we have some empirical evidence that this is far from inevitable. In the Netherlands, where active voluntary euthanasia for the terminally ill has been legal for some years now, there has been no indication of any tendency to go further and extend this practice to non-terminal cases. A second point is that as many checks and balances as are needed to avoid going down such a slope can be put in place – things such as, by *law*, needing at *least two* doctors' opinions on the patient's prognosis, *explicit written* request from the patient, *cooling-off periods* for reconsideration, *offer of palliative care* instead, and so on. With passive and active euthanasia hedged around by these safety measures, provided we aren't complacent, there are no real grounds for alarm.

The final test of assessment will be the comparison of what divine command theory advocates with what people's normal intuitive feelings are about what should be done. Well, if a recent Yougov poll is to be believed, over 70 per cent of people in the UK are in favour of legalizing passive euthanasia, with the appropriate checks and balances, so this is not an auspicious start for the divine command theory.

Furthermore, many if not most people in the UK have discarded traditional Christianity's beliefs concerning the moral authority of the Bible, the existence of a human soul, and the existence of a God who created us, as opposed to our evolving from lower animals. Life doesn't have so much sanctity these days, and many see this as a good thing, since this has in the past resulted in millions of terminally ill people having to suffer in agony, without the benefit of a quick and easy death, in the misguided belief that this reflected our concern for human dignity as stemming from having been made in God's image.

It seems to me – if I might be allowed to express my intuitions for a moment, in the hope that they may be representative of the majority view – that, if we're not prepared to let a pet dog die a pointlessly lingering and painful death when we can do something about it with a vet's painless but lethal injection, then all the more should we be willing to do the same for a human being in a similar situation who firmly and repeatedly wishes us to do this for them. If strict laws were set in place to protect this right to die with dignity, by legalizing active voluntary euthanasia, I fail to see how this could be anything other than a huge improvement in our quality of life, and a huge reduction in the fear of death, for I think this fear is more to do with the painful *process* of dying than with *death* itself.

Therefore, it seems that divine command theory, as applied to euthanasia, is an inadequate guide to action because it's contrary to our basic intuitions. It is also based on a highly dubious set of theological 'facts' which don't even provide clear guidance, because the two 'divine' commands most relevant in this area – 'Thou shalt not kill' and 'Love your neighbour' – seem to be at odds with each other.

Utilitarianism

Now for something completely different. The general utilitarian approach doesn't bother about divine commands and doesn't rate intentions as morally significant, but focuses instead on the consequences in terms primarily of the patient's happiness – the balance of pleasure over pain, and the wider impact on the relatives, doctors, nurses, the law, and the public. Again, the utilitarian approach rejects both the doctrine of double effect and the acts/omissions distinction, since, regarding the former, intentions are neither here nor there, so it's irrelevant, and regarding the latter, if the consequences are the same, it doesn't matter whether they're brought about by an act or an omission.

Act utilitarianism

Each individual case is treated on its own merits, with calculation of pain and pleasure outcomes determining what should be done. An act utilitarian would support *voluntary active* euthanasia if this results in less pain than passive euthanasia, which tends to extend the last days and hours of suffering, and even if the patient is pain-free, the anxious waiting of the relatives, the cost of the extra drugs and nursing time, and the fact that a hospital bed can't be used for some other needy patient will all be factors to be taken into the calculation, adding extra support for active euthanasia.

In non-voluntary cases the patient's wishes can't be taken into account in the calculation, unless they made a living will, so the joint decision of the closest relatives, along with the doctors, as to what to do in the best interests of the patient and all concerned will determine what is to be done. Act utilitarianism would probably advocate *active* euthanasia in most of these cases, avoiding the fruitless and expensive delays consequent upon the *passive* option.

Where the patient is able to express their wishes, and prefers passive euthanasia in the event of their falling into a coma, or if they opt against euthanasia altogether and prefer palliative care only, then their wishes would be respected as a key contributing factor to their happiness and peace of mind.

Rule utilitarianism

Rule utilitarianism won't consider each case on its own merits because it's more interested in adopting general rules that generate maximum happiness if *widely accepted by society.* Individual actions only get tested indirectly via their adherence to social rules. Now, a very good social rule that's widely accepted and is great for producing lots of happiness all round is the rule that we shouldn't go around killing innocent people. So rule utilitarianism will approach euthanasia with this rule in mind and advocate only forms of euthanasia that conform to it or, at the very least, don't tend to undermine it.

So although each individual *act* of active euthanasia might decrease a patient's pain more than any other alternative, such as passive euthanasia or palliative care, rule utilitarianism would probably reject active euthanasia across the board on the grounds that, if *widely adopted* as a medical routine in our hospitals, then among the general public, and in the longer term, this gradual whittling away of a good rule not to kill will cause more unhappiness than happiness. Think of the jitters millions of people would feel at the prospect of the rule 'not to kill' being eroded to something so thin that it afforded no protection at all. Plus, there would be widespread fear that the system may be abused and corrupted to such an extent that people would come to view hospitals with loathing and fear as 'death' houses rather than places of healing.

Because of its fear of rule-eroding slippery slopes, rule utilitarianism is suspicious of passive euthanasia too in case, with a change in the law to allow it, its widespread use infects and undermines people's readiness to adhere to the rule not to kill. Recall that utilitarians don't see any significant moral difference between acts and omissions, between killing and letting die, which adds extra weight to this worry. So there's likely to be a significant disagreement between act and rule utilitarianism in their approach to euthanasia.

Preference utilitarianism

The focus here is, of course, primarily on the *preferences* of the patient but also on those of the relatives and doctors, since these are also affected by any decision. So in cases of voluntary euthanasia, where the patient, relatives, and doctors all agree on this, then it's an open and shut case – it should be done, either actively or passively, according to the patient's *preference*. Where the patient disagrees with the relatives and/or doctors, then it's more problematic. How does one decide how much weight to give the patient's preference, in contrast to that of several close relatives, and in comparison to the expertise of the doctors? Or does the patient get an absolute right of veto over anyone else's preference, since it's their life after all?

In non-voluntary euthanasia it will obviously be the relatives in combination with the doctors who decide in the light of their preferences regarding what's in the best interests of the patient. In none of these situations does preference utilitarianism make any moral distinction between active and passive euthanasia or bother with the doctrine of double effect. If the decision is made to proceed with a request for euthanasia, the doctor should be entirely free to administer a lethal injection, the clear purpose of which is to end life in accordance with the patient's wishes.

Assessment of utilitarianism

While seeming to be an eminently down-to-earth, commonsense approach, utilitarianism nevertheless has some worrying counter-intuitive aspects which count against it. For instance, none of the versions canvassed above is concerned about the motives and character of the relatives and medical staff. It doesn't really matter if they have ulterior self-serving motives for what they do, as long as the greatest happiness or least pain is achieved. But this would encourage corruption of the whole business of euthanasia, and perhaps turn it into a kind of scam for those on the make. Act utilitarianism, in particular, would even seem to advocate involuntary euthanasia if the pleasure of the relatives and doctors outweighed the fear and pain of the unwilling patient.

Rule utilitarianism scores over act utilitarianism in this respect, because this sort of thing is devastating to tried-and-tested social rules against murder, and rule utilitarianism's strength is in protecting these and rejecting individual acts which undermine them. But, on the other hand, rule utilitarianism would also reject some individual acts of euthanasia that would unequivocally and significantly reduce a patient's agony without tending in the least to undermine traditional, happiness-protecting rules banning killing, and this too seems unacceptable to ordinary folk's moral intuitions.

But preference utilitarianism improves on act utilitarianism by outlawing any possible type of involuntary euthanasia provided it gives the patient's preference a veto over all others. On the whole, utilitarianism is a big improvement on divine command theory as applied to euthanasia, because it chimes in better with most people's moral intuitions concerning patient welfare, and because it comes free of the highly contentious, supernatural baggage that continues to drive, yet dog, the divine command theory. The latter protects the alleged sanctity of human life at the cost of a world of pain and indignity. Most people these days prefer less pain and more dignity to the dubious benefits of being made in God's image.

Kant's moral theory

As a deontological theory, Kant's moral position is not interested in consequences, but only in the actions themselves and their motives or maxims. Accordingly, we shall apply the categorical imperative to the problem of whether to perform euthanasia and see what his theory advises. Taking active voluntary euthanasia first, given what he says about suicide (the voluntary taking of one's own life to avoid pain) as a serious breach of the categorical imperative, it seems clear that Kant would condemn this out of hand as even worse than suicide, because *another* person, the doctor, is taking a life, and in Kant's book this makes it murder. The formula of universal law bids us universalize our maxim, which would be something like, 'When my life is nothing but pain and is running out, I'll ask someone else to kill me painlessly.' Kant would argue that this is not consistently willable as a universal law because you would have to will that reason universally kills off reason, which is a contradiction in conception. It therefore breaks the moral law and *must not be done ever by anyone.*

The formula of ends, which bids us treat persons as ends in themselves and never only as a means, agrees with this outcome because it would condemn the patient's abuse of his autonomy in breaching the formula of universal law, and would forbid others from aiding and abetting this immoral decision. The patient is *using* his very own *rational* nature, the *source of the moral law*, as a *mere means* to avoid pain, and is therefore not treating himself as an end in himself, thereby breaching the formula of ends.

Non-voluntary active euthanasia is also banned under both formulations of the categorical imperative because, again, it's the killing of a rational moral person by another rational moral person, and reason is not logically or morally allowed to kill an instance of itself. Also, this would not be treating the patient as an end in themselves but purely as a *means* to reduce pain. Such an action looks to the consequences, whereas according to Kant morality is not founded on this.

It's more difficult to see what Kant would say regarding passive euthanasia, whether voluntary or non-voluntary, because the categorical imperative deals only with positive actions, not passive inactions or omissions. On the one hand, from what Kant says about the notorious axe murderer incident, you must do your duty to tell the truth, even though it means passively letting the murderer kill his victim who is hiding in your house. So, in some circumstances, Kant does not have a problem with letting other people die, as long as you yourself don't actively kill them. But, on the other hand, there are aspects of passive euthanasia that aren't particularly inactive. Pulling the plug on a life-support machine is, after all, an action, and the withdrawal of food to a patient is a particular decision with its own maxim, so the categorical imperative should cover both of these cases, and it would seem to say that each decision, whether to stop food or to switch off life support, was done with the deliberate intention and maxim of shortening a life that would otherwise have continued for longer. This, again, would be a case of reason terminating reason and therefore wrong; but perhaps not. Take the following example.

Surely someone who is in an irreversible coma, or suffering from advanced Alzheimer's and doesn't know what day it is or who they are, let alone have the capability of rational moral thought, is no longer, or ever will be again, a rational source of the moral law; in other words, they're not a person or end in themselves in the Kantian sense – not even *potentially* so. If this is the case, then we don't have a duty to treat them as such, so it should be okay with the categorical imperative to perform passive euthanasia on them; this is not a case of reason killing reason, or of treating an end in itself as a mere means. In fact, why not resurrect the possibility of *active* non-voluntary euthanasia on the Kantian grounds that we are killing a non-rational human? The categorical imperative says nothing about how we should treat this type of being. They are therefore beyond the moral sphere, being even lower functioning than many animals.

Assessment of Kant's moral theory

Kant is strong on human dignity and the respect owed to persons, but worryingly unconcerned about human suffering and the consequences for the patient. I suppose Kant would have no objection to a patient being given pain relief on request, but it would seem that he can't consistently advocate pain relief that induces a coma-like state or even mental confusion or befuddlement, because this interferes with a person's reason and autonomy. Would Kant then have the patient keep his conscious reason while screaming in pain? It would appear so.

Even stranger results occur if we try to defend Kant's position by attempting to bring euthanasia into line with the categorical imperative under the description of 'helping others when they are in need', instead of Kant's notorious suicide example. Kant thinks it an imperfect duty to help others in need, because not to do so is to will a universal law where no one helps anyone else, which means willing that you yourself would not be helped when you want and need it. This is a contradiction in will since, although we can conceive such a possible world, we can't will such a world because, as rational but vulnerable beings, we will at times need help to continue living, and willing such a world would deny us this help. So, if it is an imperfect duty to help others in need, shouldn't it be an imperfect duty to help others in need of an easy and painless death?

There are two problems with this line of defence. One is that, in any clash between imperfect and perfect duty, perfect duty always wins. This means that, if it's a perfect duty not to kill or let die a rational being in pain in order to ease their pain (euthanasia, in other words), then trying to defend euthanasia on the grounds that it's an imperfect duty to help others will always lose out to the absolute prohibition against euthanasia, based on our perfect duty not to kill. The second is that, even if it *is* an imperfect duty to perform euthanasia, with no opposing perfect duty not to do so, this still results in the absurdity that you only have to perform euthanasia some of the time, and you get to pick who gets help and who doesn't, because imperfect duties don't require universal obedience at all times.

A weakness in Kant's theory is that it doesn't always give us clear or consistent moral advice regarding euthanasia. A further weakness is that it's contrary to our strong intuitions concerning the desirability and rationality of reducing pain and ending life when the alternative is a living hell.

Virtue ethics

The focus here will be on the virtues in play – the character of the patient, their family and friends, and the doctors involved – because, if the decision to have euthanasia performed stems from a virtuous character, then euthanasia will be a good thing, a noble act, whether active or passive, voluntary or non-voluntary. Virtue ethics is also concerned with the vital question as to whether euthanasia encourages the eudaimonic flourishing of life. This sounds paradoxical, because how could a decision to end life more quickly possibly contribute to a flourishing life? However, this conundrum is easily resolved by considering that, if the alternative to euthanasia is a steady, dismal, painful, undignified decline of one's faculties, such that in the end you can't control your bladder or bowels, you're gasping for breath, in and out of drug-induced stupefaction, and raving incoherently, then anything that avoids this nightmare has got to be flourishing by comparison.

But to die at the right time, when it feels right, and still to have your wits about you and be able to recognize your family and friends – this would seem to be a much more affirmative way of rounding off a life. It's also life-affirming and eudaimonic for your family and friends, for they will retain happier memories of you and not be plagued by horrible thoughts of your last days. So virtue ethics would favour a noble and dignified exit rather than have you dragged off stage kicking and screaming just because you want an extra few minutes in the limelight.

Being interested in virtuosity of character rather than the action itself, virtue ethics doesn't bother with the doctrine of double effect or the acts/omissions distinction, because it's the *nature of the agent* which is central to the morality of the killing or letting die, and the intending or foreseeing death, not the nature of the act or non-act. Virtue ethics doesn't lay down any rules concerning the right time for euthanasia, for this will differ from person to person according to their circumstances; rather, it's *cool with **any** type of euthanasia*, provided it's done *virtuously*, and if someone can die with dignity without euthanasia, e.g. peacefully asleep with drug-controlled pain, then this is fine too.

A patient facing a decision about euthanasia needs courage to die at the right time, because lingering on to the bitter end is symptomatic of cowardice (a vice of deficiency), and wanting to die too soon, e.g. as soon as you've heard the diagnosis, would be rash (a vice of excess).They would also need the virtue of pride in order to treat with contempt the indignities that would be heaped upon them throughout a humiliating physical and mental decline. Wisdom is needed to know when the right time is. Friendship is needed in order to be concerned for what your family and friends would have to go through if they had to witness the gruesome spectacle of your lingering and agonizing death.

Virtues appropriate for the medical staff are professionalism, compassion, and wisdom. Too little of these and you get the corresponding vices of incompetence, callousness, and stupidity. Too much and you get the vices of officious bureaucracy, bleeding-heart emotionalism, and cleverness in a bad sense. Virtues useful to family and friends are, in non-voluntary cases, the same as those needed by the patient in voluntary cases. But in voluntary cases they need to be friendly and supportive of the patient's decision while being prepared to advise the patient if they think he or she has made the wrong decision. This, of course, means that family and friends will also need wisdom to advise well.

Virtue ethics would advocate tough and detailed procedures to avoid any slippery slope that might result from its endorsement of active euthanasia, but these are only for the particular benefit of the vicious and unscrupulous who would be tempted to extend euthanasia to people who had lots of flourishing life left. The virtuous don't need such rules because they'll do the right thing by nature.

Assessment of virtue ethics

Although virtue ethics is mostly in line with our moral intuitions, I suspect that its advocacy of active euthanasia would make a lot of people uneasy. Public opinion is still quite conservative on this question. Another possible weakness is that virtue ethics doesn't tell us when, precisely, is the right time for euthanasia, and merely contents itself with saying rather vaguely that it differs from case to case, and that the wise patient will know when the time comes. Clashes between different virtues might make a decision impossible. For example, what if courage was leading you to go for euthanasia now, but compassion for your friends, who can't bear to see you go yet, leads you to want to postpone death? What do you do? I suppose if you have the virtue of wisdom this will sort out the dilemma, but again there's no specific guidance on how this is done, because no rules can be laid down.

Applying the normative theories to the two case studies

The case of Dr Cox

Theory	Verdict on what was done
Divine command theory	Bad
Utilitarianism (act)	Good
" (rule)	Bad (probably)
" (preference)	Good
Kant	Bad
Virtue ethics	Good

The Tony Bland case

Theory	Verdict on what was done
Divine command theory	Good (just about)
Utilitarianism (all)	Good
Kant	Good (probably)
Virtue ethics	Good

It seems to me that what was done in both cases was good, so in the Dr Cox case my intuitions strongly disagree with divine command theory, rule utilitarianism, and Kant. With regard to these three theories, this seems to me like a classic case of rule fetishism denying humane relief to a being in dire distress. I think Dr Cox was right to take the legally risky, yet morally heroic decision to terminate Mrs Boyes's life. In the Tony Bland case all four theories agree by and large, and I suspect most people's intuitions also agree on this, but would we all agree that using a lethal injection would have been even better? Divine command theory would definitely oppose it on the grounds that it is killing an innocent person; their *soul* is still there, after all, and finishing life is God's prerogative, not ours. The others, I think, would all support such an action, and so would I. But it's not clear what the general public would think of this, so the theories might get a mixed reception here.

5   Abortion

'Abortion' can be defined as 'the deliberate termination of a pregnancy by killing the foetus'. I shall generally use the word 'foetus' to refer to the unborn child at all stages of its development, from conception to birth, so as to leave the discussion open as to whether the foetus is or becomes a person at any time during this period. This question has been seen as one of the crucial issues in the problem of abortion because, if the foetus does become a person at some point, any subsequent abortion might be classed as murder – the wilful and wrongful killing of an innocent person. The problem of deciding the moral status of the foetus, in terms of whether it is or is not a person, arises because of the difficulty in drawing a definite person-defining line cutting through the continuous trajectory of foetal development. Various attempts have been made to define or pinpoint the 'magic' moment, but all are more or less arbitrary and controversial, and have run up against seemingly insurmountable difficulties.

Here's a list of the main suggestions and the problems they face. The foetus becomes a person:

1 *at conception.*
Problems:
  i)   A sardine is higher functioning than the foetus at this stage, yet we don't call it a person.
  ii) If it's replied that the foetus, unlike a sardine, is *potentially* higher functioning, and so a *potential* person, then:
      a) this in effect admits it's *not* a person *now, at conception*, thus the definition is refuted.
      b) it can also be objected that potential people don't have the rights, (e.g. the right to life) of *actual* people, and shouldn't therefore be treated as if they had. I am *now* a potential corpse but that doesn't mean I ought to be buried alive as I write this.
      c) since each sperm is a potential person, the potentiality argument would lead to the absurd conclusion that masturbation is mass murder, and that therefore half the human race should be given life sentences.
  iii) If it's replied that the foetus is special because it has a *soul* from the

moment of conception, and that's what makes it a person, unlike sperm, then:

a) we're embroiled in the philosophical difficulties of what the word 'soul' is supposed to mean; the seemingly insurmountable problem of how a completely immaterial entity, such as the soul, could possibly attach itself to a material body and causally interact with it; and whether there is any evidence for our possession of such a thing

b) it should also be pointed out that the Bible is completely silent on this issue. Nowhere does it state, or imply, that the foetus is a soul from the moment of conception.

2 *when it possesses a recognizably human shape (around eight weeks).*
Problems:

i) Surely being a person has to do with the possession of mental qualities such as self-awareness, the ability to reason, and a moral capacity of responsible decision-making, and not just a human physical form. So having human form is not a necessary condition of personhood; that's why we can immediately recognize 'ET' as a person, though not a human one.

ii) It's not a sufficient condition either, because we could easily imagine an alien with a human form which behaves just like a monkey, yet we wouldn't call it a person. So the foetus may be a human being physically speaking, without being a person yet.

3 *when it is sentient, i.e. at the point when it can feel pain/pleasure.*
Once the nervous system has developed, i.e. from eight weeks onwards, sentience appears possible.

Problem: This is not a sufficient condition of personhood, because rabbits feel pain but aren't people, and it's not a necessary condition either because, if a person was under general anaesthetic but retained consciousness, they would not cease to be a person during such a state.

4 *when it is viable, i.e. when it has the ability to survive independently outside the womb.*

Problem: Since, for our purposes, 'viability' means 'independent survivability with *technological aid*' such as incubators and intensive care facilities, this would mean that a foetus would be classed as a person if the mother lived in a high-tech society but not if she lived in a low-tech one. However, it seems absurd that the personhood of the foetus should depend on the availability of equipment and medical expertise in the local hospital – that the close proximity of certain machines has the power of turning you into a person.

5 *at birth.*

Problems:

    i) This has the counter-intuitive consequence that it would be permissible to abort an *eight*-month-old foetus *still unborn,* but wrong to kill a *seven*-month-old foetus *born prematurely,* **despite the former being more developed.**

    ii) Spatial location inside or outside a womb seems totally irrelevant to the question of personhood. Surely the self-same organic being does not suddenly become a person on emerging from the dark warmth of the womb into the bright chill of the room. Personhood doesn't depend on 'geography'.

But if not here, when? When is there present a sufficient degree of self-consciousness, rationality, and all the other person-making qualities? At age one, two, five, ten? But then infanticide prior to the magic age of personhood would not be murder, and this seems highly objectionable. The question of infanticide is simply at the extreme end of the problem of where on the slopes of the developmental continuum to set up camp for personhood.

Types of abortion predicament

Abortion, like most things, comes in all shapes and sizes. Reasons for abortion range from:

- causes of pregnancy due either to rape or to contraceptive failure
- the condition of the foetus, e.g. anencephaly (no brain)
- the condition of the mother, e.g. under age, health at risk, adverse social conditions such as poverty, drug addiction, abusive partner
- other issues, e.g. having the baby would spoil the mother's holiday, or figure, or career chances.

Taking sides?

The two main sides in the abortion debate are the pro-choice advocates at one end of the spectrum and the pro-lifers at the other. Pro-choice focuses on the rights and happiness of the mother, arguing that these are more important than those of the foetus. This position would allow abortion as morally permissible in most if not all cases. It is sometimes given the name of 'abortion on demand'. Pro-life focuses on the rights of the foetus, or 'unborn child' as they prefer to call it, arguing that its right to life overrides anything, or almost anything, that may be cited in the mother's favour. These are the conservative thinkers who argue that abortion is wrong in most if not all cases. Although advocates of each of our four moral theories may be found throughout the range of opinion, from pro-choice to pro-life, I think it's safe to say that the bulk of divine command theorists are at the conservative pro-life end, whereas the bulk of the utilitarians are liberal pro-choice thinkers. Kantian deontologists may be found in either camp, depending on how they interpret and apply the categorical imperative; more on this later. Finally, the virtue ethicists, as you would expect from recalling their doctrine of the mean, generally find themselves in the middle, veering from a more pro-choice to a more pro-life position depending on the circumstances of each case and the relevant virtues that would apply.

Now for the application and assessment of the four normative theories. We'll cover them in the following order:

1 utilitarianism
2 divine command theory
3 Kant
4 virtue ethics.

1 Utilitarianism

Act utilitarianism

Since, for act utilitarianism, the name of the game is for each action to produce as much pleasure or happiness all round as possible, the rights and wrongs of abortion will be decided by these kinds of consequence as they vary from one abortion to the next. Whether the foetus becomes a person at some stage in the pregnancy is of little significance in itself, because persons are expendable in the pursuit of maximum utility: recall that, according to hedonistic act utilitarianism, pleasure is the only good in itself, so what counts is the degree of *sentience* possessed by the foetus at different stages of development, and how this balances against that of the mother and any others affected by the decision.

In cases of rape, for instance, it all depends on how the mother feels about having a baby conceived in such a manner. If she wants it badly enough and can distance herself and the baby from the rape, perhaps with the help of counselling and family support, then it would be wrong to have an abortion, because her distress at the abortion would outweigh her happiness if she had had the child. But if she feels disgust or hatred for the foetus, regarding it with loathing as a sort of virus or parasite implanted within her, which she feels merely continues and exacerbates the rape and would blight her whole life, then, unless she would be happy to have the baby adopted, abortion is clearly the obvious choice, morally speaking.

Similar considerations would apply in cases of contraceptive failure. It's not likely the mother would feel disgust – more likely she'd be shocked – but, again, whether an abortion would be right depends on the calculations of the pleasure and pain resulting from the alternatives. The mother should be allowed to choose an abortion if she wants, because to forbid this would have much greater traumatic consequences for her happiness and state of mind – and for that of the baby, born unwanted.

When we come to severely handicapped and defective foetuses the pleasure/pain calculations, while clearly including the mother and her family, centre even more on what's in store for the foetus. Again, each case will differ, depending on the severity of the disablement, the mother's mental state, and the doctors' prognosis. In general, the more severe the foetal defect, the more likely is the act utilitarian to recommend abortion as a moral obligation, because if all the foetus has to 'look forward to' is a life that's 'nasty, brutish, and short,' then it's better to cut its losses with an early abortion.

Again, regarding the mother's social conditions, the worse these are, the stronger the case for abortion. In every case the calculation must be whether the overall happiness of the foetus, the mother, and all concerned will be increased or decreased by an abortion, and then decide accordingly.

In life-threatening conditions such as ectopic pregnancies (these are where the fertilized egg lodges in the fallopian tube; without an operation to remove it the mother will die), because the mother's life is subject to much more intense pleasure and pain than that of the foetus, and because both will die anyway if nothing is done, act utilitarians would advocate an abortion as obviously the right thing to do. The mother is much more self-aware, has hopes for the future which death would dash, and so would suffer more, whereas the foetus knows nothing of this or itself, and so would suffer less. Provided the mother agrees to the abortion, the calculations are easy. The foetus dies painlessly and the mother survives to live a long life. The alternative is that both die and the mother misses out on all that happiness.

Where the mother is under age, the significance of her condition may escape her. The hedonic calculations would need to be done by others and a decision about whether to abort made on her behalf. Yet again, these calculations would need to take into account her age, lack of knowledge, lack of responsibility, state of mind, and the family and social context, and a decision made based on her and her child's best interests. Act utilitarians would probably go for abortion in these cases.

Lastly, in cases where taking the baby to term would clash with the mother's plans or values, and she favours an abortion to solve this problem (which basically leads to abortion on demand), then the act utilitarian would still advise the abortion, provided the more or less trivial or at least manageable 'pain' of the mother (ranging from the inconvenience of a spoilt holiday to the undermining of her career prospects) resulting from not aborting would exceed the relatively painless death of the foetus were the abortion to go ahead.

Preference utilitarianism

The usual problems of calculating pleasure and pain will of course continue to bemuse act utilitarians. Preference utilitarianism side-steps these difficulties by, instead, finding out the preferred outcomes of all the relevant parties – an easier task altogether. However, the one party at the centre of the problem, namely the foetus itself, clearly doesn't have a say, since it can't have a preference one way or the other. This is a disadvantage compared with the act utilitarian approach, because at least that could accommodate the pain/pleasure of the foetus in the overall calculations. At least the foetus had a 'say'.

Problems also arise when it comes to weighing preferences. For example, although it's obvious the mother's preference is most important, how is one to weigh the preferences of the medical staff if they differ from those of the parent? However, in most cases things should be pretty straightforward if all or most agree on their preferred outcome, and this will apply to all four categories of predicament. Since family and doctors tend to support the mother's preference, whatever she wants will be deemed the right thing.

Rule utilitarianism

Finally, rule utilitarianism will look at the results of applying certain rules or policies of action to abortions and judge its advice on its assessment of these. Would there be more or less harm done to society if there were a rule aborting foetuses produced via rape? Probably less, so abortion in these cases is right. The same could be said for failed contraception, severely handicapped foetuses, ectopic pregnancies, and dire social conditions; abortion seems right in all these cases under such a rule, notwithstanding the odd exception, which the rule would *overrule* anyway.

But I think rule utilitarians might baulk at allowing a rule to abort in trivial cases in which the mother, say, at first wants the baby and then afterwards changes her mind because she's worried about getting stretch marks, for the message this sends out to society as a whole is that human life is extremely cheap at its inception – of even less importance than stretch marks. If this kind of attitude were to spread to human life in general, not just at its inception, we would be on a slippery slope to social chaos, and much greater long-term unhappiness than the short-term happiness of a woman without stretch marks. So it's better to have a strict and exceptionless utilitarian rule here, even if there may be individual cases where the mother is so paranoid about her stretch marks that, were an abortion allowed, there would be a positive balance of pleasure over pain in that *particular* instance.

In summarizing the general utilitarian approach, it's worth noting that in none of the above discussion was there any talk of the sanctity of life, or the rights of the foetus and the mother, the reason being that this is deontological language and has no place in utilitarianism, which is concerned only with consequences and not the so-called intrinsic value of the person, action, or motive.

Most forms of utilitarianism, most of the time, will allow abortion on demand in all four categories, subject to the law, which in the UK is that after twenty-four weeks abortion is illegal unless the physical or mental health of the mother is under threat or there is severe foetal abnormality.

Let's assess the utilitarian position. One of its strengths is that it addresses many of our concerns regarding the welfare of the foetus and mother. It has their interests at heart, and its down-to-earth, common-sense approach has a lot in common with our intuitive responses when considering abortion. Still, utilitarianism has four aspects that are particularly worrying, and which compromise its acceptability as a normative, action-guiding theory in this matter. They all boil down to one big defect at the heart of the theory, namely a serious undervaluing of the foetus.

i) Abortion is permissible for the flimsiest of reasons (spoilt figure; an irritation on holiday), leading to abortion on demand, or even on a whim, provided the slight discomfort of the mother outweighs the painlessness of the aborted foetus. This dismissive, throwaway attitude to human life at its inception is too cavalier.

ii) More evidence of this attitude is the ease with which utilitarians appeal to the replaceability of the foetus, were it to be aborted. The attitude seems to be, 'there's plenty more where that came from', so if a woman aborts a foetus because it's going to spoil a holiday, that's okay, if she intends to get pregnant again afterwards, thus replacing the lost foetus. But this is demeaning to human life. The foetus is treated like a commodity that may be disposed of if proves to be a nuisance, like a car you get tired of and replace with a different model.

iii) In a similar vein is Singer's comment that, until the foetus is capable of feeling pain, 'an abortion terminates an existence that is of no "intrinsic" value at all' (*Practical Ethics*, p. 151). This overlooks the special relationship that the foetus has, as a potential son or daughter, with the mother – the depth of emotion involved, it being part of *her*. This is not like losing a tooth, or having a haircut. Singer also remarks that it's hard to get upset over the termination of a few cells. Again, this might be true of him but, to a mother contemplating an abortion, these few cells would be the *child she never had*. Singer misses the poignancy of this, and the heartache involved.

iv) Another worrying symptom of the utilitarians' disregard for the foetus is Singer's defence of infanticide on the grounds that it can't be murder, or indeed wrong in any other way, because a) the child, not being self-conscious, is not yet a person; b) if it were killed painlessly, the parents' preference would outweigh that of the child, which in fact is too young to have a preference. This is callously counter-intuitive.

Not all utilitarians are quite this dismissive of the foetus. Rule utilitarians, as we've seen, would draw the line at abortions for flimsy reasons. However, the focus of their attention is the *happiness* of the foetus, not the foetus *itself*, for it has no intrinsic value. It's just the wrapper; the *happiness* is the more valued chocolate inside. This attitude mislocates the proper source of the foetus's value. So utilitarianism can't give us what we seek.

2 Divine command theory

On the face of it, applying this theory to abortion should be straightforward: just find out what God commands us to do about abortion, and then do it. All you need worry about are the divine rules, never mind the consequences. So what does God say, taking the Bible as our source? Well, God never comments *directly* on the question of abortion or in what circumstances, if any, it should be carried out. There's no unambiguous command such as, 'Thou shalt not kill a foetus, or potential person.' The nearest thing we have is the fifth commandment, 'Thou shalt not kill', interpreted as 'Don't kill people', plus a number of verses indicating God's creative activity in the development of the foetus in the womb (see Psalm 139:13) and Jesus's welcoming attitude to children (see Mark 10:13–16).

Given this raw data, divine command theorists have generally interpreted these verses to mean that the foetus has a soul from conception and is therefore a person from the word go. Personhood does not depend on self-awareness, rationality, and so on, but on being essentially an immaterial, spiritual entity called a soul, which animates its bodily vehicle. So this makes the command not to kill refer not only to innocent adult persons, but also to foetuses from conception onwards. From conception, all human life is sacred because made in God's image right from the start. So what we get when we apply divine command theory is practically *a blanket ban on all abortions throughout all four categories* – the very opposite of a utilitarian approach. In all cases the foetus, qua person, has an absolute, sacred right to life, which it is wrong to violate.

Abortion would be unthinkable in relatively trivial cases of ruined holidays and stretch marks, but even in rape cases the innocence of the foetus precludes its murder, which is what an abortion would amount to. Rape is bad enough, but to follow it up with a murder would be outrageous. It's true that the mother has a right to decide what happens to her own body, but the foetus's right to life trumps this and, anyway, the foetus's *soul* can't belong to its mother's body.

In cases of severe foetal deformity, the foetus should be carried to term and, depending on the level of severity, in terminal cases it should be kept comfortable until it dies. This is tantamount to passive euthanasia. In non-terminal cases it should be kept comfortable indefinitely. Under no circumstances should it be actively killed, i.e. aborted, either in the womb or outside it.

There is perhaps only one circumstance where an abortion is permissible, and this is where the mother will die if the pregnancy is taken to term. In ectopic cases this will happen if no abortion is performed, and since the mother's right to life is as important as the foetus's we have a dead heat. Now, if nothing is done, both will die, and this is lose–lose. But divine command theory uses the doctrine of double effect as a way round this dilemma, because if the surgeon performs the life-saving operation by removing the fallopian tube containing the egg, with the *intention of saving the mother's life*, while merely *foreseeing* the unavoidable death of the foetus, then the surgeon has done no wrong, because it's the *intention* that determines the moral status of the act. In all cases where the refusal to abort brings about unhappy consequences for the mother and foetus, these should be ameliorated as far as possible via social services. Options such as adoption and fostering should be considered, but the consequences, be they ever so bad, aren't morally relevant.

But what about the command to 'Love your neighbour'? Doesn't this pull in the opposite direction, especially in cases of severe foetal abnormality? Isn't it clearly an act of love to reduce someone's pain as much as possible, and if the foetus has only a short painful life to 'look forward' to, isn't it better for it to die a sooner pain-free death than a later pain-wracked one? The essential dilemma at the heart of the divine command theory is that God is giving marching orders in opposite directions at once: don't kill, but ease pain through killing. As with euthanasia, many, if not most, divine command theorists assume the command not to kill takes priority, and resolve the dilemma in this way, reinterpreting 'Love your neighbour' as meaning ease pain *except* through killing.

Others take the other line, especially in really severe cases of foetal abnormality, e.g. where the foetus, if not aborted, will result in a baby without a brain and no hope of conscious life. An abortion here would be a loving act that draws the curtain down on a being that has such a minimal quality of life as to be barely existing at all in human terms. Aborting or killing it would not be killing in the full-blooded sense of depriving a conscious being of its life, or even the half-blooded sense of depriving a potentially conscious being of the possibility of a full life.

Assessing divine command theory

Unlike utilitarianism, because of its stance on the absolute value and sacredness of human life, divine command theory would never condone abortion on flimsy or whimsical grounds. This is a real strength, because it squares with many people's intuitions concerning the dignity of human life and the seriousness of any decision to abort.

Unfortunately, it appears to take foetal life too seriously for the mother's and the foetus's own good. The mother's rights and welfare come a poor second to those of the foetus, and the interests of deformed and damaged foetuses are not sufficiently taken into account. Because of the absolute ban on abortion due to the soul superstition, in many cases this leads to terrible hardship, suffering, and unwanted babies. I don't think 'superstition' is too strong a word for this belief that there are such things as souls created by God at conception, and united with fertilized eggs, one per egg. A superstition is a deep-seated but irrational belief in paranormal or supernatural forces operating in everyday life. No reputable moral theory should depend on such an ill-founded belief, and people certainly shouldn't be made to suffer because of it. There are several reasons for thinking it's superstitious to believe that the fertilized egg has a soul.

Firstly, there's no evidence for it. The only one who could tell us either doesn't exist, or is silent on the matter, and this is one reason why the church's greatest thinkers can't agree. Augustine (AD 354–430) thought the foetus acquired a soul at forty-six days. Aquinas (AD 1225–1274) thought that male foetuses get a soul after forty days, but female ones, for some reason, have to wait ninety days for theirs. The modern church generally settles on the moment of conception, no doubt guided by the Holy Spirit, but apparently this doesn't make for infallibility either. Only the pope enjoys that, and he, like God, has not made any official, ex cathedra pronouncement on the matter.

Secondly, it's a complete mystery how a completely immaterial entity such as the soul, whatever that is, can causally interact with any physical body, including a fertilized egg, since the two have absolutely nothing in common. We have no well-founded experiences of forces external to the universe, yet we would have to believe that such a force attends every sex session that results in conception and performs a miraculous intervention of the laws of nature by 'injecting' a soul (yet another supernatural entity) into the zygote. Descartes (French philosopher, 1596–1650) tried to get round the causal problem plaguing this relation of soul to body by suggesting that the soul was somehow 'mixed in' with the body. But a ball bearing lobbed into a soufflé has more chance of becoming 'mixed in' than a soul, 'lobbed' by God, has of mixing with a zygote. At least both ball bearing and soufflé are material objects; a soul isn't even that. Replying that God has all power and can perform mysteries such as this is an explanatory cop-out, and is as philosophically unsatisfying as an author explaining that the trussed-up hero facing a firing squad escaped 'with a mighty bound'.

Thirdly, let's grant, and it's a big grant, the soul is somehow 'in' the blastocyst (this is the name for the bundle of cells into which the single-cell zygote develops as a result of cell division). At this early stage the cells, are as yet undifferentiated, which means that, being stem cells, they have the potential to form *any* bodily tissue. But it follows from this that the soul is mixed in with cells which will form *the placenta*, the *amniotic sac*, and the *umbilical cord*, as well as the *foetal cells proper*. Does this mean that, when the non-foetal cells eventually actualize their potential, the soul unmixes with them (how does that work?), but that until that time the potential umbilical cord, along with the placenta, is a sacred person?

Fourthly, from conception up to fourteen days a number of blastocysts split into two and either stay split, forming identical twins, or reunite, forming the original individual. This poses a number of dilemmas for the soul superstition.

i) Souls, being simple (i.e. not made up of parts), cannot split, so for blastocysts which split permanently, God must either lob in another soul at the time of the split to cover the second blastocyst, or settle for just the one soul, in which case a person will grow up without a soul, which is impossible according to divine command theory. So it looks like we need another soul here.

ii) However, if so, then in cases where the divided blastocyst reunites to become the original again, we'll have a soul going spare, so God would have to remove the extra soul to avoid the absurdity of this particular adult possessing two souls instead of the regulation one – yet another miracle, making some women's wombs rather busy thoroughfares for supernatural transactions.

To avoid such silly extra miracles, divine command theorists might reply that God's omniscience would allow Him to predict which blastocysts will split permanently and which will reunite, thus allowing him to allocate the reuniters only one soul and the permanent splitters two souls at the start, so that the extra one is available to move over with the bit that splits off. But this just leads to more superstitious absurdity, because

iii) it would be okay to abort the bit that splits off from a reuniter since, while it is split, it doesn't have a soul and therefore isn't a person. Divine command theorists won't want to admit this possibility

iv) as regards permanent splitters, if an abortion occurs before it splits, this would amount to a *double* murder because of the two souls making two people inside the tiny bundle of cells. This seems equally implausible.

In view of this divine comedy, it appears the soul is more of an arcade idea than an arcane one. When making decisions in life, and especially life-and-death decisions such as whether to have an abortion, it's much better to avoid things such as touching wood, blowing on dice, or playing the soul card. The soul is as reliable in morals as Lady Luck is to gamblers.

3 Kant

Before applying Kant's theory to abortion we need to clear up a possible ambiguity in his concept of rationality. This is necessary, as he never explicitly addresses the question of our duties towards *potentially* rational beings. He doesn't, as far as I know, comment directly on abortion, and clearly the healthy foetus is potentially rational in that, barring accidents, and if not aborted, it will become a normal human person capable of rational moral choice. Much hangs on our interpretation of Kant here because, if he's only interested in beings who are *actually* rational, regarding only these as ends in themselves, then foetuses won't have moral value and can be disposed of, much like animals; we have no duties towards them since, according to Kant, the categorical imperative doesn't apply. To kill or abort a foetus won't, then, be a case of reason killing reason (in *this* sense of *actual* reason) and, not being rational, the foetus can be used as a means to our ends because the second formulation of the categorical imperative only prohibits treating ends in themselves in this way, and non-rational beings aren't ends.

If this is the way to interpret Kant, then *the categorical imperative won't apply to abortion and so would allow abortion on demand*. But it may be arguable that a different interpretation is better, one wherein Kant sees reason not just as actual, but as *potentially* available to a rational person, and that a being can be deemed a rational end in themselves if at any time it only has the *potential* to be rational.

Here's the argument:

Premise 1: If Kant thinks of rationality as having to be *actual* for us to have duties towards rational beings, then we would have no duties towards people who are asleep, have fainted, are under anaesthetic, have been knocked unconscious, are in a coma or a drug/alcohol induced stupor, or are temporarily insane, and so on, because they aren't *actually* rational during these episodes.

Premise 2: This would be an absurd consequence, because then we could kill them, eat them, experiment on them, as we do animals. Anyone wanting to bump someone off just has to wait for them to fall asleep and then do it. But Kant would never allow this.

Intermediate conclusion: Therefore, Kant can't think that being rational means *only* having to be *actually* rational.

Main conclusion: Therefore, he must think being rational includes being *potentially* rational.

This argument, *if it works*, opens the door for the categorical imperative to apply to healthy foetuses, in which case Kant's moral theory will impose a ban on all abortions except those performed on foetuses that are so badly deformed that they don't even have the potential to be rational – for instance, anencephalic foetuses or those who, despite having a brain, won't live long enough to use it.

Any abortion in any other category will be condemned as murder by the categorical imperative because it is a case of reason killing (potential) reason, and of treating a (potential) person as a mere means rather than as an end in themselves. Bad, unhappy consequences as a result of not aborting don't count; and, of course, any decision not to abort is only right if it's also done merely because it's right. If any other motive, such as love for the child, drives your decision to keep the baby, then your decision is not moral.

Assessment of Kant

A major strength of Kant's theory is that, on the 'potential reason' interpretation, the status of the foetus as an end in itself protects it from being aborted on flimsy grounds, thus avoiding the utilitarian line while, at the same time, unlike divine command theory, not having to pay for this protection by basing it on the flimsy grounds of the soul superstition. Unfortunately, there are five problems undermining his theory as it applies to abortion.

i)   The major strength mentioned above is available with only *one* interpretation. The other 'actual reason' interpretation allows abortion on demand, and then Kant is lumbered with the utilitarian position. But it's not certain which interpretation is correct.

ii) The argument used to support the 'potential reason' interpretation may be flawed because based on a false analogy with the cases listed in its first premise. Sleeping adults may not be actually rational in the sense of *currently* engaging in rational activities such as doing maths, but they are *actually* rational in the *dispositional* sense of, even during sleep, *actually* having the *capacity* to do maths if woken, which makes it *true* to say of them *even while asleep* that they have the *rational belief* that $2 + 2 = 4$. **This is not the same for healthy foetuses.** They aren't actually rational even in the dispositional sense, because it's *not* true to say of them that they *now, while unconscious in the womb,* have rational beliefs about things such as maths. They have no rational beliefs at all, only the mere long-term potential to acquire them. This would allow Kant to condemn the murder of a sleeping adult while not condemning the abortion of a healthy foetus, because the former is *actually dispositionally* rational and therefore protected by the categorical imperative, whereas the latter is *not actually* rational in *any* way, but merely *potentially* so, and so lacks moral protection. The argument for the 'potential' rationality interpretation is therefore invalid, resting as it does on a false analogy which in turn, was generated by an equivocation on the term 'potential'. The unconscious foetus and the sleeping adult are not the same because the potential rationality of the former is *mere potential,* whereas the potential rationality of the latter is an *actual disposition.*

iii) As a result of this analysis, each interpretation is equally plausible as a reflection of Kant's intention, giving Kantians the unpalatable choice of either living with the inconsistency of adopting both, or adopting one and lurching to either the utilitarian extreme or the divine command extreme, depending on which interpretation is favoured.

iv) Another problem with the 'potentially rational' interpretation is that it leads to the two formulae of the categorical imperative contradicting each other. The formula of ends demands respect for the potentially rational foetus, so it's our moral duty not to kill it or use it as a means.

But when we apply the formula of universal law we get a different story. The mother will ask, 'Can I universalize my maxim to abort this foetus in these circumstances of severe spina bifida?' The answer is 'yes', because such a world is easily imaginable and logically possible. There is no contradiction in nature, because it wouldn't lead to universal abortions and therefore the cessation of the human race and rationality. That *would* be a contradiction, of reason killing reason. Instead, it would lead only to universal abortions for severe spina bifida cases, and that's not self-contradictory. But is universalizing this maxim a contradiction in will? No, because for that to happen there'd have to be the possibility that the mother would end up on the wrong end of her maxim and herself become a foetus with spina bifida. This is not even theoretically possible, because she'd have to imagine herself as a foetus with a will, but foetuses don't have will that can be contradicted and, even more out of the question, they can't logically be adults and foetuses at the same time. Therefore the universalized maxim to abort is a contradiction neither in nature nor in will and so is morally permissible, which clashes with what the formula of ends tells us to do.

v)   Kant's one-dimensional focus on duty and respect for the moral law, as the *only* morally praiseworthy motive, dehumanizes the relation between mother and foetus. He must ignore the intimate and raw feelings of love and the instincts of protective care mothers have for their babies. These very emotions might lead a woman to decide on an abortion if the foetus, her baby, is likely to suffer considerable pain in its short life. Their moral value doesn't register with Kant, yet surely these feelings are not just morally relevant but ethically crucial to any decision to abort. This is *her baby* we're talking about, not just some abstract rational source of future categorical imperatives.

4 Virtue ethics

The holistic nature of virtue ethics provides it with an approach to abortion which contrasts with all the other theories. Neither foetus nor mother are treated as utilitarian shells containing precious pleasure, or as Kantian generators of rational moral principles, or as the bloodless souls of divine command theory, but as flesh and blood human beings with an immensely complicated array of conflicting emotions, desires, thoughts, and social relationships, trying in trying circumstances to make their way in the world as best they can.

The virtues are essentially future looking because they are means to the eudaimonic, flourishing telos of life, and are valuable because they help one achieve one's potential. It's only natural, then, that it's the foetus's *emotional significance to its mother*, along with its *potential* as a *flourishing human being*, which is the focus of attention here, rather than the red herring of whether the foetus is a *person* at any time during pregnancy.

This stance is supported by Thomson's thought experiment of the famous violinist (see Rachels, *Moral Problems,* pp. 130–50). The story goes that you have been kidnapped by the society of music lovers and wake up to find yourself in hospital, with a famous violinist plugged in to your kidneys. He's suffering from a rare and fatal blood disease, and if he doesn't have the use of your kidneys for nine months he'll die. Thomson argues that, although it would be very nice of you to allow this, especially after the way you've been treated, you're not morally obliged to do so, and would do no wrong if you unplugged yourself from the violinist and let him die, despite the fact that he's a ***person with a full right to life.*** His right to life does not give him the right to use your body against your will. This judgement would also apply if, instead of being kidnapped, you had merely wandered into the ward by mistake and been taken for a volunteer 'plugee'.

The relevance of this to cases of rape or contraceptive failure will be obvious. Even if the foetus is classed as a person on a Kantian or religious basis, it wouldn't make much difference to the morality of an abortion in such circumstances; it would still be morally permissible because the foetus's right to life would not give it the right to use the woman's body against her will, so she may 'unplug' it.

Virtue theorists only have to ask themselves two questions to decide whether an abortion is good or not.

- Can it be performed virtuously – that is, as a result of one or more of the virtues, e.g. compassion, wisdom?
- Can it be done so as to enhance eudaimonia or a flourishing life for the agent (the mother's eudaimonia *incorporating*, rather than overriding, that of the foetus)?

If the answer to both is 'yes' then such an abortion is good; otherwise it is bad. Let's see how this pans out when applied to different cases.

i) Regarding pregnancies caused by rape or contraceptive failure, since a woman's eudaimonia would be more enhanced via a wisely chosen voluntary and planned pregnancy, than by one foisted on her, especially by a rapist, virtue theory in the vast majority of these cases would be likely to recommend an abortion as the virtuous thing to do.

ii) Cases of severe foetal abnormality, e.g. an anencephalic foetus, will generally lead to an abortion, based on the virtues of compassion for the child and the wisdom to see that such a short, painful, low-quality life would be futile and anything but flourishing, and would have a major negative impact on the well-being of all concerned. In such cases, an abortion is good. But there may be mothers with less severely deformed foetuses that have non-life-threatening abnormalities (perhaps Downs Syndrome, or autism, or milder forms of spina bifida) who choose not to have an abortion because they think they can give the child a loving, supportive, and happy life. Displaying courage, patience, loyalty, dedication, and a string of other virtues, she may feel she is all the richer for having this experience and that her child, though not able to flourish in the full sense of an able-bodied or sound-minded human being, nevertheless has been given the chance to realize *its* potential in flourishing, which wouldn't have been the case had she had the abortion. In this situation, an abortion is bad.

iii) In terms of the mother's condition (social, mental, physical) in general, the harsher the social conditions, the less chance there is for a eudaimonic life for the baby and mother. A wise mother, seeing this, and having compassion for the foetus, may decide to abort it – a decision virtue ethics would tend to support – but social conditions can vary so markedly that very little specific advice can be given in advance. Everything has to be decided on a case-by-case approach rather than by reference to strict principles, for the virtuous mean will shift relative to each different situation.

In an ectopic pregnancy if nothing is done, both mother and foetus will die, so a case such as this is one of the few areas in which virtue ethics gives us an unequivocal answer. Abortion is definitely the only wise and eudaimonic option. With under-age mothers, given the likely psychological, physical, and familial effects on a young girl of giving birth and rearing a child when she's barely out of childhood herself, it's likely that virtue ethics would advise the decision-makers to go for abortion. They'd need to have the wisdom to get advice from the best medical, and possibly psychiatric, experts but, of course, it all depends on the details of the case. If the mother isn't too young (say, fifteen), and if she's relatively mature, has a supportive partner and family, and wants the baby, then perhaps the wise thing to do, the eudaimonic thing, is not to abort. Both mother and baby would likely thrive.

iv) When other issues are involved, we have women at this end of the spectrum who might abort a foetus, previously wanted and planned because, let's say, the opportunity of a nice holiday has come up, and to continue the pregnancy would spoil it. Virtue ethics would condemn such a mother as callous and selfish, and hence vicious. She is concerned only for a two-week period of her life, and not its *overall* flourishing, and is willing to eliminate all the eudaimonic possibilities of a lifetime for her baby. *A virtuous agent would not literally **kill** for a good holiday.* An abortion in such circumstances is bad.

But now let's take a less superficial reason for abortion. Let's say a woman has all her life been aiming for, and working towards, a career goal – an Olympic gold medal, for instance. This will obviously give her a deep sense of fulfilment if achieved, and many virtues will have gone into trying to attain the dream. Now suppose she's been passed over by her country's selectors, a silly error of judgement on their part. She thinks her last chance has gone and so gets pregnant as the start of an alternative family career, when, suddenly, through the letterbox drops a letter from the selectors inviting her to the Olympic Games in the place of Miss X who has had to drop out. I can't see virtue theorists blaming her for having an abortion so as to take her one big chance to compete for that gold medal. Since this is something she has lived and breathed since she was a little girl it's not like a two-week holiday, but goes much deeper into her *being*. She *is* an athlete. Not having an abortion would empty her life of any meaning it had had. Her eudaimonia throughout her life, for years after the Olympics, would be compromised by a deep feeling of frustration at a personal telos forever unfulfilled. So virtue ethics would support a virtuously motivated abortion in such circumstances, prompted by the virtues of proper ambition and physical prowess, aiming for the glory of being the best in the world, but would expect her to feel proper regret and a sense of loss that the foetus had to pay that price.

Assessment of virtue ethics

One advantage of virtue ethics is that, through its concern for both the foetus's and the mother's eudaimonia, it can share all the benefits of the utilitarian approach without being stuck with its drawbacks. There are two main drawbacks to utilitarianism as applied to abortion.

- It permits lightweight, superficial reasons for abortions, leading to abortion on whim, never mind demand.
- It demeans both mother and foetus by treating them as containers of pleasure/pain, rather than as concrete individuals having value in themselves.

Virtue ethics avoids the first by insisting the mother make a virtue-driven decision that's not selfish, thoughtless, and light-minded and avoids the second by taking seriously the mother's character, her emotional attachment to her baby, and the deeply significant relationship they have with one another. This honest embracing of the messy complexity of human nature and its situation in the world also side-steps Kant's shallow, rationalistic, Mr Spock approach to mother and foetus as actual or potential logical generators of morals; and, needless to say, the soul superstition is given a wide berth.

The flexibility of virtue theory can also be seen as a strength, allowing it to avoid the all or nothing extremes of the utilitarian and divine command theory approaches, with Kantians lurching from one to the other, depending on which interpretation of Kant is in play. The flexible reflection of complexity embodied in the many virtues and vices is more likely to 'get it right' than the attempt by the other theories to reach the right decision armed only with one principle and a cardboard cut-out picture of human beings.

However, it's possible to be so flexible and amenable that you end up saying nothing, and consequently giving no real advice on what to do regarding an abortion. It's as if virtue theory merely supplies a shopping list of relevant virtues and allows the customer to choose the ones that suit her. For example, in rape cases, if the woman favours justice for herself, she can abort the foetus out of justice, but if she feels justice and compassion for the foetus, she won't abort. People seem to want more concrete guidance from a normative moral theory than virtue ethics is prepared to give, so its vagueness is a disadvantage.

It might be replied that it sees normativity as merely providing a *framework* of ideas and virtues within which people are left to make their *own* decisions, arguing that, far from being a weakness, its vagueness is in fact a strength, because it treats people as mature adults capable of making their own decisions rather than paternalistically hectoring them with moral principles.

6   Animal Rights

The following two chapters have a different feel to them compared with the more traditional ethical debates surrounding euthanasia and abortion, because the centre of gravity shifts to the non-human issues of animals and the environment. New theories are introduced, the arguments go deeper, and the issues become more complex. Both are hot topics. Both are relatively new.

The animal rights chapter is the longest in the book because in it I try to develop a sustained challenge to the philosophical basis of the animal rights movement, while yet giving animals much more moral protection than they have had hitherto. It requires more time to go into the detail with rigour yet with the level of clarity demanded of an introduction, but the pay-off is that here we may have found the most defensible animal ethic of the lot.

Although some people may regard the moral problem of how we should treat animals as of much less importance than the issues of euthanasia and abortion because, after all, they're 'only' animals, many have come to see this as of equal or indeed more importance, if only because of the sheer scale of deliberately induced killing and suffering. Even limiting statistics to the food industry and animal experimentation laboratories, just in the USA and UK – let alone taking a global perspective – the figures run into billions. So we'd better be sure we're doing the right thing – that we've an adequate moral justification ready to defend our actions. And it's not just the sheer scale of killing and suffering that might give us pause for thought, but also the added worry that our behaviour might be no better than that of sexists and racists: that, in giving preferential treatment to the human species over animal species *simply* because we're human, we're no better than sexists who think men superior to women *simply* because they're men, and racists, who think whites are superior to blacks *simply* because they're white.

We shall see later on that Peter Singer, the most famous and influential contemporary utilitarian thinker in this area, accuses us of this very thing. If he's right we'll need to change our ways radically – our eating habits for a start. But is he right? We'll only be able to answer this once we've examined all the relevant normative moral theories with regard to our treatment of animals. To that end, the theories will be covered in the following order:

1 divine command theory
2 Kant
3 utilitarianism
4 Regan's rights-based theory
5 virtue ethics

Note the addition of a theory not previously encountered in this book – that of Tom Regan (American philosopher, b. 1938). He merits his place on account of the influential and radical nature of his thought, which we'll consider in more detail later in this chapter. Three limitations will be placed on our examination of this issue.

i)   Discussion of our dealings with animals will be confined to the food industry and animal experimentation, owing to their size and severity.
ii) The kind of animals relevant to our discussion will be restricted to mammals and birds.
iii) Discussion as to whether these sorts of animals can suffer is curtailed. By now, there should be enough evidence to convince all but die-hard sceptics that animals do really feel pain and pleasure. Their screeches are not on a par with the noises made by a squeaky wheel.

1 Divine command theory

It's remarkable that, in scouring the Bible from Genesis to Revelation in search of an explicit, unambiguous command concerning the treatment of animals, we come away empty-handed. We've nothing definite to go on because the commands 'Thou shalt not kill' and 'Love thy neighbour' don't seem to apply to animals. The former is interpreted as applying only to humans – it tells us not to murder; and when Jesus was asked to specify who our neighbour was, he told the parable of the Good Samaritan, illustrating how a *human being* who'd been mugged was helped by the Samaritan. The message is clearly that *all* human beings are your neighbour. Jesus doesn't explicitly exclude animals, but he doesn't include them either, so again we're in the dark. This is a worrying silence, because God's reticence seems to leave divine command theorists with nothing to say on this major moral issue, so it's vital they dig up something resembling God's will on the matter. However, all is not lost because, although no *explicit* command is given us on how to treat animals, God does give a number of fairly strong but *implicit* suggestions. Based on various statements and events in the Bible we can reasonably extract, and Christianity *has* extracted, a pretty clear but inferred directive from God as to the moral status of animals. Unfortunately, from an animal's point of view, it doesn't look promising.

Taking the Old Testament first, right there in the opening chapter of the opening book, in Genesis 1:26 are found the crucial words spoken by God that have reverberated down the ages: 'Let us make *man* in our *image*, after our likeness; and let them have *dominion* over the *fish* of the sea, and over the *birds* of the air, and over the *cattle*, and over all the earth, and over *every creeping thing* that creeps upon the earth' (emphasis mine). For the past two thousand years conservative Christianity has taken the words 'image' and 'likeness' to be references to our possession of an immortal soul which is the seat of the God-like attributes of reason, moral conscience, free will, and all the rest of the things that we thought made us lords and masters of creation, and justified the dizzying chasm between the value of human life and the lives of animals. This latter thought has been taken to be implicit in the use of the word 'dominion' – that is, that animals are ours to do with as we please. Genesis 9:2–3 is even more emphatic; it says: 'The *fear* of you and the *dread* of you shall be upon every beast of the earth, and upon every bird of the air, upon everything that creeps on the ground and all the fish of the sea; into your hand they are delivered' (emphasis mine).

It's easy to see where this verse is headed. 'Fear' and 'dread' are dark words, threatening very unpleasant experiences for any animal at the hand of man, and we've been only too eager to take God up on His offer. The rest of the Old Testament confirms the message – the Jewish sacrificial system, wherein millions of animals were slaughtered as offerings to God, the annual Passover meal in which every family killed and ate a lamb, and the famous tradition of 'killing the fatted calf' for special celebrations. So it's safe to conclude that God's people weren't exactly vegetarian. But we've yet to see what the New Testament has to reveal about God's will.

With its perceived emphasis on gentleness, and on God as infinite love, people naturally expect the New Testament to take a softer line. They're in for a surprise. Regarding animals, it's not merely business as usual; if anything, an even harsher line is taken. In terms of 'business as usual', the temple sacrifices continue and are not condemned; as a Jew Jesus keeps the Passover, so eats lamb. He's seen eating a fish breakfast with his disciples after his resurrection. He wasn't a vegetarian, and believed it was alright to kill animals for food. He also doesn't have a problem with carelessly killing animals for no reason at all, as the incident of the Gadarene swine illustrates (see Mark 5:1–13), in which he gives permission for numerous demons to enter into the pigs in a nearby field who then, in a state of frenzy, run over a cliff and are all killed. What's Jesus playing at – doing favours for Satan's cronies at the expense of 2000 innocent pigs? Peter Singer went so far as to observe, bluntly but accurately, that 'The New Testament is completely lacking in any injunction against cruelty to animals, or any recommendation to consider their interests' (*Animal Liberation*, p. 191).

In response to this, many Christians will want to register a strong protest against this understanding that God's attitude is that animals don't have any rights. Their argument goes something like this. Animals are God's property, and we must respect God's property so we must respect animals. Moreover, the word 'dominion' in Genesis 1:26 can be interpreted as meaning 'Having stewardship over', which is a more caring role than the more authoritarian construal. Furthermore, in Genesis 1:29 God said to Adam and Eve: 'Behold, I have given you every plant yielding seed which is upon the face of the earth, and every tree with seed in its fruit; you shall have them for food.' No mention of eating animals here. It seems God had prescribed them a vegetarian diet in Paradise, and only after the Fall, when they sinned, were they allowed to eat meat, the point being that vegetarianism and the consequent protection of animals was God's ideal (plan A), whereas the meat industry is ultimately a second-rate result of sin (plan B). This vision is confirmed by the picture of life in Paradise regained, as depicted in Revelation, where 'the lion will lie down with the lamb', as opposed to tucking into it.

We could for the sake of laying out the arguments call such Christians the 'doves' and nominate as the 'hawks' those who interpret God's attitude to animals as callous. So how are we to judge between these rival 'hawk' and 'dove' interpretations? I'll argue below that, despite the laudable sentiments of the Christian doves towards animal welfare, logic and evidence strongly favour the hawk position, and that therefore God's will allows us to be callously cruel to animals. 'Callous cruelty' is defined as 'indifference to, or pitilessness in the face of, severe suffering or distress'. Leaving aside, for the time being, the tussle over the meaning of 'dominion', all the doves have going for them are some gestures towards animals as God's property, the generally meek spirit of Jesus, and a couple of references to vegetarianism in Paradise at the beginning and end of time. But, obvious though it may seem, it needs to be pointed out that we're not in Paradise now, so different, non-vegetarian rules apply and, in addition, we haven't even been given commands to promote vegetarianism in the hope of bringing about Paradise in the future; plus Jesus doesn't provide a vegetarian role model for the interim period. This disposes of the 'Paradise argument'. To defeat the doves' ' "meekness of Jesus" argument', the hawks can appeal to Jesus's role in the pig massacre and his use of the Good Samaritan parable, tacitly implying that animals aren't covered by the 'Love your neighbour' rule.

The doves' 'God's property' argument proves too much because, if that's the reason we should respect animals, then by the same token we should also respect every grain of sand and bit of muck and drop of water in the universe, because they're *all* God's property. But sand on a beach doesn't have rights. Against the doves' remaining meagre defences are ranged Paul's cynical attitude to the welfare of animals (see 1 Corinthians 9: 9, where he has the nerve to argue that an Old Testament verse about feeding oxen properly is actually God's way of saying that the church should pay him more money!), the sacrificial system of animal blood-letting, and 'dread' and 'fear' for the animals to look forward to. What wouldn't the doves give for a miracle story where Jesus resurrects a herd of cows, or heals a poor man's pet dog, or has the Good Samaritan rescue a chicken instead of a mugging victim? What wouldn't they give for a verse where Paul quotes an Old Testament passage about feeding the poor, and then goes on to inform us that what God really means is, 'don't let your cat starve'? What wouldn't they give for some positive, clear-cut guidance from God about treating animals decently? But there is none. So the core argument must reflect the hawk attitude to animals allowing, on God's authority, callous cruelty towards them.

From now on, when setting out philosophical arguments of this kind, P means 'premise'; IC means 'intermediate conclusion'; and MC means 'main conclusion.'

Divine command theory's core argument regarding animal rights

P1: Whatever God commands is right.

P2: God commands us not to kill (interpreted as applying only to innocent humans, not animals).

P3: God also commands us to rule the animal kingdom by giving us dominion over them.

P4: The biblical evidence for the hawks' attitude to animals is significantly stronger than for that of the doves.

IC1: So, we're justified in applying the authoritarian hawk interpretation to 'dominion', entailing 'fear' and 'dread' for animals, *not stewardship*.

IC2: So animals don't have any right to life.

MC: Therefore, it's morally permissible to kill animals for food and in medical experiments, and to deliberately inflict severe pain on them in the service of science and mass-produced food. In other words, callous cruelty is morally fine.

Given the practical nature of these issues, it's important to consider the likely impact of each theory on the meat industry and animal experimentation. In the case of divine command theory, impact is likely to be negligible. Though the overwhelming majority of animal deaths and suffering are inflicted for cheap meat and safe drugs, the use of inhumane and callously cruel methods can't be condemned by divine command theory. There's certainly maltreatment and lack of concern in keeping millions of hens in small wire cages for the entire span of their lives, never seeing the light of day, or being able to spread their wings. There's clearly a lack of care, to say the least, when toxic substances are dropped into the eyes of rabbits (particularly useful animals as they have no tear ducts to wash these fluids away) in order to test shampoos. But divine command theory condemns none of this as immoral. We can conclude with an assessment of this theory and its weaknesses.

Problem 1: Lack of consistent normative guidance

The mixed message sent out by the dove v hawk dispute is bound to weaken the moral authority of divine command theory in this area, since it indicates that Christians themselves aren't sure what God's will is, and hence aren't sure of the moral principles that are supposed to operate here.

> P1: A normative theory that offers contradictory moral guidance is flawed.
> P2: Divine command theory offers contradictory moral guidance.
> Conclusion: Therefore, divine command theory is flawed.

Problem 2: Any guidance it does give is counter-intuitive

Taking the hawk interpretation of God's will as the most plausible, we at least get a tolerably clear picture of the divine command regarding animal rights, but the problem here for a lot of people is that it's unpalatably negative, and doesn't offer animals sufficient protection from the depredations of mankind (attaching 'kind' to 'man' is almost oxymoronic in this context). Are battery hens, veal crates, and cosmetics testing really part of God's plan for the world? Should they be? Animal treatment under these conditions amounts to callous cruelty and a morally objectionable preparedness to make as big a profit as possible, ruthlessly using any means necessary, in catering for gourmet palates and the desire for the cheapest possible chicken. And should any animal have to suffer agonies just so humans can smell a bit better?

Insofar as our intuitions rebel against this undervaluing of animal life; insofar as we have the intuition that animal suffering counts for something in itself and cannot be overridden so easily; and insofar as we, since the acceptance of the theory of evolution, no longer think we are so high and mightily removed from animal status ourselves, then to this extent will people reject divine command theory's guidance as morally disreputable. It goes too deeply against the intuitive grain. So, in conclusion, I submit that divine command theory should be rejected either as an ineffective moral guide or as an effective, immoral guide.

2 Kant

Kant holds that we have duties only to other rational agents so, because they aren't rational, animals have no rights and no moral status of their own, and this means we can use them as we see fit; they aren't ends in themselves, but only means to our ends.

There are only two exceptions.

i) If the animal belongs to someone, then it's wrong to hurt it because this is *damage to property*.
ii) If treating an animal cruelly has a bad effect on *your* character, which will lead you to *treat other human beings cruelly* too, then you do wrong.

Kant's core argument regarding animal rights

P1: The categorical imperative says one shouldn't act irrationally by willing contradictory universalized maxims, or by treating people, i.e. rational, moral agents, as mere means instead of as ends.

P2: Animals are not rational, moral agents.

P3: A universalized maxim of killing animals is not a contradiction in conception because such a world is easily imaginable, and it doesn't involve reason killing reason.

P4: And it's not a contradiction in will, because there's no way you'd ever turn into an animal and end up on the 'wrong' end of your maxim (as in Kant's example of the man who wouldn't help others).

IC: So killing animals and using them as means to our ends is morally permissible, because maxims to this effect pass the categorical imperative. We have no direct duties to animals, only to humans.

P5: Since we have duties only to humans, the only time it's wrong to damage or kill an animal is either when it's owned by someone, in which case it's wrong only because it constitutes damage to property and is a breach of our duty to the owner; or if its harsh treatment by us makes us more likely to be cruel to other people, in which case it will lead to a breach of our duty to treat other people as ends not as means.

MC: Therefore, *we can treat animals any way we like* as long as it neither damages other people's property nor leads to our being cruel to humans.

As before, we should move to consider the likely impact of Kant's theory on animal welfare. As with divine command theory, Kant has no impact whatsoever on welfare, as his moral theory totally supports the status quo in the meat industry and animal laboratories. It's only cruelty *for fun* that he objects to, and these industries are not in the game for *that* reason.

Let's conclude this section with an assessment of Kant's theory regarding animal rights. We'll see that criticism of Kant conveniently focuses on the two exceptions (in P5 of the core argument), where it's wrong to harm an animal.

Animals as property

What Kant's theory brutally boils down to is that, were you to poison your neighbour's cat with weed-killer for a laugh, so that it dies in agony, this is no worse, morally speaking, than pouring weed-killer on his lawn and ruining the grass, or pouring it on his car and ruining the paintwork, because these are equally his property, and painful consequences don't register on Kant's moral radar. The wrong is done to the *neighbour, not* the cat. The cat *itself* doesn't matter morally, only the cat as *property*.

What's wrong with this is that, *no matter what you do* to an animal, you can't do wrong to *it*, but only to *other human beings* such as the owner. The problem we have with Kant here is that the *suffering* of the animal *in itself* is *completely irrelevant*, whereas most people see this as the *heart of the matter*. On this issue Kant's theory is strongly and fatally counter-intuitive, and a related intuition is also violated, namely the instinctive feeling that a cat's welfare matters more than grass or the paint job on a car, yet Kant treats them all the same. Kant is right about the action being wrong, but he is wrong about the *reason* that it's wrong, his theory focusing on a relatively trivial side issue of *property* rights, instead of the *cat* as the *proper* moral focus.

Cruelty to animals as **bad-habit forming**

If the cat belongs to nobody, or to you yourself, it's still wrong to get sadistic fun out of harming it. Again, this is not because you've done any wrong to the cat *itself* but because, according to Kant, you have duties to the *rest of humanity*, and your cat-bashing habit is likely to generalize and transfer from cats to other humans as your targets. Kant argues that you would be failing in your moral duty to *other people* by putting them at extra risk of being disrespected via gratuitous violence, and *this* is what makes it wrong to hit the cat, not the *hitting* of the cat itself. For example, the more often you take a baseball bat to your own or an unowned cat, the more likely you are to take one to your neighbour, and you owe it to your *neighbour, not* to the stray cat, not to beat it to a pulp. The cat's pain, even the cat's life, is of no consequence morally speaking.

There are no fewer than three serious problems with Kant's theory and its implications in this matter.

i) He relies on a very shaky psychological doctrine of the supposed proneness of the human mind to generalize cruelty from animal to human, but there's very little evidence for this, and Kant certainly never cites any. There's no evidence, for example, that butchers and fishermen have a greater statistical tendency to violence towards other humans than people in gentler trades. Kant's armchair psychology is less than helpful to his theory here.

ii) Kant's position also implies that, if you *don't* happen to be the kind of person whose animal-torturing habits tempt them to torture humans, then the categorical imperative has no problem with you blow-torching as many cats as your heart desires, so long as they're yours or have no owner. This is so counter-intuitive it hardly needs further refutation.

iii) It's plausible to suggest that the very opposite might be closer to the truth, that is, that 'taking it out on' the cat might make you *less*, not more, violent to other human beings. David DeGrazia (professor of philosophy at George Washington University, Washington, DC) makes an amusing reference to this: 'Perhaps kicking his sheep around will allow the shepherd to blow off some steam, making him less likely to rough up his wife and kids' (*Animal Rights*, p. 18) – in which case we have the moral absurdity of Kant having to say that kicking his sheep was not only permissible but actually a moral *obligation* based on his duty to his family. His theory doesn't offer animals enough protection because it doesn't give them sufficient recognition, seriously underplaying their moral status. We can therefore conclude that Kant's moral theory, in permitting counter-intuitive and cruel actions towards animals, should be rejected as a moral guide in this area.

3 Utilitarianism

In addressing the question of what makes animals morally relevant, Bentham famously said, 'The question is not, Can they reason? nor Can they talk? but Can they suffer?' At one stroke this brings animals in from the cold and places them firmly within the charmed circle of our moral concern. What entitles animals to serious moral consideration is simply their capacity for pain and pleasure, because that means they're covered by the principle of utility, which tells us to maximize pleasure and minimize pain – never mind whose, or what species they belong to. Pain is pain, whether felt by a child or a chimp. Utilitarianism grants animals *equal* moral consideration to humans. The strongest and most influential arguments for this utilitarian approach have been made by the aforementioned leading animal rights philosopher Peter

Singer, so we shall examine these more closely in the remainder of this section, taking Singer as representative of utilitarianism as a whole.

Singer's 'principle of equal consideration of interests'

Singer, a preference utilitarian, interprets the classic utilitarian principle 'each should count for one and no one for more than one' as instructing us when we work out the likely consequences of our actions to give *equal weight to everybody's preferences*, and 'everybody' includes animals. Preference utilitarianism looks to preferences, but only because they are indicative of interests. It's really the interests that Singer is concerned in satisfying. Verbally expressed preferences are merely pointers to these, so the fact that animals can't verbalize their preferences doesn't really matter as long as we can understand what their interests actually are.

Applying 'equal consideration of interests' to animals

Singer acknowledges that you can only have *equal* consideration of interests where there are *comparable* interests on *both* sides, and that the principle doesn't apply where this isn't the case. For example, humans have an interest in voting, whereas animals don't. It would therefore be an absurd objection to Singer to accuse him on the basis of equal consideration of interests of arguing that animals have the right to vote – absurd precisely because these aren't comparable interests. But where there's parity of interest, this crosses the species barrier. Since only interests count with Singer, lack of membership of the species Homo sapiens is of no moral relevance when it comes to deciding how to treat animals with similar interests to ours. So, what interests *do* we have in common with them? Singer concentrates on the two crucial ones, namely,

- avoidance of pain/pursuit of pleasure
- avoidance of death.

Singer illustrates the application of his equal consideration principle by comparing a slap to a horse and a slap to a child (*Practical Ethics*, p. 59). If you had to choose, then, in giving equal consideration to the pain of each, you should slap the horse because it will feel less pain than the child, having a thicker skin. But if hitting the horse with a big enough stick caused it to suffer more than the child, then you should slap the child instead, so as to minimize the pain caused. It doesn't matter *whose* pain it is because *pain* is all that counts; species is irrelevant, and if you prefer to hit the horse with the big stick, causing it more pain than the child would have suffered had it been slapped, on the grounds that the child is human, after all, and the horse is only a horse, then the principle condemns you for being unfair and prejudiced. Singer would accuse you of 'speciesism'. This is the name he gives, following Richard Ryder, to the prejudice of preferring one's own species when it comes to a choice between humans and animals. Singer argues that, like racism and sexism, speciesism is morally repugnant, because it employs similar arguments, and for similar purposes. This is what's known as an *argument from analogy*. Arguments from analogy have the following form:

> P1: x has features 1, 2, 3.
> P2: y has features 1, 2, 3.
> P3: x also has extra feature 4.
> Conclusion: Therefore, since y is analogous to x in so many other ways (sharing features 1, 2, and 3), it's probable that y also possesses feature 4.

These arguments never lead to a knock-down proof. They're always only more or less probable, but, generally speaking, the more features y shares with x the stronger the argument, and the fewer features, the less strong the argument. An example:

> P1: Alex 1) has a runny nose, 2) sneezes, 3) has a sore throat.
> P2: Ben, too, suffers from 1), 2), and 3).
> P3: Alex also has extra feature 4), a cold.
> Conclusion: Therefore, since Ben is analogous to Alex regarding all the other symptoms 1), 2), 3), it's probable he also possesses feature 4), i.e. it's likely he has a cold too.

The more symptoms in common, the stronger the conclusion, and the fewer symptoms, the less strong – e.g. if Ben had a rash but Alex didn't, this disanalogy would weaken the argument. Back to Singer's argument from analogy. I've constructed a version of it below:

> P1: Racists (e.g. white supremacists) possess:
> > feature 1): they think pain felt by a black person is less important than pain felt by a white.
> > feature 2): they're particularly harsh to blacks, killing and enslaving them.
> > feature 3): they justify their racism by citing some morally irrelevant characteristic such as extra intelligence, culture, power, technology, art, science, etc., that *all* whites are supposed to have and blacks don't.

feature 4): they're inconsistent in giving whites who don't have these features, e.g. the insane or the brain damaged, respect and rights that more intelligent and cultured blacks aren't allowed.

feature 5): when this inconsistency is pointed out, they say that these disadvantaged whites are the '*kind*' of thing that's superior; in other words, they come clean and admit it's just because they have white skin that they're treated so much better.

P2: Speciesists share all five features with racists.

 i) They regard animal pain as less important than human pain.

 ii) They're particularly harsh to animals, killing, eating, and hunting them, when they wouldn't dream of doing such things to a human being.

 iii) They justify their speciesism by citing morally irrelevant features such as greater intelligence, language, and technology that *all* humans are supposed to have but animals don't.

 iv) They're inconsistent in giving humans who don't have these features (e.g. the brain damaged) rights and protection far above those given to higher functioning animals.

 v) When this inconsistency is pointed out to them, they say these are the *kind* of thing that's superior and deserves rights, which is to admit that it's just because they walk on two legs instead of four, have smooth skin instead of fur, etc., that they're treated so much better.

P3: Racism also has the extra sixth feature of being morally repugnant.

Conclusion: Therefore, since speciesism is closely analogous to racism in that it shares all its other five features, it's highly likely that speciesism shares the sixth feature too, and so is also morally repugnant.

This has been a very influential argument for animal rights, for giving animals the equal consideration which speciesism immorally denies them. The following examples highlight the comparison between racism and speciesism.

Suppose it comes to a choice between a black man's life and a white man's car, and you decide to sacrifice the black man's life; this is blatantly racist and wrong, because the black man's life is a *major* interest to him which you are sacrificing for the *minor* interest of a white. To treat skin colour as in any way relevant here is immoral and unfair, because you're not giving the black man's interests equal consideration with those of the white man. But the same goes when it comes to a choice between the life of a chicken and a tasty chicken dinner. A *major* interest of the chicken, namely its *life*, is sacrificed for a *minor* interest of a human, namely a *nice meal*. We can live without the meal, but the chicken can't live without its life. This bias against the chicken's interests is what makes its treatment as unjust as racism and sexism; this is what makes it speciesism; and this is what makes it wrong, according to Singer.

The core argument of utilitarianism for animal rights

P1: The principle of utility tells us to promote the greatest happiness of the greatest number.

P2: This number includes all sentient beings.

P3: Animals are sentient beings.

IC1: So we ought to promote the happiness of animals.

P4: The **principle of equality of interests** tells us to give equal consideration to the comparable interests of all sentient beings no matter what their species.

P5: Animals' interests in pursuing pleasure and avoiding pain and death are comparable to ours in this respect.

IC2: So animal welfare (pleasure/pain) is of equal importance to that of humans.

P6: This means that, if we cause an animal more pain than we get pleasure, or we deprive an animal of a long and happy life (a *major* interest of the animal) in order to promote a *minor* interest of ours, e.g. the pleasant taste of its flesh, or yet another safe perfume, then this is **speciesist and is morally wrong**.

P7: Insofar as we kill animals for food, when we could be vegetarians; insofar as we use them to test perfumes and detergents, which we don't need, and for trivial, pointless 'scientific' experiments, we do them wrong.

MC: Therefore, because the major part of our dealings with animals, including factory farms, veal crates, slaughter houses, and most animal experimentation, sacrifice major interests of animals for minor human interests, and cause infinitely more pain than pleasure, the principle of utility and the principle of equality of interests condemn them as speciesist and morally wrong.

In this next section we will, as for divine command theory and Kant, assess this core argument and consider its weaknesses. As this argument seems valid, the only remaining way of putting it under pressure so as to avoid its conclusion is to query the truthfulness of one or more of its premises. The most plausible targets are P4, with its principle of equality, and P6, with its assertion that speciesism is immoral, so the dance of debate will be focused here. As we'll be going backwards and forwards between Singer and his critics, each section is signalled as either Singer's critics' response to his arguments or his continued reply to them.

Singer's critics: initial rebuttal of P4

Starting with P4, Singer's opponents argue that the principle of equality, as applied to animals and humans, has got to be false given the overwhelming superiority of human beings. We can reason, appreciate and create beauty, write music, use language and technology, and make moral decisions. Animals can't do any of these things so our interests deserve to be given priority over those of animals because we are more important than they. Equality can only apply among equals. Animals aren't equal to humans. Therefore, the principle of equality of interests can't apply, so P4 is false. This also means that P6 is irrelevant because speciesism only applies where the principle of equality *ought* to be adhered to and isn't. Since it has already been shown that this principle is inapplicable here, treating animals as inferior is not speciesist, so it's okay to eat them and use them in experiments.

Singer's reply

Let's move on to consider how Singer might reply to these criticisms. We can begin by looking at what is known as *the argument from marginal cases.* This argument appeals to the fact that there are millions of 'marginal' humans, such as babies born with no brain, people with irreparable brain damage, PVS patients, coma victims, severe Alzheimer's sufferers, and so on, who don't possess or have the potential to possess any of the features cited above – features such as reason, creativity, language, tool use, self-consciousness, and moral responsibility. If Singer's opponents are seriously arguing that animals can be killed, eaten, and experimented on because they don't have these features, then the argument from marginal cases seems to indicate that his critics are committed to denying the most vulnerable humans basic human rights and, in the name of consistency, should also deem it morally permissible to kill, eat, and experiment on these unfortunate human beings! Since their position leads to such moral outrages, they must be wrong to justify their treatment of animals on the basis of particular superior features possessed by most humans.

Critics' response to the argument from marginal cases

Since it's out of the question for Singer's critics to 'bite the bullet' and accept the horrible implications of their argument, namely that it's okay to eat the insane and do experiments on severely disabled babies, their fall-back position is to assert that these 'marginal' humans are still considered superior to all animals, and therefore safe from being eaten and experimented on, because, unlike animals, they're the **kind** of thing that possesses these superior features, even though many of the higher mammals are higher functioning than these 'marginal' humans.

Singer's reply

The above response is blatant speciesism, because basing the protection of 'marginal' humans on the fact that they're the *kind* of thing that has superior qualities is tantamount to appealing to their biological nature as members of the *species* Homo sapiens. But appealing to the fact that they have two legs, opposable thumbs, smooth skin, and no tail as grounds for preferential treatment over animals is as absurd and morally irrelevant as the racist appeal to the white colour of one's skin as grounds for preferential treatment over blacks. It's worth making it clear that Singer is not advocating downgrading 'marginal' humans to the level of animals so we can perform experiments on them and indulge in cannibalism, but is rather advocating the upgrading of animals to the protected moral status currently accorded to marginal humans. All that's needed for equal consideration is a shared interest in avoiding suffering and death, and animals do share this interest with marginal humans along with the rest of humanity. So if we're not prepared to kill, eat, and experiment on 'marginal' humans, we shouldn't do these things to animals.

Response to Singer

Singer's position leads to the moral absurdity of holding a chicken's life as of equal value to that of a human being, because each has a comparable interest in living, and his principle of equality of consideration of interests insists that each should be given equal weight. This is completely counter-intuitive; people won't stand for it. But it gets even worse. It seems, as a utilitarian, Singer would have to agree that, given a choice between saving *two* chickens and saving *one* human being, since each life gets *equal* weight, we should save the chickens and let the human die.

Singer's reply

Singer can counter this seemingly fatal objection by insisting that it misrepresents his position. It's not so much the *lives* he's interested in as the *amount of suffering* the loss of these lives would cause. Superficially, two chicken lives would seem to outweigh one human life in terms of sheer numbers alone, but when we look at the 'cash value' of these lives in terms of the utilitarian currency of suffering, it's not hard to see that the human being would suffer immeasurably more at the prospect of losing their life than two chickens. The self-conscious awareness of the human being, and the knowledge of what death means, would give rise to dread, intense fear, despair, and dashed hopes of a happy life ahead. Chickens, on the other hand, don't suffer from existential angst, so it would seem that we have a much greater stake or interest in our lives than chickens have in theirs. Ours mean more to us, which is why we would suffer more at the prospect of being killed, which is why the principle of utility would advocate killing the chickens rather than the human being, and this lets Singer off the hook.

Response to Singer

Actually, he's not off the hook yet. His argument above was only a temporary respite but leads to more trouble. In relying on the extra suffering that higher states of consciousness may involve to justify saving the higher functioning human life over that of the lower functioning chicken, his argument seems to entail that, had the choice been between saving a normal chimp or a severely retarded baby from a cauldron (imagine there are no grieving relatives), Singer would be committed to saving the chimp. Why? Because its higher level of consciousness compared with that of the baby makes its life more important to it. The chimp would suffer more, so it has a weightier interest in being saved, which means the principle of utility and equal consideration of interests both back the decision to save the chimp and let the baby die. I think it's safe to say that most of us would be appalled at this decision, but does this prove Singer wrong?

Possible reply by Singer

Singer could reply that our appalled reaction is simply the result of deep-seated species prejudice and we just have to try and get over it rationally, just as white supremacists ought rationally to examine their appalled reaction to the thought of a white woman marrying a black man. Just what is wrong with this? Is it just because she's white and he's black? Is it just because it's a baby rather than a chimp? But human life is no more sacred than animal life; we're just more complex animals, that's all, and, in this *particular* case, *less* complex. It's worth considering that, given the choice between saving a brain-damaged white baby and a normal black baby, white racists would save the white baby. Singer would argue that our appalled reaction to saving the chimp instead of the baby is the same as a racist's appalled reaction to saving the black baby instead of the white one, because speciesism springs from the same poisoned well.

Final assessment

Singer's argument is hard to crack, and there's a lot at stake here because, if Singer is right, then vegetarianism becomes a moral obligation for most of us – apart from pockets of meat eaters such as the Inuit – and all but the most promising and necessary animal experiments will be banned. The meat industry and our whole restaurant culture would be slammed for being as immoral as racism and sexism.

So what other ways might there be to attack Singer's position? Well, we could reject the first premise of his argument (P1), thus rejecting his utilitarianism. This would do the trick, and in fact Regan's deontological theory, which we cover next, does this very thing.

4 Regan's rights-based theory

Tom Regan is an American philosopher who takes an uncompromising deontological approach to the defence of animal rights. He follows Kant in emphasizing our duty to treat beings that are ends in themselves with respect, in recognition of their inherent value, but unlike Kant he extends this duty of respect beyond fellow humans to all the animals we kill, eat, and experiment on. This presupposes that these animals have inherent value just as humans do, and that therefore the respect due them engenders an absolute duty not to use them as a mere resource, as means to our ends, whether for food or experimentation. But how does Regan justify this widening of the moral net to include animals?

Explaining 'subjects-of-a-life'

Regan rejects Kant's idea that it's the possession of moral reason which grounds moral rights, and replaces it with being what he calls a *subject-of-a-life* as the only viable basis for such rights. So what does he mean by a 'subject-of-a-life'? As it happens, Regan kindly provides us with a checklist of ingredients, including perception, memory, desires, a sense of the future, emotions, sentience, the ability to initiate action in pursuit of goals, the sense that life can go well or ill, and psychophysical identity over time. If you're missing *any* of these features you're not a subject-of-a-life, and if you have them *all* then you are.

Next, we need to understand what Regan means by 'inherent value'.

Explaining 'inherent value'

Inherent value is value that's possessed independently of anyone else's interest in you or your usefulness to others. You either have it 100 per cent or you don't have it at all; there's no sliding scale of inherentish value in between. Inherent value can't be earned, lost, or given away. It's inalienable, and every creature that has inherent value has it *equally*. Finally, it's not the sort of thing that can be traded off against utility calculations. In other words, you're not allowed to violate or disrespect a creature's inherent value even if doing so helps maximize utility. Any being possessing inherent value is therefore an end in itself, not a means to an end or a handy resource having only instrumental value for the benefit of others. Having explained these two crucial concepts we can now begin to examine Regan's argument.

Steps in Regan's argument

Regan begins his argument by *reminding us of our moral intuitions* concerning justice and the fact that, in the name of justice and equality, we ascribe to all human beings basic moral rights, such as the right not to be tortured, killed, eaten, or experimented on. I think we'd all sign up to this. His next move is to look for the *best explanation for these intuitions,* for instance, our insistence on human dignity, and respect for others, including the insane, the old and senile, young children, the mentally retarded or damaged, and so on. We grant basic human rights to *all* of these people. Why?

Regan's answer is that the best explanation for this is that they all have *inherent value,* for if they didn't they would be vulnerable to all sorts of abusive, demeaning treatment and exploitation. So far, there's nothing startlingly new in Regan's theory, for divine command theorists and Kant would both agree that all human beings have inherent value and basic moral rights. It's the step Regan takes next that makes all the difference between his and the other moral theories.

We now have to ask *what **explains** our belief that **all human beings** have* ***inherent value.*** In other words, we need to find out on what inherent value is based, for it can't remain, as it were, hovering inexplicably in the air, and we can't explain it by reference to our intuitions of justice, because that would be to argue in a circle. You can't have intuitions of justice being explained by inherent value and inherent value being explained by intuitions of justice; that way, neither gets explained. So we need a *third* option that will adequately ground and explain our ascription of inherent value to all human beings.

Regan's next step is to offer *being a 'subject-of-a-life' as the explanation* we're looking for, and to argue for this by showing that all rival explanations are flawed, thus leaving only the 'subject-of-a-life' explanation standing, winning by default as the only plausible option. So what are these rival explanations for humans having inherent value, and thus rights, and how does Regan attempt to refute them?

1 We are rational sources of morality (Kant).
2 We have other rational features such as language, tool use, etc.

3 We have a divinely implanted soul (divine command theory).
4 We all belong to the species Homo sapiens.
5 We are persons.
6 Utilitarianism.

Regan's rejection of the rival explanations

Target 1): We are rational sources of morality

Regan rejects Kant's position by applying the argument from 'marginal' cases, for if Kant were correct about the capacity for moral reasoning being the basis of human rights and inherent value, then it would follow that non-rational human beings devoid of the capacity for moral responsibility, e.g. coma cases and mentally retarded babies, would not have any rights at all because they fail Kant's qualifying condition, so we would have no moral duty to treat them with respect as ends in themselves. In other words we'd be free to use them as we wish, just as we do animals. Since his view entails this absurdly outrageous conclusion, Kant's explanation of inherent value must be wrong.

Target 2): We have other rational features

Features such as language use, using and making tools, abstract reasoning in maths and science, artistic/aesthetic creativity and appreciation, and the capacity to make, understand, and honour contracts have all been employed at one time or another to account for the uniqueness of human beings in the animal world, as the basis of our inherent value, our human rights and privileges. However, just like Kant's failed attempt, each in turn succumbs to the seemingly unstoppable argument from 'marginal' cases. For example, it hardly takes a moment's thought to realize that language use won't apply to coma victims, or any of the others on our 'marginal' list. Does that mean they have no inherent value and therefore can be experimented on, eaten, and killed because they have no right not to be so treated? Of course not, so language can't be the basis of inherent value.

The same goes for making and using tools, doing maths and science, creating art, and drawing up contracts. Have you ever heard of severely brain-damaged babies doing any of these things? No. But we nevertheless believe that 'marginal' cases such as these have basic human rights preventing their use as experimental subjects and as food, so this belief in their inherent value and rights must rest on a different foundation.

Target 3): We have a divinely implanted soul

Each human being possesses a soul made in the image of God, which makes human life sacred, thereby giving it inherent value and moral rights. No animal has a soul according to Christianity, so animals don't have rights, which means they can be killed, eaten, and experimented on as a means to our ends.

Now, the interesting thing here is that the argument from 'marginal' cases can't touch this claim, because even PVS patients, along with all the other 'marginals' – in fact *all of humanity without exception* – have souls, so there are no marginal cases that Regan can use as counter-examples against the soul explanation of inherent value. In addition, since not a single non-human animal has a soul, divine command theory is able to draw the protective moral line of rights neatly round all and only humans, thus leaving animals without rights and without inherent value.

How does Regan counter this? Interestingly, he doesn't try to prove that souls don't exist. Instead, he makes a more modest but telling methodological point that, if your method of defending an already controversial position is to appeal for support to an *even more* controversial theory, rather than shoring up your beliefs, you end up undermining them even further.

Regan's basic point is that there's far more agreement on (and evidence for the belief that) humans being subjects-of-a-life than there is for the belief that we have immortal souls, and that therefore Regan's subject-of-a-life explanation provides much more solid support for inherent value and rights than divine command theory's soul explanation, and should therefore be preferred to it.

Target 4): We belong to the species Homo sapiens

Against this line Regan can't use his earlier arguments because there are no marginal cases of human beings not being of the species Homo sapiens (we all possess the same human genome, and DNA doesn't lie). Nor can he use the argument that worked against the soul explanation, because the belief that all humans belong to the same species is markedly less, not more, controversial than our beliefs concerning our inherent value.

Instead, Regan's response is to stamp this explanation as blatantly speciesist. It chooses an arbitrary feature, our genetic structure as designated by the term 'Homo sapiens', and tries to rest inherent value and rights on this; but this is a prejudice akin to racism and sexism. The latter argue in an analogous way by appealing to arbitrary genetic features that determine white skin and male gender as justification for denying rights, respect, and dignity to blacks and women, leading to their wholesale exploitation. Since we reject racism and sexism as immoral, and speciesism is like them, we should also reject speciesism. Regan, in effect, is using Singer's argument from analogy against speciesism in order to reject this explanation.

Target 5): We are persons

Is being a person what generates inherent value and human rights? Persons are ends in themselves. Animals aren't persons, so they don't have inherent value, and hence can be eaten and experimented on. But what is a person? Here are the best attempts to define what a person is.

- To be a person is to be able to formulate rational moral principles and act on them.
- To be a person is to have a capacity for reason exhibited in such things as language, technology, creativity, self-consciousness, science.
- To be a person is to have a soul.
- To be a person is to be a human being.

None of these definitions of 'person' can adequately explain why persons have inherent value while non-persons don't because, as you can see, these four definitions coincide with the first four rival explanations of inherent value which Regan has already disposed of. So, what seemed an additional, fifth, rival explanation, the appeal to personhood, turns out to be merely a rehash of all the others. There remains to be discussed one other rival to Regan's theory of human and animal rights, but it's not a rival in the *same sense* as the other theories of inherent value.

Target 6): Utilitarianism

The reason the rivalry of utilitarianism is different from the others is that it doesn't even pretend to explain how we come to have inherent value, for the simple reason that it doesn't think we have inherent value at all. It doesn't recognize the very concept of inherent value as applied to human beings, and hence doesn't use the language of rights. What it does recognize is the inherent value of pleasure, or preference satisfaction; but these aren't the same thing as people – as humans. They are better understood as what people or humans 'contain', and this is what utilitarianism uses as the bridge linking humanity to the other animals. Whether it's pleasure or preference satisfaction that has inherent value as the contents of human life-experience, these are shared equally by all the other animals that are processed as food by the meat industry and experimented on by the pharmaceutical companies. As we've seen, it's in this way, in terms of our shared interests in pain avoidance and preference satisfaction, that Singer argues for equality of animals with humans.

So, Regan the deontologist and Singer the utilitarian largely agree that animals should be treated much more humanely than heretofore and on extending the protection of morality to other species of animal besides us. Those who don't are guilty of speciesism. Where they differ, and this is where the rivalry of utilitarianism comes to the fore, is on how to *justify* this extension of the magic moral marker to cover animals. On the one hand, Regan argues that humans and animals have *inherent value*, and that's what their rights are based on, with inherent value itself arising from their being *subjects-of-a-life*. On the other, Singer argues that neither humans nor animals have inherent value; what they have is *shared interests* in avoiding pain and death, and these are what it's important to satisfy, thereby generating *equality of consideration* for animals and humans. So how does Regan see off the utilitarian approach to animal 'rights'?

Regan versus Singer

Regan's basic argument is that utilitarianism's denial of inherent value for humans has absurd consequences and is therefore wrong. He uses the thought experiment of "Aunt Bea" to illustrate this type of absurdity, (see Hursthouse, *Humans and other Animals*, p. 228). To cut a long story short, utilitarianism would say that you ought to kill your rich Aunt Bea and give her money to charity because it's the resulting beneficial consequences in terms of pleasure and preference satisfaction that count, not Aunt Bea's life, since the latter has no inherent value whereas pleasure and preference satisfaction do. Regan appeals to our intuitions that this killing is absolutely morally wrong because we believe that it is *Aunt Bea herself* who has inherent value, *not* the pleasurable consequences, and so her inherent value cannot be overridden for the sake of greater utility.

The very meaning of inherent value is that you shouldn't be treated as a mere resource for others. Rights would be worthless if they didn't stop this sort of thing happening. As Regan points out, 'A good end does not justify an evil means. Any adequate moral theory will have to explain why this is so. Utilitarianism fails in this respect and so cannot be the theory we seek' (Hursthouse, *Humans and other Animals*, p. 228).

With the apparent demise of his sixth and final rival, utilitarianism, the way seems clear for Regan's account of animal rights to claim victory as the only explanation still remaining on the battlefield – his account being that animals should share the basic rights accorded to human beings, such as the right not to be killed, eaten, or experimented on, because these rights are founded on being a subject-of-a-life, and animals are subjects-of-a-life, just like humans.

Regan's core argument
P1: We ascribe basic rights, such as the right not to be killed, eaten, or experimented on, to all human beings.
P2: We do this on the basis of their inherent value.

P3: The argument against utilitarianism supports P2 and thereby disposes of utilitarianism itself as a rival hypothesis to Regan's.

P4: Regan's hypothesis is that the best way to explain and justify this inherent value and thus human rights is with reference to our being subjects-of-a-life.

P5: The argument from marginal cases, the argument against speciesism, and the argument against the soul explanation refute the other five rival explanations of inherent value and rights.

IC1: Therefore, this confirms Regan's hypothesis that being a subject-of-a-life is the right foundation for inherent value and basic human rights.

P6: But all the animals we kill, eat, and experiment on are also subjects-of-a-life and so have inherent value *equally* with humans.

IC2: Therefore, they too ought to share equally in these basic rights, prohibiting their being killed, eaten, and experimented on.

MC: Therefore, it's morally wrong and an unjust violation of animal rights to do these things to them, and we must stop this immediately.

In contrast to some of the theories we considered earlier in the chapter, Regan explicitly intends his position to have a direct impact on our treatment of animals. Regan states very clearly what he wants to see happen; he says:

> I regard myself as an advocate of animal rights – as part of the animal rights movement. That movement, as I conceive it, is committed to a number of goals, including:
>
> - The total abolition of the use of animals in science;
> - The total dissolution of commercial animal agriculture;
> - The total elimination of commercial and sport hunting and trapping. (Hursthouse, *Humans and other Animals*, p. 222)

When we consider and assess Regan's core argument, it seems he has put together a strong case for animal rights – a case that would have devastating implications for the meat industry, the pharmaceutical companies, and human lifestyle in general. The core argument looks solid, especially P5, in which he convincingly sees off all his rival moral theories, leaving his own as the only viable option. He uses the argument from marginal cases as a kind of gallows to string up his opponents, and those that try to wriggle free get skewered by his anti-speciesism argument.

However, contrary to appearances, P5 is actually the weak link in the argument, because Regan himself falls foul of the argument from marginal cases. Here's how. You'll recall that memory, emotions, perception, and the ability to initiate action in pursuit of desires and goals were among the many characteristics a thing must have in order to be a subject-of-a-life, and thereby have inherent value and, so, rights. Well, babies born without a brain, PVS cases, and coma victims all fail to satisfy these criteria, and so cannot be subjects-of-a-life. In other words, Regan's theory implies that marginal cases such as these do not have inherent value and therefore do not have rights, and hence can be killed, eaten, and experimented on. The irony is that he finds himself strung up on the very gallows he prepared for his rivals. And, as if this were not enough, he has a further problem: that of *the case of the baboon, the brainless baby, and the lab*. The question posed by this case is: which should we experiment on? Most people would be appalled at the prospect of experimenting on the baby, and would plump for the baboon, but Regan, counter-intuitively, would have to select the baby for experimentation on the grounds that it fails to qualify as a subject-of-a-life, and so has no protective rights, whereas the baboon, being sufficiently higher functioning to be a subject-of-a-life, does have inherent value and rights, which impose on us the duty not to use it as a means to our experimental ends. That Regan ends up here indicates that his theory is wrong. In eliminating his rivals he has inadvertently eliminated himself.

5 Virtue ethics

For the past thirty years or so a battle royal has taken place between the culturally dominant Christian hawk attitude to animals, aided and abetted by Kantianism, and the animal rights movement led by Singer and Regan, which has been making inroads into the majority opinion. It's a battle for hearts and minds, between two polarized views, the former according animals little or no moral status, and the latter according them equal moral status with humans. Perhaps this all or nothing attitude is a false dilemma. The middle ground is left completely unoccupied – the middle ground in which animals could be accorded more or less moral status depending on how highly functioning they are in terms of degree of sentience, self-awareness, and emotional and social sophistication. Perhaps a better, more excellent, virtuous approach would be to look for the mean between these black and white extremes, and accord animals moral status on the basis of a hierarchical value system or sliding scale of consideration depending on the rung each species occupies on the evolutionary ladder. The more evolved and sophisticated they are, the more consideration a wise, virtuous person would accord them. Perhaps the one moral position we have not yet considered in this chapter, virtue ethics, can occupy this position in the middle ground. If so, it will avoid both the callous cruelty of Kant and the divine command hawks, at the one vicious extreme, exhibiting deficient compassion for animals, and also the overly sensitive line taken by Singer and Regan at the other extreme, exhibiting an unwise, over-inflated misjudgement of animals' equal status with humans and resulting in absurd outrages such as the decision to save the chimp from the cauldron and experiment on the brainless baby. My purpose in what follows is to try and provide, on behalf of virtue ethics, the justification it needs to grant animals less than equal consideration compared with all human beings, but stopping well short of granting them none or a minimal amount, as Kant and the Christian hawks would have it.

The problem virtue ethics must solve

Speciesism is the Berlin wall dividing the two camps. Kant and the divine command theorists think there's nothing at all wrong with speciesism, because either God or the categorical imperative says it's right, and this is proof enough for them.

Singer and Regan on the other side of the wall are agreed that speciesism is always and totally wrong, because their principle of equality stamps it as an immoral prejudice analogous to racism and sexism, and is as outrageously unjust as them.

The problem virtue ethics must solve in order to make room for itself in the middle ground of the mean is to transform the Berlin wall of speciesism into a half-way house, and it can do this only if it can show that *both* sides are wrong – that speciesism is neither always wholly bad nor always wholly good, but may *sometimes be good.*

To achieve this goal virtue ethics needs to do three things:

1 to show that not all speciesism is, like racism, an immoral prejudice, but that instead some form of speciesism is virtuous and, therefore, good
2 meet the argument from marginal cases against speciesism
3 avoid the kind of hard-edged, callously cruel speciesism purveyed by Kant and divine command theory, which justified almost any treatment of animals because they weren't of our species.

What follows is an argued account of how modern virtue ethics can succeed in meeting all three challenges and thereby justify its place as the leading moral theory in this area.

The first challenge: the case for applying virtue ethics to animal rights

The first challenge is to show that not all speciesism is an immoral prejudice, but that some form of speciesism is virtuous and, therefore, good. The first step is for modern virtue theory to distance itself from its founder, Aristotle. He was an out-and-out speciesist because he misread nature as being there *simply to serve us*, and misread human nature as having *absolute authority* over all non-human animals on account of our reasoning ability. These errors led him to the conclusion that '. . . *any* form of money-making that depends on . . . animal husbandry is for all men *in accordance with* nature' (*The Politics*, p. 46, emphasis mine), which is tantamount to saying that we can make money in *any way we like*, using animals in *any way we please*.

I'm not sure that even the Kantiest Kantian or the hawkiest Christian hawk would sign up to this. Even they would draw the line at taking a blow-torch to a cat and charging admission to the 'show', yet Aristotle's absolutist stance of mind over matter gives us the leeway to do this sort of thing. This is the high road to racism, sexism, and the vicious sort of speciesism so rightly despised by Singer and Regan. Modern virtue ethics, by adopting a modern scientific, evolutionary understanding of nature, human nature, and animals, opens the door to the possibility of a more benign type of speciesism, but more work needs to be done to dissociate it from racism and the like. Recall that Singer and Regan used a seemingly powerful argument from analogy to tie speciesism to racism and thereby stamp the former as immoral.

How do you fight an argument from analogy? One way is to try to loosen the ties, i.e. weaken the analogy, by finding so many differences or disanalogies between speciesism and racism that speciesism is more unlike racism than like it, leaving speciesism in the clear. Accordingly, this is the method we'll use.

We can begin this work of distancing good or virtuous speciesism from the prejudice of racism with a thought experiment devised by the British philosopher Mary Midgley, which I'll call the zookeeper argument. The particular disanalogy between race and species that this argument is intended to underline is that racial distinctions are relatively insignificant when it comes to knowing how to treat other human beings, whereas differences in species are absolutely crucial in dealing with animals. As Midgley points out,

> A zoo-keeper who is told to expect an animal, and get a place ready for it, cannot even begin to do this without far more detailed information. It might be a hyaena or a hippopotamus, a shark, an eagle, an armadillo, a python or a queen bee. Even members of quite similar and closely related species can have entirely different needs about temperature and water-supply, bedding, exercise space, solitude, company and many other things. (*Animals and Why They Matter*, pp. 98–9)

But it hardly needs to be said that no human of whatever race can fly unaided like an eagle, or breathe under the ocean like a shark, or live on dung like a dung beetle. There's no biological bar to interracial breeding, unlike the emphatic biological bar to inter-species breeding. You could test this rule by having sex with a sheep or a chicken or even a rhino, but I wouldn't advise it, and dung beetles are definitely out. The point of the zookeeper argument is that, unlike racial difference, species difference is very real, which gives us good grounds for *preferentially* discriminating between our species and other animal species, but no ground at all for *prejudicially* discriminating between one race and another. Preference and prejudice aren't the same thing.

Now, although this begins to weaken the analogy between racism and speciesism, we need more than just one disanalogy to do any real damage. However, by adapting several of Midgley's points to virtue ethics, we can strongly argue for no fewer than four further disanalogies between racism and a good version of speciesism.

1 Good speciesism stems from the virtues, whereas racism is vicious

The argument defending this point involves setting up a rival analogy to Singer's and Regan's. The rival analogy is that good speciesism, being a partiality or bias in favour of our own species, is far more analogous to our perfectly honourable partiality or bias in favour of our own family and friends. Such partiality, far from being vicious, is deemed virtuous and praiseworthy the world over. The main virtues involved are friendliness, love, gratitude, and loyalty, these being excellent dispositions that affirm people's self-respect, security, and sense of belonging.

What's wrong with the virtue-driven bias that leads you to buy presents for your family and friends at Christmas but not for strangers, or to save your mum rather than a stranger from drowning? Nothing. Home is where the heart is, and rightly so. Home is the home of the virtues; it's where they are first taught and practised. Hursthouse has labelled this positive and admirable bias to one's nearest and dearest 'familyism' (see *Humans and other Animals*, p. 150) So how does good speciesism stem from the virtues of familyism?

It seems that these strong feelings favouring our closest family spread and thin out, becoming less intense as they expand to include community, nation, and finally the whole human species. Charity may begin at home, but it doesn't have to end there. The additional virtues of compassion and justice can lead us to give money to aid agencies to help total strangers without expectation of recompense, and to protest against the injustice of illegal wars and state oppression affecting countless and nameless people on the other side of the world.

It's this virtue-inspired sense of being part of the human family in its widest sense that justifies our good, Homo sapiens bias when it comes to a choice between favouring our species over other animals.

The reason racism is not like good speciesism or its genesis in familyism is that it stems not from the virtuous mean of friendship, love, loyalty, and gratitude, but from the vicious excess into which these virtues can degenerate, namely the corresponding vices of cliquishness, obsession, fanaticism, and obsequiousness. With these vices in operation we get a vicious familyism, better named 'Mafiaism', that will stop at nothing to protect its own. So you give the job to your ill-qualified nephew rather than the better qualified stranger; you perjure yourself to give your dad an alibi when you know he's guilty of rape and murder; you take a job as a hit man just for the money so you can send your children to better schools and enjoy exotic family holidays.

Racism is vicious familyism writ large. Justice and compassion for 'foreigners' is nowhere to be seen; violence, abuse, exploitation, slavery, and murder are the order of the day. Good speciesism can degenerate into vicious speciesism if not driven by the virtues, in the same way that familyism can degenerate into 'Mafiaism' and racism at a more general level.

Singer and Regan make the mistake of thinking *all* speciesism is vicious speciesism and therefore like racism. They fail to show that you can't have the virtue-driven good version – good speciesism that's like familyism, and not like the generalized Mafiaism that is racism.

2 Good speciesism is instinctive or innate

Since good speciesism stems from familyism, if we can show that familyism is *instinctive or innate*, it will provide strong evidence that this is also true of good speciesism, coming as it does from an innate source, whereas racism is *learned later* on in life.

Here are four arguments, briefly sketched, which support this difference. Each argument on its own may not appear sufficiently convincing, but taken together they form a powerful cumulative case.

i) *The argument from universality* – If feature x is found universally in all members of a species, this makes it more likely that it's a natural, innate characteristic of that species than an accidentally acquired property, for accidents, by their very nature, come and go more or less randomly. The ball falling on red in the roulette wheel is an accident because sometimes it doesn't happen and sometimes it does. If there were a universal run on red we'd immediately think the wheel was rigged, making red, in a sense, 'innate' to that wheel. But familyism is such a universal feature of humanity that it's like a million spins at roulette all ending in red. As far as I know, anthropologists have yet to discover a culture or race that frowns upon partiality to one's family and friends. *Everyone* has special people in their life whom they value above others, so it seems *everyone* is a familyist. The best explanation is that familyism is innate, that human nature is rigged for *this*, *not* for racism, which is not universal. *Not* everyone is a racist – not even *nearly* everyone is a racist – therefore racism is more likely to be an accidental feature of one's cultural upbringing.

ii) *The genetic explanation of familyism* – You can hardly get more innate than genetics, so if it can be shown how emotional bias towards our family is based on the 'selfish' gene's drive to replicate itself in the next generation, whereas racism is culturally conditioned, then it will strengthen the case for this particular disanalogy with racism.

A gene's best chance of replication is through reproduction, because each parent passes 50 per cent of their genes on to their children; hence genes 'program' the emotions that fuel the sex drive. But this on its own would be leaving too much to chance, for what if the parents, having satisfied their genetically inspired sexual urges, didn't give a toss about their children? The children would have a significantly lower chance of surviving to the mating age at which they can continue the genes' replication. So the genes meet this requirement by predisposing us to familyism, i.e. to love our children intensely and to do everything in our power to protect them. This significantly increases their chances of survival to mating age and helps fulfil the genes' 'agenda'. Evolutionary psychologists call this 'kin-directed altruism'.

Since the human genome contains the fundamental biological 'code' for human nature, any emotions that rest on it would properly be called innate, so familyism is innate. Race also is innate because determined by genetic structure, but *racism* isn't. A child may be born black or white, with the parents' unconditional love for the child also there at the birth, but nobody is born genetically coded for racist attitudes.

iii) *Anecdotal evidence of children as non-racist* – I'm sure a thousand stories would support this, but I'll make do with only one, taken from my own experience as a parent.

On one occasion when I was out of the house, a knock came at the door. So my wife picked up our daughter Julia, who was about eighteen months old, and went to open the door, which revealed a very tall (6'6") black guy who was there to read the gas meter. Julia immediately pointed at him and called out 'da da', causing general amusement. Clearly, to her, his race and colour were as irrelevant as his height when it came to thinking he was her dad.

It might be replied that she didn't really understand the concept 'da da', confusing it with men in general, hence her mistake when a strange man comes to the door; but this only supports my point because, if a child can't yet grasp the abstract concept 'man', they won't be able to grasp, at that young age, the abstract concept 'race'. They couldn't possibly be racist without the prerequisite understanding of what it is: it would be like someone claiming to be against votes for women who, when asked what they understood by a 'vote', pointed to a camel. You can't be against something if you don't know what it is.

But a further reply might argue that this proves too much, because if this is so then you equally can't be *for* something if you don't know what it is. Julia's confusion over the concept 'da da' shows she doesn't know what it is, so she can't be *for* her da da and therefore, like all children, can't be familyist, proving it's not instinctive but, rather, acquired later on when the concepts of mum and dad are understood.

However, this objection can be met by distinguishing between how children get to know their parents and how they get to know what 'race' means. A child's knowledge of its parents is knowledge by *acquaintance*, involving myriad, everyday concrete personal, and emotional, interactions. This is **pre-conceptual**, thereby enabling children to have emotional bias towards their parents, in other words, to be *for* their da da without needing to know the concept 'da da' or being able to distinguish it from the concept 'man'. That's why, had I been present, Julia would have gone to me, been *for* me, rather than the black guy, despite misapplying the concept 'da da' to him.

Now admittedly, by the same token, it's also true that at the level of knowledge by *acquaintance* you can be **pre-***conceptually* **against** something without knowing *what* it is in the sense of its *conceptual* classification. For example, you might taste something disgusting on your plate (you know it's disgusting by personal *acquaintance* with its taste) and therefore be *instinctively and emotionally against it* without knowing what it is, i.e. you *don't possess the concept* with which to classify it.

However, this argument cannot be used to show that children can be pre-conceptually and instinctively racist, i.e. be disgusted by or *against* a particular race, because such pre-conceptual pro and con attitudes regarding x can only obtain where (x) is known by *acquaintance*, and race x is far too *abstract and general* for knowledge of it to be acquired through personal *acquaintance*. It would be absurd to suggest that a child could have *personal acquaintance* of a *whole race* of people, and so know what race is on this basis. Therefore race can only be known conceptually; the concept needs to be learned and understood before talk of racist attitudes can make any sense.

This means that familyism *can* be innate or instinctive, because the pro attitudes it inspires may be had pre-conceptually by very young children, based on the knowledge by acquaintance they have of their parents, whereas racism cannot be instinctive or innate, because anti-race attitudes can't be had pre-conceptually by very young children through knowledge of what race is, since this has to be acquired conceptually rather than by acquaintance, and must come later with the acquisition of language and cultural upbringing. That is to say, racism is artificial, learned, and thereby a cultural product, not instinctive like familyism.

iv) *Mencius' story of the child and the well* – Lastly, as an example of how this innate, instinctive care for one's family can be seen as a more general, species-wide instinct, the following example by Mencius (Meng-tse, *c*. 372–*c*. 289 BC, greatest Confucian scholar after Confucius himself) is hard to beat.

> Suppose a man were, all of a sudden, to see a young child on the verge of falling into a well. He would certainly be moved to compassion, not because he wanted to get in the good graces of the parents, nor because he wished to win the praise of his fellow villagers or friends, nor yet because he disliked the cry of the child. (*Mencius*, p. xviii)

The man's compassion can be seen as instinctive because it occurs 'of a sudden', before he has time to think it over and find some self-serving motive. It's not his child; it could be *any* child – i.e. any human being. If this is typical of human(e) reaction to a child in danger, then we can plausibly argue such emotional protective ties bind us to humanity, not just to our own family. This neatly exemplifies the journey from familyism to good speciesism, both being instinctive.

Hence, in the light of the cumulative case mounted by the foregoing four arguments, it's plausible to conclude that good speciesism is innate or instinctive, this constituting yet another disanalogy between it and racism.

3 Good speciesism stems from emotional bonding

Typical racist arguments rest on some sort of appeal to an alleged *rationally* based evaluation involving a particular distinguishing feature separating one race from another. Thus various values, such as intelligence, knowledge, superior religion, technology, and the fine arts, have been enlisted by white racists as reasons for treating blacks as *essentially* inferior.

Midgley agrees that this is a bad logical move in aid of a bad moral cause, because it's wide open to the argument from marginal cases, which either refutes it as inconsistent or forces such racists to come clean and admit it's only because they're white that they think themselves superior. This is of course ludicrous, as skin colour has nothing to do with superiority of any sort.

However, Midgley, instead of grounding it on some value akin to those listed above, and being shot down by the marginal cases argument, bases good speciesism on the *pre*-rational instinctiveness of the emotional bonds that tie together, firstly, families and, secondly, human beings as a whole, thus giving them priority over animals in general. She says that this bonding is 'an emotional, rather than a rational, preference for our own species . . . a necessary part of our social nature, in the same way that a preference for our children is, and needs no more justification' (Hursthouse, *Humans and other Animals*, p. 252).

At this instinctive, emotional level, good speciesism is *too deeply rooted* to be a *prejudice*. Laughter, tears, love of music and beauty, play, language, and so on, are as instinctive a part of human nature as familyism, and we wouldn't call *them* prejudices – merely deep-seated natural dispositions – so why call good speciesism a prejudice if it's based on an equally instinctive emotional bond?

Prejudice can only obtain at the more superficial level of *reflective* reasoning in which one engages in argument and assessment of evidence for and against your case, and is bad because it's the *deliberate* ignoring or distorting of *evidence* which counts against you. You thereby *pre*-judge matters *ahead* of the evidence.

But at a deeper pre-rational level, where reason doesn't even enter into decision-making, at the emotional bonding level, you don't need reasons to love your children – you just do; you just *have to*. Nothing here is *self-consciously judged* as *rationally justified* one way or the other, so there can be no *pre*-judged position and therefore no such thing as *pre*judice at this level. Just as 'inside' can't exist without 'outside', their being polar concepts, so 'pre-judgement' can't exist without 'judgement', and since judgement doesn't exist at the pre-rational, emotional bonding level, neither can *pre*-judgement, and therefore *pre*judice.

So if good speciesism rests on emotional bonding between humans, and emotional bonding goes too deep to be a prejudice, and racism is a prejudice, then emotional bonding can't be analogous to racism in this matter, and so good speciesism probably isn't either, being caused by a source that's disanalogous to racism.

4 Good speciesism is essential for our survival and therefore our eudaimonia

It's pretty clear that we won't achieve eudaimonic self-fulfilment if no self survives to be fulfilled, so whatever aids survival aids eudaimonia. Genes, under pressure from the evolutionary process, compete for survival via better adaptedness to the environment, so the emotions that underpin familyism are genetically 'inspired' because of familyism's effectiveness in contributing to the genes' survival via replication in children. But since good speciesism stems from familyism, it also must be essential to the survival of our genes, and hence our survival as a species, and further hence, our eudaimonia.

By contrast, the divisive nature of racist attitudes detracts from rather than contributes to the survival of humanity by undercutting the human solidarity promoted by good speciesism. But merely existing is not enough to live well, and survival is mere existing, so what is the more that's needed to turn surviving into thriving? Well, I think the virtues of familyism have a dual role here: the virtues of love and loyalty that hold families together as *surviving* units also significantly contribute to the *joy and worthwhileness* of life, as do the more wide-ranging virtues of justice and compassion on which good speciesism relies. Without these, instead of our good speciesist tendency towards solidarity, we'd have a destructive 'war of all against all'. There is also a strong prudential element of mutual self-interest involved in good speciesism that helps promote eudaimonia all round. This virtue is captured nicely by evolutionary psychology in its concept of 'reciprocal altruism', which applies to humanity on a more general level, i.e. to good speciesism rather than familyism's kin-directed altruism. Reciprocal altruism is a kind of genetically inspired habit of 'you scratch my back and I'll scratch yours', whereby everybody's back gets a scratching, thus promoting eudaimonia. Genes have more chance of replicating via the production of future offspring if, rather than everyone being at one another's throats, there is general cooperation. Through aeons of time, when it was primitive man as a species versus faster, fiercer, stronger animals, the virtue of self-interested prudence was at a premium on account of the group or species solidarity it encouraged.

It's the virtues needed for this kind of species-wide cooperation that give us all the goods and services of society, the arts, music, literature, science, education, entertainment, technology, the economic structures of trade and industry, our legal framework, and so on – all the things, in fact, that go to make life not only viable, but also a richly flourishing enterprise.

You could even say that, whereas evolution produces the *survival of the fittest*, the virtues produce the *fittest of the survivors*.

The only race that's relevant to both these goals is the *human* race. The only kind of 'racism' that good speciesism is analogous to is human racism; in fact, they're identical. Good speciesism is a perfectly virtuous preference or bias in favour of the human race over other animal species, but this doesn't have to involve a vicious, hard-edged attitude towards other animals, as we shall soon see. In fact, now that we've established that '*good* speciesism' is not immoral, not like racism, and therefore not the same as 'speciesism', I think it's justifiable to use a new term to designate 'good speciesism' more conveniently and to distance it from any association, even verbally, with the word 'speciesism'.

I suggest the word *'specielism'* (pronounced spee-shell-ism) as a replacement for 'good speciesism', because it captures the specialness of family and friends, from which it originates, but at the same time contains a positive phonetic reference to our preference for our species as a whole, without explicitly using the negatively loaded 'speciesism'. So, from now on, for 'good speciesism', read 'specielism'.

Specielism is tied to virtue ethics by many conceptual strands, making it plausible to claim that it is in fact *the* virtue theorist's stance on animal rights. For example, in contrast to the other normative theories, virtue ethics promotes both the **emotions** and **partiality** for people **special** to you rather than an abstract egalitarian approach to others – a **self-interested** stance that openly and unashamedly recommends the **virtues** as good for you, the agent. It's based on **human nature** and its **natural environment**, and aims at achieving a **eudaimonic** life.

Now, from what has been said, it's obvious specielism fits this profile like a glove. It's based on **emotional** bonding, stemming from familyism – a form of **partiality**, driven by the **virtues** which are themselves derived from the genetic structure of **human nature** and its **environment**. The extension of these attitudes of family partiality leads from kin-directed altruism to reciprocal altruism at the general human level, which reciprocity is tantamount to the virtue of **enlightened self-interest**, or **prudence**. Finally, all of this is conducive to **eudaimonia**, and since the virtues' job is to enhance this, and specielism also enhances this, the pro-attitude to humanity encapsulated by the word 'specielism' must also be virtuous.

So it seems virtue ethics, with its specielist stance to animals, has met the first challenge by disposing of the charge that specielism is like racism.

The second challenge: virtue ethics must meet the argument from marginal cases against speciesism

A big advantage that specielism has over the speciesism so effectively criticized and castigated by Singer and Regan is that it avoids the problem of marginalized humans, because the emotional bonds that tie humans together in mutual solidarity extend to *all* human beings *qua human*. In other words, there are no humans marginalized by specielism, so it's immune to this criticism.

The third challenge: virtue ethics must avoid the kind of hard-edged, callously cruel speciesism purveyed by Kant and divine command theory

How does specielism avoid this vicious speciesist attitude so reminiscent of racism? There are four features, central to specielism, which constitute an emphatic rejection of speciesism's hard-hearted, prejudiced stance towards animals.

1) – Specielism, unlike speciesism, can grant different degrees of independent moral status to animals according to their position on the evolutionary sliding scale, registering different levels of biological, social, and psychological sophistication. This is because each species has its own *objective* good derived from the biological facts of its evolved nature and from its potential to achieve its own kind of eudaimonia. Animal eudaimonia is as objective as human eudaimonia because both are based on the natural characteristics and potentialities of their respective species. For example, it's as much a fact about rabbits that they like to hop about and gnaw things as it is a fact about humans that they like to hear music. So, in the absence of a pressing reason, stressing 'pressing', to interfere with the rabbit's gnawing activities, such as the observation that it's gnawing through your chair leg, or your own leg, then out of consideration for the eudaimonic good of the rabbit, virtue ethics would recommend the wise, virtuous person should leave it alone to enjoy its well-being in its own way. The wide range of virtues that virtue ethics allows, including wit and intelligence – virtues far beyond the narrow moral pale of the deontologists and utililtarians – allow it to include rabbit 'virtues' such as gnawing and hopping as virtues in the context of rabbithood, precisely because they're conducive to the rabbit's eudaimonic telos of what a rabbit should be. These are virtues at the instinctive level, operating beyond moral praise and blame, but still good in the broader sense of good, as embodying excellent means for achieving the good life as a rabbit. In this way moral goodness is an utterly natural characteristic tendency of all organisms, which 'strive' to achieve the status of being an excellent specimen of their kind.

For virtue ethics, this is the real moral law – not Kant's categorical imperative, or God's ten commandments, or the principle of utility – the law to become a better example of your species than you are. The virtue of respect for that law will engender respect for animals' 'attempts' at living a flourishing life.

2) – Specielism acknowledges the closeness between humans and the higher animals as revealed by evolution, the extent of shared DNA, and animal studies, which have shown them to have complex psychology and social relations. This precludes any hard-edged divide between us and them. For Kant, Christian hawks, and Aristotle, the difference between humans and animals is like a *cliff edge*, with no quarter given to non-human animals beyond the edge of safety.

But for the specielist, sliding-scale stance of virtue ethics, it's more like a *slope* running between humans and the great apes, and then further on down to the lower mammals, ensuring that an animal's interest in living a eudaimonic life cannot simply be dismissed as irrelevant and of *no* importance in itself.

3) – Hard-edged, brutal speciesism is condemned by the specielist approach as stemming from the vices of callous cruelty and selfishness, which have led to the ruthless exploitation of animals in laboratories and factory farms in the pitiless pursuit of cheap food and safe cosmetics. In sharp contrast to these dark vices, specielism appeals to our natural and instinctive sense of compassion to reach out to other animals, easing their suffering and enhancing their chances of a eudaimonic life. The virtue of sympathy, for instance, can transcend the species barrier, blurring its edge with a soft focus lens of virtue perception that sees other animals as fellow travellers having their own eudaimonic stake in the world we share with them.

In the same way that partiality towards our family doesn't bar us from having a wider sense of justice and compassion for the fair and decent treatment of other human beings, so specielism, while supporting partiality towards our own species, doesn't bar us from exhibiting virtuous behaviour towards the wide world of non-human animals, ensuring they're treated humanely.

The virtue of sympathy – the excellent ability imaginatively and emotionally to put oneself in another's shoes – is central to this and, as a result of seeing with their eyes, to act wisely and kindly towards them. This seems to be a universally instinctive characteristic of human nature, evidentially supported by children's automatic response to animal suffering. Take, for example, the stressful reaction of children to the death of Bambi's mother. Granted, the heavy anthropomorphism is tantamount to people in animal suits, but still the point stands that the conscious life of real animals is not *that* far removed from this. We now know that animals feel pain, get stressed and anxious, can mourn the loss of parents and young, and have emotional bonds with their group, so our sympathy for them is not misplaced. In fact, as the following anecdote reveals, children's instinctive sympathy for non-human welfare can extend even to inanimate objects, never mind sentient animals.

My daughter Claire was about two years old at the time, and we were driving home on a moonlit night. She was happily pointing at the moon, saying, 'Look daddy! Moon, lovely moon!' All was fine until a dark sliver of stratus cloud slid in front of the moon, appearing to cut it in half like a cracked egg. Claire immediately burst into tears and cried, 'Daddy! Moon broking! Moon broking!!' She continued to be very distressed, despite assurances that it was just a cloud and that the moon was really okay. It wasn't until the cloud had finally passed and the moon was restored that she calmed down again.

Now the point is that she was too young to have *learned* this kind of response, and my wife and I had never sat her down and instructed her about how the moon might possibly suffer, and she wasn't crying because she wanted the moon and couldn't have it, so this kind of self-interested motive was ruled out. Rather, it seems to have been an entirely spontaneous, natural, emotional response of sympathy for the moon's 'plight'. It was precisely the kind of natural response we all have when we're horrified at cruelty to animals. Our articulate objections are really our adult way of saying, 'Look! Veal calf broking! Battery hen broking!' And it's not just the animals that don't fare well with this kind of treatment, although it is *particularly* them. *We* don't fare well in witnessing this sort of treatment, even if it's for our benefit. This is why the meat industry and the pharmaceutical companies have been so sensitive and secretive about the conditions in which animals are kept and what they do to them. As far as they're concerned, the less we know the better.

By encouraging the virtues of sympathy and a wise understanding of what's going on in the meat industry and in animal laboratories, virtue ethics can hold to a soft-edged specielism that eases the burden on these animals by demanding significant improvements in their treatment.

4) – Finally, despite specielism being soft-edged and therefore virtuously considerate towards animals, it's still *specielist* and therefore also pro-human in a partial, prioritizing sense. Basically this means we can use animals for our own ends provided it is done virtuously. The relevant virtues on which our priority rests include the fundamental ones constituting the emotional human bond, e.g. love, sympathy, loyalty, and compassion, but also the virtue of prudence (enlightened self-interest).

So much for the kind of *attitude* these specielist virtues encourage towards humans and animals. What about how this pans out in actual *practice*? How do we strike the virtuous mean between the vicious extreme of cruel and ruthless exploitation, on the one hand, and the extreme of supine hypersensitivity, on the other, which allows animals to walk all over us?

Applying virtue ethics to our treatment of animals

How should a virtuous person react to the sight of a shedful of thousands of battery hens? To disregard their suffering and distress would be callously cruel, and to delight in it would be sadistically cruel, neither of which vices belong to a virtuous person. To inflict that amount of pain and deprivation on an animal for the unnecessary and short-lived pleasure of a chicken dinner would seem cruel and utterly selfish.

While avoiding these vices, the virtuous person, speaking more positively, would exhibit the virtues of compassion and kindness – compassion in the sense of feeling distressed for the animals' plight and wanting to alleviate it, and kindness as the desire to help the animal achieve its telos and the eudaimonia appropriate to its species.

So what makes for a thriving, flourishing eudaimonic hen? Here's a plausible list:

- room to roam around in some sort of enclosure
- protection from predators
- sunshine rather than artificial light
- to be able to peck seed from the ground
- grass or soil under foot
- room to spread its wings
- the chance to mate
- being with other hens, not separated by cages
- appropriate food and water, not some artificial concoction designed to make them so overweight their legs can't hold them up
- living to maturity and enjoying maturity for some time.

Virtue ethics would favour traditional, free-range, family farms rather than the intensive factory farms of modern agribusiness. The virtuous person would take a similar line regarding animals being used in experiments. There's one crucial difference, though, and that is that some of these experiments are essential to the pursuit of human eudaimonia – that is to say, those that are likely to contribute to the fight against lethal and debilitating diseases such as cancer. It's at this point that the virtue theorist's evaluation of the human telos, as being of more importance to us than an animal's, begins to bite. A choice needs to be made: them or us?

Virtue theory chooses us, i.e. our eudaimonia, and is prepared to sacrifice some animal eudaimonia to that end on the basis of the primeval and instinctive emotional human bonds that make for human solidarity as a species. But this, of course, should be done in as virtuous a way possible, with due care for animal welfare in the use of anaesthetics, living conditions, etc. Trivial animal testing for such unnecessary and frivolous purposes as having yet one more perfume or detergent on the market would be dubbed viciously selfish and callous. This should be stopped.

Going back to animal husbandry, does this mean that, since eating meat is unnecessary for human nature to thrive – we could do just as well in terms of nutrients with a vegetarian diet – virtue ethics would insist that the virtuous person should be a vegetarian? The answer, I think, is not necessarily. Given the superiority of human eudaimonia over that of chickens, cows, sheep, and the rest, although eating meat from these animals is not *necessary* for our eudaimonia, it does provide us with nourishment and pleasure, which contributes to a flourishing human life.

So, provided the animals concerned are given a eudaimonic, though shortened life, on free-range family farms, then they can be eaten with a good conscience by the virtuous person, knowing they have been treated humanely and enjoyed the life they had, a life they would not have had at all if we hadn't bred them to be eaten. In this way, we do right by the animal and also by ourselves, our happiness having greater priority than theirs.

As with all our other theories, we need to assess and consider any weaknesses of the approach taken by virtue ethics. It seems virtue ethics has successfully met all the challenges necessary to be a viable moral guide to our treatment of animals, and it's the only theory to have done this, so it seems safe to conclude that it's the moral guide for us. It avoids the nasty cruelty on one side of the 'wall' and the supine sentimentality on the other.

However, it's not out of the woods yet. The following three objections need to be dealt with.

1 Specielism may lead to racism and sexism.
2 The naturalness of emotional bonding doesn't make it right.
3 The 'pets before people' objection.

1 Specielism may lead to racism and sexism

Couldn't a white racist, arguing along similar lines to a virtue theorist, hold that the same emotional bond which justifies partiality to family and extending to our species also justifies partiality to one's race along the way, and the discriminatory treatment of all blacks that goes with it? Similarly, sexists might appeal to emotional male bonding as being 'in the genes', like familyism, and justifying chauvinist partiality to men and discrimination against women.

Virtue ethics would reply that this objection is unfair, because it doesn't draw a line between the kind of partiality to members of one's ethnic group, race, or gender which is virtuous and good and the vicious kind that is fanatical, discriminatory, and unjust. Instead, it lumps them both together. This line needs to be drawn because virtue ethics is okay with the virtuous kind of partiality towards gender and ethnicity, but condemns the vicious racist and sexist sort. The virtue of wisdom would know where to draw the line in these sorts of cases. Vices, not virtues, lead across this line.

For example, certain ethnic preferences are entirely natural, right, and proper, and foster eudaimonia – such as the preference or partiality of immigrants of all races to live together in their own communities, where they feel more at home, sharing a language, culture, family, memories of home, religion, cuisine, and a host of other subtle bonds. Thus spring up places such as Chinatown, Little Italy, English expatriate communities in Spain, Asian communities in Birmingham, and the Irish in Liverpool.

Again, it takes wisdom to be a fine judge of these matters, maintaining the proper mean or balance between, on the one hand, turning these neighbourhoods into ghettos of alienated citizens and on, the other, assimilating them wholesale into the wider host culture, thereby losing their distinctive identity and heritage. The middle road is the most flourishing for all concerned.

Likewise, gender partiality may sometimes be virtuous or innocuous rather than discriminatingly sexist. For example, stag nights and hen nights are openly exclusive to only one sex, yet no one thinks these are objectionally sexist. And it's not sexist for a woman to prefer, on entering a room full of men, to make her way over to the only other female in the room and strike up a conversation. There's nothing wrong in preferring to associate with your own 'kind', just as there's nothing wrong with preferring the company of your friends and family, as long as this doesn't degenerate into the vicious extreme of discriminating unfairly against 'outsiders'. This objection wrongly assumes virtue ethics can't tell the difference. It can.

2 The naturalness of emotional bonding doesn't make it right

This could also be called the 'feels so strong, can't be wrong' objection. Doesn't virtue ethics appeal to the deep-seated, instinctive nature of our emotional bonds tying us to family and species, in order to show that these feelings are right? However, we also have equally deep-seated emotions and instincts for violence and hatred, yet that doesn't mean it's right to express these features of human nature. If being natural doesn't make them right, the same goes for our emotional species bonds.

Again, let's consider the virtue ethics reply. It's true that, just because something is natural, this does not automatically make it good. However, virtue theory doesn't hold this doctrine, so the objection is a straw man fallacy, which caricatures the virtue ethics position. Naturalness of emotion is the *starting* point – the given, at which education in the virtues begins to train the individual in expressing these emotions in line with the mean. If virtue ethics held that naturalness was sufficient for goodness it would make itself redundant, because training in the practice of the virtues would not be needed. Natural traits merely have *potential* for goodness, but also for badness. For instance, eating is a natural desire, but this doesn't automatically make it good because, if it's not directed by the virtue of wisdom, you'll eat things that aren't good for you and, if not guided by the virtue of temperance, you'll miss the mean by eating either too much, leading to obesity, or too little, leading in extreme cases to anorexia.

Equally, though our emotional human bonds are a natural desire, if not guided by virtue they'll either be deficiently developed, leading to us caring about nobody – a nihilistic nightmare – or excessively developed, leading to fanatical tribalism and constant warfare. Virtue ethics merely claims that natural dispositions such as emotional human bonding are a *necessary* condition of goodness and eudaimonia. This objection accuses it of holding that they're a *sufficient* condition, so the objection is misguided.

3 The 'pets before people' objection

Virtue ethics seems to be saddled with the absurd consequence that the much-vaunted emotional bonds that ground the virtues of familyism may also justify the vice of 'petism', e.g. putting your pet dog before other people because the dog is deemed a 'member' of the family. What if it's a choice between saving, not your mum this time, but your pet dog, as opposed to a stranger, from drowning? Wouldn't saving the dog be immoral, and since virtue ethics may sometimes support this, isn't it immoral too?

The rather surprising and robust reply from virtue ethics is to insist that, while agreeing that saving the dog is in *many* cases *immoral*, it does *not deny* that saving the dog is *sometimes right*. (This is a case of sucking the bullet rather than biting it.) Our judgement of these cases will differ according to the circumstances. Saving the dog is sometimes virtuous, sometimes vicious. In fact, by appealing to our intuitions in this matter, virtue ethics can turn this objection into an advantage. For example, say the stranger is Saddam Hussein: who would save him rather than their pet dog merely because he's human? Suppose your dog is having a swim in the river and a stranger starts insulting you and throwing stones at him just for a laugh, but then falls in and both the dog and he get into difficulties. Would we blame you for saving your dog *first*? And how many people spend more on pet food than they do on Oxfam? Is this immoral too?

In the film *Dances with Wolves*, when the soldiers take pot shots at Dunbar's adopted wolf Two Socks and kill him, if you had a choice, who would you prefer to see killed, the soldiers or Two Socks? My intuition is to kill the soldiers and save the wolf. I have a much stronger emotional bond with it than with them. So the leeway virtue ethics gives us *sometimes* to put pets before people may turn out to be a strength rather than a weakness – a point you can verify if your intuitions agree with any of mine above.

7 Environmental Ethics

Environmental ethics can be defined as 'a systematic account of the moral relations between human beings and their natural environment' (DesJardins, *Environmental Ethics*, p. 11). Debate continues as to whether these moral relations entail duties to all life forms, including insects, trees, and grass, and perhaps extending even to non-living categories, such as species and ecosystems with their inorganic elements – rocks, rivers, rainfall, and suchlike. Another way of putting this is to ask whether the natural environment itself has not just instrumental value, as a set of resources we can use as means to our ends, but intrinsic or inherent value on a par with humans. Is it only good *for* something, or is it good *in itself*?

This chapter will form a brief introduction to this most crucial question of practical ethics: How should we treat nature? I'd go as far as to say that, in the long run, maybe in the not-so-long run, all other moral problems take second place to this one, because what is at stake is nothing less than the future of humanity, and of the planet. This may look like scaremongering but I don't think so.

They say the ice caps are melting and the forests disappearing. They say species upon species are dying out, and that global warming will bring environmental catastrophe. They say it's our fault, and that time is short and getting shorter all the time. They might just conceivably be wrong – but I wouldn't bet on it. You see, 'they' happen to be the overwhelming majority of the most hard-nosed, experienced, scientific experts in the field. For the longest time we thought the Earth could take whatever we threw at it – it was an infinite fountain of resources and a bottomless sink for pollution – but no longer. The sombre scientific statistics tell another story – a story of Earth's limitations and the repercussions which will be visited upon us if nothing is done to stop the environmental rot. But back in 1968, when the warning voice of science was just a whisper, before the whisper became a fire alarm, we got an early inkling of our vulnerability courtesy of Apollo 8 and the beautiful picture it sent back. The blue-white living Earth, hanging in the blackest black of lifeless space, recalled the fragility of a Christmas tree bauble; it has since turned out that this impression was not far from the truth.

It is vital that we take a long hard philosophical look at our moral relations with regard to nature, because it may be that our traditional moral theories have got this badly wrong. Perhaps instead of providing a solution to the problem they are in fact part of the problem. Could it be that what we need is an altogether different ethical approach to the environment? There are three fundamentally different types of environmental ethics:

- *anthropocentric* (human centred): 'light green'
- *biocentric* (life centred): 'mid green'
- *ecocentric* (ecosystem centred): 'deep green'.

These are distinguished according to the kinds of thing to which they ascribe intrinsic or inherent value as opposed to merely instrumental value. Recall that for a thing to have inherent value is for it to be valuable in its own right, or for its own sake independently of any usefulness it might have for us. To have inherent value is to be morally considerable.

The *anthropocentric* approach regards only humans as being morally considerable; all else has merely instrumental value. Because of this, humans are therefore seen as *superior* to all other forms of life on the planet. The *biocentric* approach differs from the anthropocentric in that it regards not just humans, but all individual life forms as being morally considerable, including worms, insects, trees, grass, and micro-organisms. No non-living thing, such as rocks, chemicals, and water, including systems of things such as species and ecosystems, has inherent value. At most they have only instrumental value in virtue of their usefulness to living things. (It may help to distinguish a species from an individual living member by considering that an individual cat can breathe, eat, purr, move, and sleep, whereas the cat *species* can do none of these things and so is not alive.)

Finally, the more radical *ecocentric* approach holds that not only individual living things but also *non-living systems*, comprised of living and non-living things, possess inherent value, and *even more so* than any living individual. These non-living systems include all species and ecosystems, encompassing their physical locations – lakes, mountains, oceans, forests, wetlands, deserts, moorlands – and perhaps even the Earth itself, as a biosphere or self-regulating super-ecosystem. That leaves the *less* valuable *individual* things to provide the instrumental value which serves the needs of the relevant ecosystem seen as an end in itself. For example, if a population explosion of rabbits threatens to destroy an ecosystem by eating all the grass, they can be culled to protect it.

All four of our normative theories fall squarely in the anthropocentric camp because, as we've seen, they hold that only humans have inherent value and are superior to all other life forms. Utilitarianism, however, does extend its anthropocentrism a little because, despite regarding humans as superior to trees and rocks, they're not seen as intrinsically more valuable than sentient animals, since sentience is the only relevant moral feature, and they share this with humans. In order to evaluate the strengths and weaknesses of the three categories of environmental ethics, each will be challenged from its rivals' point of view with respect to its ability to provide a defensible moral guide to the kind of sustainable equilibrium with nature that's essential in securing the long-term future of life on this planet. With that in mind, let's begin with the anthropocentric theories.

Anthropocentrism

Far from easing our environmental difficulties, our four anthropocentric theories have instead been accused, by rival biocentric and ecocentric theorists, of stoking the environmental fire. Because the only things in which they were ever morally interested were human beings, since only these had inherent value, the natural environment was treated as simply a morally irrelevant backdrop to the ethical arena where humans took centre stage. It literally was just the scenery, having only instrumental value. None of these moral theories thinks we have any duties to forests, grasslands, insects, or ecosystems. It's impossible to do moral wrong to them no matter what you do, be it mining, burning, flooding, or polluting, because they're not moral beings (Kant), don't have souls (divine command theory), and can't rationally practise the virtues (Aristotle) or feel pleasure and pain and have preferences (Bentham, Mill, Singer). Thus anthropocentrism not only permits, but actively encourages, exploitation of nature in the service of humanity, and only now, when the huge scale of our environmental impact has begun to have serious adverse effects on *us*, has the anthropocentric camp started to take any notice. Recommendations to recycle waste, use low-energy light bulbs, build more wind farms, cut down on car use, are suggested to protect the environment, more for *our* sake than for *its*. The mid- and deep greens say that light-green recommendations such as these are not enough, and accuse anthropocentrism of having all along misunderstood our relationship to nature by completely undervaluing it. It's this attitude, they argue, that has helped get us into our current mess, aided and abetted by rapid population growth, the widespread desire for an affluent consumerist lifestyle, and a powerful industrial technology.

It appears we're in the middle of the greatest extinction killing binge since the dinosaurs died out over 60 million years ago. Estimates indicate it's continuing at well over 1000 times the natural background rate of extinctions that would normally occur through natural evolutionary processes, but this is the first one to be caused by a single species – us. By 2050 it's estimated that over a million species will become extinct as a direct result of climate change (see Curry, *Ecological Ethics*, p. 12). Extinction is for keeps; it does exactly what it says on the *tin*. We're turning biodiversity into biomonotony. Surely it's a morally bad move to generate a degenerate, cringingly boring Earth heaving with humans, but where the only tigers you'll ever see are on celluloid, yet anthropocentrism seems to encourage the kind of dismissive attitude to nature that has led to this nightmare.

Our four normative theories are well and truly in the dock, and the question we must ask is whether they have sufficient philosophical resources to meet the charge of environmental incompetence laid against them. Are they adequate to meet the need of a sustainable future, or do we require a different ethic, one which topples humans from their moral throne by locating inherent value *at least equally* in a non-human source? To answer our question we'll begin by taking a look at the case for a more radical ethical approach to the environment, namely the mid-green stance of biocentrism.

Biocentrism

Paul Taylor (American philosopher, b. 1923) is the best-known biocentrist, so we'll take his thought as representative of this position and focus our discussion on him. Taylor believes he can make a good case for *biocentric egalitarianism*, that is, that *all life has inherent value and has it equally*. If he's right, then this will mean major changes to our obligations and behaviour towards nature. For example, if pests have as much inherent value as humans, then farmers won't just be using pesticide, they'll be *committing* pesticide. But is he right? To help answer this question we'll first explain and assess Taylor's normative theory, and secondly look at its practical application.

Explaining biocentric egalitarianism: the theory part

According to this, having inherent value is an all or nothing thing. There are no grades in between. You either have it or you don't, which entails that, if you do have it, you have it equally along with all other inherently valuable things. The next step is to find out what quality you need to have in order to possess inherent value. According to Taylor, what you need to have is 'a good of one's own'. You can't have inherent worth without this.

What is it to have a 'good of one's own'?
There are four essential ingredients:

i)   A thing must have a biological organic goal or telos which belongs to the kind of thing it is, and at which it 'aims' in order to realize its potential. This is to be what Taylor calls a 'teleological centre of life'.

ii) The realizing of a thing's potential must be in its interests.

iii) Reaching this goal must be good for the entity concerned, without reference to any usefulness it might have to any other thing.

iv) It must be a *living* thing because non-living things don't have any interests, and are not on their way to realizing a telos which is their optimum state.

An example should help clarify these ideas. An acorn's good consists in fulfilling its potential to become an oak tree. That's its telos. An acorn is therefore a teleological centre of life, and it's in its interests to become an oak. It can be harmed by being prevented from fulfilling this potential through being cut down or burned, but it's important to realize that the young oak does not *take* an interest in this, not being a conscious being; nor does it need to take an interest in order to *have* interests. It doesn't *care* one way or the other, nevertheless it's an *objective biological fact* that it's bad for the oak *itself* to be cut down, because this damages its potential and its good, and this is true merely with reference to *its own* welfare, never mind that of any other thing. That's the sense in which it has a 'good of its own'. Only living things have this dynamism from start to finish. A pile of sand, on the other hand, can't be harmed because it's not going anywhere, has no telos, and is not alive. There's nothing you could do to a pile of sand that would make it any better or worse off than it is, because it not only does not take an interest in anything, nothing is in its interests at all. Wet, dry, hot, or cold, it's all the same to it because it has no welfare and is totally inert. In sharp contrast, if you deprive plants of nutrients, sunlight, and water, they'll wither and die. These are known objective facts, not subject to opinion, as any gardener will tell you.

Now, although a plant having a good of its own is a necessary condition of having inherent worth, it's not in itself sufficient for this, because inherent worth is a value *we* ascribe to living things in virtue of their having a good of their own, and without us having the *right attitude* to the plant, there's no reason to ascribe inherent worth to it. Without the right attitude, we could simply accept that it's 'trying' to grow, but be *totally* dismissive of this if it gets in our way – say a weed growing in the middle of our lovely lawn – and hence accord it no inherent worth at all. To have inherent worth the plant needs us on its side, believing not only that the plant has a good of its own, but also that it's a *good thing to help* the plant achieve this. This pro-life attitude, Taylor contends, is generated by what he calls '*the biocentric outlook on nature*', and it's this plus the facts of plant welfare (i.e. having a good of their own), that generates our ascription of inherent value to all living things and the respect for nature that's been so badly lacking in the past, yet so badly needed in the future. This can be formulated as:

[('good of its own' + 'biocentric outlook')—>'inherent worth']—>'respect for nature'.

What is the biocentric outlook on nature?

This consists of four beliefs, namely:

i)   Humans are members of the Earth's community of life on the same terms as all the non-human members.
ii) The Earth's ecosystems are complex webs of interrelated elements with the health of each depending on that of the others.
iii) Each individual organism is conceived of as a teleological centre of life, pursuing its own good in its own way.
iv) We must reject the claim that humans are naturally superior to other species. It's groundless and false, and merely the result of irrational bias.

Taylor finds evidence to support points i) to iii) by appeal to the sciences of biology and ecology, and claims that point iv) follows on from them. It's on this basis that he argues that it's reasonable for all rational, well-informed people to adopt the biocentric outlook, and that this in turn makes it reasonable to regard all life as possessing inherent worth and therefore deserving of respect. This ultimate attitude of respect will be manifested in our acceptance of various prima facie duties owed to all living things equally (a prima facie duty is one which obtains unless overridden by a more important one). The explanation over, let's turn to assessment.

Assessment of biocentric egalitarianism: the theory part

Taylor needs all four components of the biocentric outlook in order to generate equal inherent value for all life and the respect for nature he's after. Points ii) and iii) look uncontroversial and well evidenced, so we can let them stand. More doubtful is the assertion in point i) that we hold our membership of Earth's community 'on the same terms' as all other life forms (it's not entirely clear what Taylor means by this), but from an anthropocentric point of view the weakest component by far is the seemingly mad fourth claim, to the effect that humans are not superior to any other life form. This will be the focus of our attention, for this is key to Taylor's theory.

Assessing the non-superiority of humans

One possible argument for biocentric egalitarianism is that our gifts, such as reason, morality, creativity, and humour, are inherited from the very *same* natural evolutionary *source* that provides animals and plants with their abilities – the eagle's sharp-sightedness, the monkey's climbing skill, the cheetah's speed – so we aren't inherently superior to them. Same source, same value. But this doesn't work because it's just like arguing that, since my Picasso was inherited from the *same source* (granny) as your inherited dot-to-dot puzzle book, it must be the case that a Picasso is not inherently superior to dot-to-dot puzzles.

A second argument is that, since our extra gifts were due to *lucky* genetic mutations and nothing else, we're not inherently superior to animals or plants. This argument also doesn't work. It misses the point because our evolutionary inheritance being lucky has got nothing to do with its inherent worth. For example, let's say there's a raffle with two prizes, a Van Gogh and a child's doodle. This is no reason for the 'lucky' winner of the child's doodle to insist that the person who won the Van Gogh didn't get an inherently superior prize merely because he got it through luck. If they reason like this they deserve to win the doodle.

Thirdly, it could be argued that even if we have superior attributes this doesn't mean we are an inherently superior species. After all, someone who's more intelligent than other people is not regarded as having more rights or inherent worth. Well, the same logic applies *between* species such as humans and worms as applies *within* the human species itself. Even granted we have superior intelligence compared with a worm, this doesn't mean we have superior inherent worth; as far as this is concerned, we're equal.

What's wrong with this argument is the invalid but crucial claim that what applies *within* a species applies equally *between* species. An analogy might help. Within the species 'chess' there may be different sets ranging from plastic to gold, but, despite the gold ones being superior in monetary value, they're not superior with regard to their inherent worth considered as pieces in a chess game. In this respect all are equal: a gold queen is no better than a plastic one in terms of its powers of movement, ability to capture, or to checkmate. This would be similar to Taylor's position regarding differences within the human species. But once we step outside the species of chess and compare it as a species of game with other species of games such as ludo or tiddlywinks, this doesn't mean we're not justified in asserting that chess, as a species of game, is inherently superior to ludo and tiddlywinks. It could be, for all this argument has shown, that as a species Homo sapiens is as superior to all other species as chess is to ludo and tiddlywinks, despite not admitting any inherent difference in value between individual humans within our species.

The final argument accuses advocates of human superiority of arguing in a circle. To illustrate this fallacy, imagine the following conversation:

Max: Ghosts exist.
Ben: Why do you think that?
Max: A ghost told me.

Good arguments move in a linear path to prove something new. Arguing in a circle is bad because you end up where you started, 'proving' ghosts exist by assuming ghosts exist. The point being made is that we can't avoid circular reasoning, because we can't claim human superiority over animals and plants without looking at things from the *human* point of view and *assuming already* that we're superior. Imagine the following conversation:

Megan: Humans are superior.
Rachel: Why do you think that?
Megan: Because we can do things that animals can't, such as maths and morality.
Rachel: But animals can do things we can't, such as run at 70 mph, or swing from tree to tree.
Megan: But our things are better than theirs.
Rachel: Not from their point of view.
Megan: But their point of view doesn't count as much as ours.
Rachel: Why not?
Megan: Because we're superior.

This clearly begs the question (argues in a circle), as you can see from comparing the conclusion (the first line) with the basic premise (last line). If this sort of thing can't be avoided in arguing for human superiority over other life forms, then we'll have to give up this cosy belief and accept that a blade of grass is as inherently valuable as any human being; we'd have to accept Taylor's biocentric egalitarianism. However, I think this argument can be refuted.

Firstly, we can avoid taking a purely human point of view, and instead take a neutral perspective. From this neutral or objective stance it's clear that humans and all other life forms have an interest in survival. Since this is common ground, and a common value, those species that can survive better and longer will be superior, since all 'want' this. It follows, then, that, since we as a species are thriving in terms of sheer numbers whilst most other species are not, we're superior to them because we have superior natural abilities that fit us for this shared goal. In this sense, we're playing the same survival game and we're better at it. This doesn't appear to be question-begging due to our relying on survival as a *species-neutral* and *shared* value.

Secondly, although there are many things animals can do better than us – an eagle's sight, a cheetah's pace, cows ruminating, monkeys climbing – at least we can do these things to *some* extent naturally. We can see, run, eat, and climb – never mind when we add our technology. Let's race a cheetah against a jet and see who goes fastest; let's see if an eagle can see something on the other side of the globe, or on the surface of Mars. On the other hand, there are things we can do of which animals have no inkling. It's not just that they can do them but we can do them better; it's that they can't even get started. What animal can even begin to do geometry or consider principles of justice, logic, science, and so on? Doesn't this demonstrate superiority?

Thirdly, it's not question-begging to appeal to the fundamental emotional human bond cited by virtue theorists as justification for our bias towards our own species. This is an evolutionary asset, is not irrational but pre-rational, and enhances our flourishing as a species. As I've already tried to show (see chapter 6), this is our fundamental moral attitude, not respect for nature in Taylor's sense, which entails believing we have no more inherent value than say an AIDS virus. While allowing us to defend ourselves by killing the virus, Taylor's position would actually commit us to the duty of promoting and protecting its welfare as long as we remained safe. This seems absurd. Surely I owe it nothing but aggression. This gestures at a possible problem with Taylor's position concerning the duties generated by the biocentric outlook. Let's look at these in more detail.

Explaining biocentric egalitarianism: the practical part

Our biocentric duties to nature
We have four prima facie duties:

1 *non-maleficence*: the duty not to harm any organism if not threatened by it.
2 *non-interference*: the duty not to interfere with the freedom of individual organisms. This means no trapping, capturing, or fencing off of wild habitats.
3 *fidelity*: the duty not to betray wild animals' 'trust', since we're all part of Earth's community of life. So there should be no fishing, as this is based on an attempt to deceive the fish into thinking the bait is genuine food, and as such it's a betrayal of the fish's 'trust'. This is wrong because it's symptomatic of a superior attitude.
4 *restitutive justice*: the duty to make up for any harm done to nature, e.g. repair any damage to habitat; return captured animals to the wild.

Being prima facie, each of these can be overridden in various circumstances – for example, let's say I'll die if I don't get something to eat soon. The urgency of my basic need to live overrides all four of these duties, which allows me to harm the fish (duty 1), by deceiving it into taking the bait (duty 3), capturing it (duty 2), and eating it, without compensating the fish in any way for its loss (duty 4).

Two problems stand out with duties 2 and 3 respectively. First, the duty of non-interference seems to pick arbitrarily on humans so as to bar them from interfering with nature, whereas so-called natural processes, such as a lion killing an antelope, which equally interfere with nature, are given the green light. But, as Taylor himself points out, we're as much a part of nature as any other living thing – the biocentric outlook, no less, says so (see points 1 and 2) – so environmental justice demands that we be equally entitled to interfere with nature. Taylor's position on this seems self-contradictory.

Second, concerning our duty of fidelity, Taylor's claim that deceiving wild creatures is wrong, because it's symptomatic of a superior attitude, puts the cart before the horse. His point is that it's wrong because we aren't *really* superior, and therefore our superior attitude is misplaced. However, one could more plausibly read this the other way and argue that the very fact that we can fool a fish into thinking bait is ordinary food *demonstrates that we really are superior*, and that our superior attitude is not misplaced at all. In fact, the problem for Taylor goes much deeper than this because, if trickery is disrespectful of nature, then nature must disrespect itself, since the survival of millions of species depends on wholesale deception of prey and predators; think of the camouflage tactics of polar bears and stick insects. Nature is justified by her children, and since we're only doing what comes naturally, perhaps it's closer to the truth to say that, along with every other living thing, our natural infidelity to other threatening or useful species constitutes true fidelity to nature's law of deception.

Resolving conflicts of interest between humans and nature

In a crowded world, conflicts of interest are bound to arise over issues such as territory, food, security, and comfort. Some of these are basic needs, e.g. food; others are non-basic, e.g. comfort. How are we to resolve these issues when all living things have *equal* inherent worth, seemingly leading to a paralysing moral stalemate between opposing claims? We need wood, but the birds need the trees, while the trees themselves need their own life; though all have equal inherent worth, there must be some winners and losers. Taylor is aware that our four moral duties don't give nearly enough guidance on these issues, so he has added a further five practical moral principles, which are outlined below.

i) *The principle of self-defence*: This applies when serious harm is threatened to humans, giving us moral permission to kill bacteria, for example.

The remaining four principles apply when there is no serious threat.

ii) *The principle of proportionality*: This says we should not favour non-basic human interests, such as building a golf course, over basic non-human ones, such as destroying hundreds of trees to make way for it. The trees have to give up their life (a basic interest) for a non-basic one (our entertainment), and this isn't fair.

iii) *The principle of minimum wrong*: This says that, if you do do wrong, do as little of it as possible, so if we go ahead and immorally build the golf course we should cut down only the minimum number of trees.

iv) *The principle of distributive justice*: This says that, in any conflict of interest between human and non-human, it's only fair that benefits and drawbacks be spread impartially between the individuals and species concerned, owing to the equal inherent worth of all.

v) *The principle of restitutive justice*: This says that, if you do more than the minimum wrong and/or the damage is one-sided, then you must make amends in some way. For example, say one hundred trees were destroyed to make way for the golf course. All the damage is on one side – nature's – so restitutive justice demands that we, as it were, pay damages to nature by planting one hundred new trees elsewhere.

Assessment of the five principles of conflict resolution

These five principles certainly give the natural environment much needed protection by severely curtailing our destructive habits. A moral ban would apply not only to large-scale activities such as polluting rivers out of convenience, fishing and hunting for pleasure, and building golf courses, but also to small-scale ones such as destroying a tree because it spoils your view. In all these cases non-human life forms are being killed for our entertainment and convenience, which breaks the principle of proportionality, so this shouldn't be done in the first place. Many who don't engage in the above activities may be tempted to react with complacency to their moral condemnation, but this would be premature. Taylor's theory has a long reach, and can reach them too. For example, I imagine almost everyone gets the Sunday newspapers. Well here's a startling statistic: 'It takes an entire forest – more than 500,000 trees – to supply Americans with their Sunday newspapers each week.' (Gore, *An Inconvenient Truth*, p. 315). I don't know of anyone who has died because they didn't read the Sunday papers, so that makes this a non-basic need being serviced by sacrificing the basic needs of half a million trees every week, and that breaks the proportionality principle, which makes it morally wrong. Planting the same number of trees to maintain sustainability helps but doesn't make up for the original wrong because it shouldn't have been done in the first place. This is like deliberately killing someone's house plant and trying to make amends by replacing it. Must we really give up our Sunday papers? No doubt Taylor's biocentric egalitarianism does some good work by making us take a serious look at things such as our management of forests and the uses to which we put them. Do we really need all those colour supplements and magazines and the wide range of Sunday papers on offer, when we could get most of this news from television and save hundreds of thousands of trees? However, the suspicion persists that biocentrism unreasonably demands too much of us. Take, for example, the case of the immoral patio (see DesJardins, *Environmental Ethics*, p. 146).

Suppose we want to build a patio – a non-basic human interest. In the process millions of micro-organisms in the soil plus countless worms and blades of grass will be killed – a basic non-human interest. Taylor's biocentric egalitarianism would see this as a *moral* dilemma. Is it really? It seems so because each and every worm, microbe, and blade of grass has as much inherent worth as any human. There's no superiority here, and given that we wouldn't be prepared to kill millions of people if they stood between us and our patio, then neither should we be prepared to kill millions of non-human life forms to do so. Building the patio breaks the proportionality principle and hence is morally wrong, because we're favouring a non-basic human interest (leisure) over a basic non-human one (life). But perhaps we can reduce the seriousness of our immorality by invoking the principle of minimum wrong. This will encourage us to minimize the damage done to nature by making the patio as small and as shallow as is compatible with convenience. However, the principle of distributive justice demands an even spread of benefits and distress among all participants, and since being dug up is decidedly 'inconvenient' for the grass and worms, perhaps morally speaking we ought to build a patio too small to be convenient for us. Taylor's principles seem to demand a pokey patio. Finally, the principle of restitutive justice requires us to make amends for the millions of lives lost, which may mean sowing extra grass elsewhere, or sponsoring a tree to atone for our wrongdoing. Still, this doesn't compensate the millions of dead individuals *themselves*. We can't patch *them* up, so things are still unsatisfactory.

Many of you by now will, no doubt, have lost all patience. Do we really have to go through all this hand-wringing palaver every time we want to build a patio? The answer is no, because these excessive moral demands stem from Taylor's undervaluing of human worth, and this has, I believe, been adequately refuted. Nevertheless, the feeling remains that Taylor may be on to something, to wit, that nature has *some* inherent value; it's just that he pushed it too far in claiming it had as much inherent value as humans. To see this, try the following thought experiment.

The last man

Imagine the last man on Earth; knowing he'll die in a few days, he decides to take a flame-thrower to a forest nearby and torch as many trees as he can. This gives him neither pleasure nor pain, and he has no particular motive, it's just something to do. Does he do a morally bad thing? As they stand, none of the four anthropocentric theories would condemn him because the trees don't count at all, not having a soul (divine command theory), virtuous reasoning (virtue theory), sentience (utilitarianism), or a good will (Kant, who respects only moralizers, not photosynthesizers). As such, they have *no* inherent worth and so are not morally considerable. Yet if your intuition agrees with mine in judging that in destroying living things for no good reason the last man has done wrong, then this can only be because the trees *do* have inherent worth. They count *in themselves* rather than merely instrumentally, precisely because, despite no one being around to make any use of them, it's still wrong to kill them.

It looks like Taylor's egalitarianism is back in business. But this would be too hasty because, in a modified version of our thought experiment, if the last man (to be) had a choice between taking an axe to the only other remaining (but anaesthetized) person, and chopping down a tree, it would be a morally worse decision to kill the human than to kill the tree. This must be because the human has *more* inherent worth than the tree, in which case Taylor is only partially vindicated, as is anthropocentrism. We seem to have justified an intermediate position which we can call *biocentric hierarchicalism*, that is, the view that living things have different *degrees* of inherent value depending on the kind of thing they are, with humans having the *most*. Since this seems like the most plausible position, our best bet for an adequate environmental ethic that accords due respect and protection to nature is the normative theory with the resources to extend its range of application so as to embrace biocentric hierarchicalism.

With this as a criterion, we can begin by ruling Taylor out because he has not made a move in this direction, and is sticking with biocentric egalitarianism. That leaves our four anthropocentric theories. Taking Kant first, it appears he also has no flexibility in the matter. Nothing on this planet can be a moral being except humans, so no other life form can have any inherent value at all. Moving on to utilitarianism, we find an equally inflexible approach. Sentience or preference satisfaction are the two qualities that bestow moral considerability, but there doesn't seem any way we could plausibly consider trees, grass, microbes, and suchlike to experience pleasure or pain or be able to express a preference, since they don't have a conscious point of view. Virtue theory seems more promising because of its focus on the eudaimonic striving to fulfil one's telos, and its recognition that all of living nature aspires consciously or unconsciously towards this goal. It's clear that Taylor has adapted this aspect of virtue theory to his own position, each organism being, in his words, a 'teleological centre of life', so virtue theory *can* accord all living things inherent value. However, unlike Taylor, it has the resources to impose on nature a *sliding scale* model of inherent value: an organism's place on the hierarchical scale would depend on such things as degree of complexity, intelligence, aesthetic qualities, and how closely we bond with it emotionally. Thus it can take a biocentric hierarchical approach to living nature, thereby giving us the kind of environmental ethic we need. The only rival remaining is divine command theory, but this doesn't look promising at all, because our conservative Christian model can't lend itself to the view that all living things have souls. Only humans do, and since you either have a soul or you don't, there being no grades in between, this rules out any graduated scale of inherent value and thus outlaws biocentric hierarchicalism. The hawk interpretation applies here too, so nature is there to be exploited. It's true that God doesn't favour wanton destruction of the natural environment, but this is not because it has inherent value; rather it's because the Earth is His property and we owe it some care out of *respect for God*, not it. There are no commands not to dig up grass or chop down trees, so we cannot do wrong to nature. Strong and peculiar confirmation of this attitude is provided by Jesus's unwarranted aggressive attitude to a figless fig tree (see Mark 11:12–21 and Matthew 21:18–22). Being hungry and spotting the fig tree in the distance, Jesus goes to it, expecting to get some figs, and on discovering it doesn't have any, in his frustration he kills it with a curse. In doing so, he unfortunately sends a very encouraging message to logging companies. Based on this incident, a neat but worrying little argument can be constructed exhibiting divine command theory's negative attitude to the environment:

P1: If trees had any inherent value, then any deliberate damage to them is morally wrong.
P2: Jesus deliberately damaged a fig tree.
P3: Jesus never did anything morally wrong in his life.
IC: Doing deliberate damage to a tree is not morally wrong.
MC: Therefore, trees don't have any inherent value.

With the failure of divine command theory, and that of the others, to provide an adequate environmental ethic which values nature for itself, it looks like virtue theory is the star player on the anthropocentric team because it is the only one with the flexibility to accommodate a hierarchical approach to inherent value in nature. Taylor's biocentrism is itself incapable of taking a hierarchical stance, being wedded to an implausible egalitarian view of things, and so is to be rejected.

Turning now to our final theory, the question that must be faced is whether any of our anthropocentric ethical theories can meet the more radical challenge posed by ecocentrism. It argues that no anthropocentric ethic can adequately reflect the true value of nature and protect it properly from human depredations, because anthropocentrism can't help but see humans as the most inherently valuable item on the planet, to the extent that human luxuries override nature's necessities. Ecocentrism castigates this as a fundamental moral error, and global warming is the price we're paying. Frankly, the stakes couldn't be higher. So who's right?

Ecocentrism

Rather like anthropocentrism with its varied normative theories, ecocentrism as a general ethical stance has its own internal differences, for example, those between the classic 'land ethic' approach of Aldo Leopold (American forester and philosopher, 1886–1948) and the 'deep-ecology' movement of Arne Naess (Norwegian mountaineer, Resistance fighter, and philosopher, 1912–2002). There are others still, but what they all have in common – the thing that makes them ecocentric – is that they believe they have strong scientific and philosophical arguments to show that *humans should be demoted to* **second** *place behind the Earth's ecosystems in the hierarchy of inherent value.*

Leopold's celebrated fundamental principle of morality sums this up perfectly: 'A thing is right when it tends to preserve the integrity, stability, and beauty of the biotic community. It is wrong when it tends otherwise.' ('The Land Ethic', in *A Sand Country Almanac*, p. 262).

This is a significant shift of moral focus, placing *ultimate* inherent value, not on individuals, even human individuals, but on *whole* biotic communities or ecosystems as *ends in themselves*. It's this *holistic* approach to the environment that marks off ecocentrism as different from both biocentrism and anthropocentrism. Holism will include as inherently valuable abiotic (nonliving) but life-supporting elements such as rainfall, rivers, rocks, mountains, and soil nutrients, which are vital to the ongoing viability of the biotic community and its complex network of interrelated species.

Let's look at the scientific and philosophical arguments for ecocentrism.

The case for ecocentrism

We will consider three arguments.

1 *The argument from ecology*

The findings of ecology, which is a science studying the relations of animals and species both to one another and to their natural environment, are a central support for ecocentric holism. No individual animal can fare well if separated from its natural habitat and all that that supplies. Just as organs get their identity and point from the function they fulfil in the body, so individuals and species get their point from the role they play in the biotic community. The reason you have a heart is to keep the body going; you don't have a body so you can have a heart. So, just as the heart exists to serve the body as an end, individuals exist to serve their ecosystem, and if it's the end they serve, then it has more inherent value, and even more reality, than they do. It's the *whole ecosystemic network* of species interrelations which is the locus of highest inherent value, not the individuals relying on it, even if they do happen to be human.

2 *The argument from quantum theory*

One of the most famous quantum physicists, Niels Bohr, said of individuals, 'Isolated material particles [individuals] are abstractions, their properties being definable and observable only through their interactions with other systems' (Fritjof Capra, *The Turning Point*, p. 69).

In other words, they cannot be defined as individual particles by attention being confined to the qualities they themselves have on their own, because these can't exist on their own. Their *essential* being, and therefore all their attributes, must be tied to others in the *system*. And if this is the case at the subatomic level of micro-particles, it must be the case at the macro-level of 'individuals', such as humans, plants and animals, because these are all made up of subatomic particles that have no real individual existence. We're more like whirlpools in a river than rocks on the river bed; take away the river and the rocks will still be there, but no river system = no whirlpool. To us Sir Edmund Hillary was a famous 'individual', but in *reality* he was just another eddy in the cosmic current – like the rest of us. The whole is not only more real than its parts, it's worth more in terms of inherent value.

3 *The argument from value-intensifiers*

Ecology has helped uncover features of ecosystems which seem to act so as to enrich or intensify inherent value. The more of these features a system or a species has, the more valuable it is. Here's a selection of such features that ecocentrists often cite as being of inherent value.

i) *Complexity*: the more complex the network of interlocking, interdependent species there are in an ecosystem, the more valuable it is. It's a kind of sophistication. Individuals could never match this.

ii) *Biodiversity:* this is closely related to complexity, and it refers to the sheer range of species available in an ecosystem – for example, tropical rainforests are amongst the most biodiverse ecosystems on Earth, and are to be valued accordingly.

iii) *Longevity:* basically, the older the better. An ancient wood has more inherent value than a forest sprung up ten years ago. Ecosystems outlast individuals by aeons. They stand the test of time better than individuals.

iv) *Stability/Equilibrium:* this is vital to ecosystems. The more their balance is disturbed, the greater the risk of collapse, so the more stable, the more inherently valuable.

v) *Naturalness:* man-made managed forests with neat rows of trees are less valuable than natural 'wild' ones. Still less would we rate a forest of plastic trees, or fake astro-turfed meadows, or factory-produced prosthetic 'rocky' outcrops.

vi) *Size:* we tend to have more respect and awe for a giant redwood or Ayers Rock than for a skimpy tree or a pebble on the beach.

vii) *Rarity/Uniqueness:* no doubt if there were a thousand grand canyons dotted all over the world, the Grand Canyon wouldn't be quite so grand. But it's the only one, so all the more precious for that.

viii) *Beauty:* we love beauty for itself, so anything that has beauty to that extent will have inherent value – for example, the Great Barrier Reef or the Matterhorn. It's worth noting that the surface quality of beauty does not detract from its importance to us, as the following exchange illustrates:

Objector: Beauty is only skin-deep.
Reply: Yes, but so is skin.

In other words, 'shallow' is not incompatible with 'vital'.

Ecocentrists argue that ecosystems have more of these value-intensifying features than any so-called individual, and this is yet another reason why they have optimum value on Earth.

Some of these features, for instance complexity, biodiversity, and equilibrium, in combination with our relative ignorance of the almost infinitely intricate workings of the biosphere and its ecosystems, lead to a principle of action, or rather inaction, strongly recommended by ecocentrism, namely, the precautionary principle. This invites us to err on the side of caution when it comes to interfering with ecosystems. Basically, if in doubt, don't. And given the sheer complexity and vital nature of the ecosystems that constitute our only home, since we're almost always in doubt, we should rarely interfere. The strong ecocentric moral preference is for *preservation* of wilderness rather than *conservation* management, because this kind of fiddling has done much more harm than good. It's like letting a child loose with pliers in a telephone exchange.

Assessing the case for ecocentric holism

Firstly, I find the general argument from ecology inconclusive. An ecosystem needs individuals as much as they need it, for without individuals there would be no species and no set of interrelations to constitute the ecosystem. You can't have relations if there's nothing to be related. Another consideration is that individuals are *alive* whereas ecosystems seem to be abstractions, sets of relations between living things rather than living things in themselves, and since conscious life is more valuable than inert relations, perhaps ecosystems don't have superior inherent value after all.

Secondly, the argument from quantum theory is invalid, committing the fallacy of composition. Just because macro-objects such as human beings are composed of micro-objects such as subatomic particles that are mere abstractions doesn't mean we're also mere abstractions, definable only in terms of our relations within the ecosystem of which we're a part. This would be as absurd as arguing that, since water at the micro-particle level isn't wet (atoms of hydrogen and oxygen on their own aren't wet), this implies that water at the macro-swimming-pool level with billions of H_2O molecules can't be wet.

Thirdly, a serious, perhaps fatal criticism has been brought against the whole value-intensifier argument. It's the charge that this whole idea is wrongheaded because it commits the *naturalistic fallacy*, which is the logically invalid move of arguing from factual premises to morally evaluative conclusions. The contention is that you can't reason from facts (even holistic facts) to values since these are completely different kinds of thing. The gap is so logically wide that you would have to jump from your factual premises to your evaluative conclusion, and it's always a bad idea to jump to conclusions. This, admittedly debatable, fallacy will be examined in more detail in the next section on metaethics, but it will suffice to illustrate it briefly here and discuss its application to ecocentrism.

Suppose I were to argue as follows:

P1: This music is loud (fact).
Conclusion: Therefore this music is good (value judgement).

As it stands, the conclusion doesn't follow from the premise, because loud music doesn't have to be good; it could be bad or indifferent. The same will go for *any* such argument that moves from facts to values; *they're all invalid*, and since the value-intensifier argument does precisely this, it also is invalid. For example,

> P1: This ecosystem is biodiverse (fact).
> Conclusion: Therefore this ecosystem is good/has inherent value (value judgement).

As it stands, this is invalid, and so for all the value-intensifiers. However, there may be a way round this problem via facts about human welfare. To illustrate this, take the following argument:

> P1: These capsules contain antibiotics (fact).
> Conclusion: Therefore these capsules are good (value).

As it stands, the conclusion doesn't follow, but if we amend it thus,

> P1a: Antibiotics are good.
> P1: These capsules contain antibiotics.
> Conclusion: Therefore these capsules are good.

then we make it valid; the conclusion now follows. But there's still a problem. We've purchased validity at the cost of going from value (the word 'good' in P1a) to value (the word 'good' in the conclusion), not from fact to value, so we need a *factual* reason why antibiotics are good. But this seems to send us back to square one, because we'll be going from fact to value again. However, there's a plausible way round this. What *kind* of facts make antibiotics good? Surely they're good because they have the natural ability (fact) to fight disease and make us healthy (good). We value health, for itself and for its contribution to our flourishing, our eudaimonia, which is our end. To will the end is to will the means, so valid reasoning can tie *factual natural means* (antibiotics' ability to fight disease) to *valued end* (health and eudaimonia), and this is how the fact–value gap is closed. Now to apply this method to one of the value-intensifiers.

> P1: Ecosystems have biodiversity (fact).
> Conclusion: Ecosystems are good/have inherent value (value):

This is invalid as it stands, but we can improve on it as follows,

> P1a: It's good to have biodiversity.
> P1: Ecosystems have biodiversity.
> Conclusion: Therefore ecosystems are good/have inherent value.

Now we have a valid argument, but it goes from value (the word 'good' in P1a) to value (the word 'good' in the conclusion), so we need a plausible factual reason (that bridges the fact–value gap) for why it's good to have biodiversity. It looks something like the following.

We humans have evolved over hundreds of thousands of years in such a way and with such a nature that we can't help but find biodiversity exhilarating, fascinating, endlessly entertaining, and energizing – the aperitif of life. Boredom and uniformity are detrimental to a flourishing life. Biodiversity does the opposite; therefore biodiversity is good for us because of its natural and factual contribution to our physical and mental well-being, to our eudaimonia. We're drawn to the rich, natural variety surrounding us, as children to a song, as the prisoners in Shawshank were drawn to a Mozart aria. If this is an integral part of our evolutionary history, it must be conducive to our well-being and survival in some *essential* way. Each value-intensifier is a chord in nature's serenade, lulling us into a true sense of security and reminding us of where we belong. The Grand Canyon is nature's rock music, the breeze in the trees its woodwind section. Perhaps this is the call of the wild – and there's plenty of evidence this call is as strong as ever. More Americans visit nature reserves such as Yosemite each year than go to all football sports events combined. And there's the rush on bank holidays in the UK to get to the sea, the forests, moors, and mountains, to go rambling, climbing, camping, picnicking, gardening. Take us away from nature and we're like fish out of water. Unlike the fish, we'll be a long time dying, but die we shall if we're not put back, and not just physically – we'll be sick at heart.

Based on this evidence, virtue theory would advocate a caring and protective attitude to nature because of its value-intensifying eudaimonic effects in enriching our lives, and it appears ecocentrism must to some extent compromise with anthropocentrism and adopt this stance if it's to avoid the naturalistic fallacy. The alternative is a logically flawed environmental ethic.

However, utilitarians may argue that to take this stance is to treat nature as having merely instrumental value as a means to our pleasure, albeit in a more subtle way. When we go for a walk in the forest we may not be exploiting the trees in the crassly instrumental sense of turning them into paper and furniture, but we're still *using* them as a means to our ends – ends such as our enjoyments of solitude, shade, fresh air, and contentment. Aren't these as much *products*, though experiential ones, as tables and chairs and, if so wouldn't ecocentrism have to abandon its view that the environment has *inherent* value?

I think this objection can be met by the *argument from irreplaceability*. An *essential* characteristic of anything with purely instrumental value is that, as long as a replacement does the job just as well, for example, replacing one screwdriver with another, then there's no loss of value. However, it seems there's no adequate substitute for nature. It cannot be replaced without suffering some loss. To test this, try the following thought experiment, a modified version of Nozick's 'experience machine'.

The environmental experience machine

If the only thing that mattered in walking through the forest was the subjective experiences you gained, then as long as you came by these you wouldn't care how. Now suppose you could plug into the 'forest walk program' in an environmental experience machine instead of actually walking in the forest; despite its giving you precisely the same feelings of peace and solitude, it would seem that something of value has been lost, because we don't just want the *experience* of the forest – we want the experience of the *real forest itself.* If it's the real thing we want, then no substitute will do; it will be *irreplaceable,* and therefore will have *more than just instrumental value* in causing pleasant experiences. If your intuitions agree with this assessment, then we must reject the utilitarian instrumentalist interpretation of nature's value.

However, is this extra value inherent in the sense that it is *totally* independent of *human* valuing? Surely it can't be, otherwise *it* couldn't be experienced and valued at all. Many ecocentrists have wanted to insist that nature's value is inherent in some such sense, e.g. either that values are out there objectively existing as some sort of ghostly attachment to things such as biodiversity, or that naturalness itself is intrinsically good, whether or not humans exist and recognize this fact. This view raises enormous metaphysical and metaethical difficulties, some of which are discussed in the next section on metaethics. Suffice it to say at this point that, if ecocentrists insist on this account of inherent value in nature, then their theory is in trouble. Their arguments from ecology, quantum theory, and value-intensifiers are far from convincing if this is what they're being employed to prove. On the other hand, the compromise with virtue ethics to avoid the naturalistic fallacy has produced a strong version of the value-intensifier argument which side-steps the pitfalls of instrumental value at one extreme and totally independent inherent value at the other. In this modified version of ecocentrism, nature possesses a 'softer' kind of inherent value which some have called 'non-instrumental value.' I prefer to call it '*adherent* value', both because this better reflects the deep psychological, dare I say, spiritual bond between us and nature that makes us adhere to its magnetic value-intensifiers, and because it meets objective inherent value half way by acknowledging that these value-intensifying qualities are out there in nature itself, but as *empirical facts*, not values in themselves.

So ecocentrism appears to have survived the pressure from both the naturalistic fallacy and utilitarianism by bending a little in the breeze, virtue ethics and adherent value giving it that extra flexibility. But ecocentrism must face a final charge, that of 'environmental fascism'.

Is ecocentrism fascistic?

Regan (in *The Case for Animal Rights*, p. 362) has accused Leopold's land ethic in particular of environmental fascism, though other ecocentric positions may also be vulnerable. As DesJardins says,

> Leopold seems willing to condone hunting individual animals to preserve the integrity and stability of the biotic community. But because he also describes humans as equal members of that community, he would seem to be committed to the permissibility of hunting humans if doing so would preserve the integrity, stability, and beauty of that community. (*Environmental Ethics*, p. 195)

In other words, humans are *expendable*, and can be culled, hunted, or sacrificed to serve the needs of the *system*. This indeed resembles some aspects of fascistic ideology, but I think the charge of fascism can be robustly countered by the following arguments.

1 Regan can't make the fascism charge stick because even if, and I stress *if*, letting the interest of the biotic community or ecosystem override the individual human interest from time to time bears a passing resemblance to *one* strand of fascist thought, this by no means justifies the charge of *wholesale* fascism. This commits the fallacy of 'hasty generalization' – basing a general claim on the insufficient evidence of only one or two examples. Going by Regan's argument, you could accuse a person of having Nazi tendencies just because they love children, for Hitler was a children-loving Nazi; or charge Churchill with fascism because he conscripted and sacrificed thousands of British citizens to serve the British state *system*. If these charges are absurd, so are Regan's. It's the 'land ethic' not the 'fatherland ethic'.

2 With this in mind, we might argue that hunting humans who despoil and wreck valued ecosystems and species may not be such a bad idea in some circumstances. First of all, we're fine with the police doing just this with criminals who jeopardize the human community or system. Of course, the police should have proper regard for human rights, which explains why we describe them as hunting *for* criminals. So while it's not like a turkey shoot, they *are* still hunted and shot if they fire first.

3 Extending this idea to greedy poachers who threaten species such as the black rhino and tiger, caring nothing for these species but only about lining

their own pockets, if it comes to a choice between a world without the tiger or black rhino, or a world without some greedy poachers, which is preferable? I'd prefer to keep the tigers and black rhinos, and lose the poachers. Capture and imprison them if we can, but if they put up an armed fight, then shoot them.

4 Extending this thought experiment even further to include mere lifeless rocks, suppose a man has planted hundreds of tonnes of dynamite all along the Grand Canyon. He's about to push the plunger and detonate the explosives, which will result in the Grand Canyon being reduced to heaps of rubble. The only way to stop him is to shoot him dead. What should you do? The choice is between no Grand Canyon or one dead human. My intuition is to kill him. This choice seems so obvious it's not even a dilemma. This is not tantamount to fascism. The sheer depth of adherent value the Grand Canyon accrues from multiple value-intensifiers such as uniqueness, size, longevity, complexity, beauty, and naturalness easily outweighs the paltry value a destructive stranger has to me. It may be tough, but it's not fascistic to be prepared to use lethal force if this is what it takes to stop rogue individuals ruining priceless ecosystems and spoiling it for the rest of us living things.

Summary of findings on ecocentric holism

Any version of ecocentrism which aims to be egalitarian is rejected, as it will face the same arguments that sank biocentrism. Of the remaining hierarchical versions, those are also rejected whose holism insists on objective inherent value for ecosystems, in the sense of it existing somehow totally independently of human valuers and human eudaimonia. The surviving versions will be the ones which admit *human valuers as essential* to the value of ecosystems, because this is adherent value. But now this looks more than just a modification of ecocentrism, because it crucially tampers with the *heart* of the theory. The locus of value is no longer in the *ecosystem itself* but in *human* eudaimonia, albeit *essentially* related to ecosystems' value-intensifying qualities. What has survived is closer to a very significant extension of a virtue ethical anthropocentrism in the direction of deep-green theory. In other words, ecocentrism was wrong to claim that we need a radically different *kind* of ethical approach to the environment, namely an ecocentric ethic. Instead what we need is an enlightened and radically extended *anthropocentric* ethic sympathetically *applied* to the environment and, of the four anthropocentric theories, virtue ethics comes closest to giving us what we need in terms of an adequate environmental ethic of sustainability.

Final summary

Now that the dust has settled in this three-way fight, we can see that biocentrism's weaknesses of underrating humans and being overly demanding make it unfit as a workable environmental ethic. Ecocentrism requires modification to survive examination, but the heart is modified out of it, transforming it into a strand of anthropocentrism in the form of an environmentally friendly virtue ethic. Since none of the other anthropocentric theories can match virtue ethics in giving us what we need to heal the breach with nature and survive climate change, that leaves virtue ethics as the most adequate ethical theory reflecting our proper moral relations with the environment.

Further Reading

Abortion
Glover, Jonathan, *Causing Death and Saving Lives*. Harmondsworth: Penguin, 1977, chs 9–11.
Hursthouse, Rosalind, *Beginning Lives*. Oxford: Blackwell, 1987.

Euthanasia
Palmer, Michael, *Moral Problems*. Cambridge: Lutterworth Press, 2005, ch. 2, pt v.
Singer, Peter, *Practical Ethics*. 2nd edn, Cambridge: Cambridge University Press, 1993, ch. 7.

Animal Rights
Hursthouse, Rosalind, *Humans and other Animals*. Oxford: Alden Press, 1999.
DeGrazia, David, *Animal Rights*. Oxford: Oxford University Press, 2002.

Environmental Ethics
Gore, Al, *An Inconvenient Truth*. London: Bloomsbury, 2006.
Benson, John, *Environments, Ethics and Human Concern*. Oxford: Alden Press, 1999.

Part III
Metaethics

Introduction

Metaethics (meta = after), as the name implies, is the branch of ethics that takes a step back from the hurly-burly of the clash between normative ethical theories and their application to the messy practical ethical disputes about things such as euthanasia. When people discuss practical moral problems and worry about which normative theory is correct, they are *doing* and living their ethics. This is ethics operating in the trenches on the front line of life. In thus engaging at first hand with the moral problems of everyday life, people use moral language to praise and condemn others and themselves, to reason about moral principles, to give advice to others, and to work out for themselves how to behave well and do the right thing.

Philosophers call this level of thinking a *first-order* activity. First-order activities are where people are actually *doing* the subject. Other examples are when historians are researching and writing history, believers are reading their Bible and praying and going to church, mathematicians are doing maths, and scientists are in the lab.

Philosophers commonly conceive of philosophy as a *second-order* activity, their job being to think about and examine the first-order level of thinking, no matter what the subject. The definition of 'philosophy' as 'thinking about thinking' captures this dual level nicely. For example, philosophy of history does not *do* history but rather, as it were, stands behind the historian looking over their shoulder examining the *concepts and principles* that they use in order to do history, and asks questions such as, 'Is there such a thing as historical objectivity?' The philosopher of mathematics won't *do* any calculations (that's first-order stuff), but will ask such things as, 'Do numbers actually exist?' The philosopher of science won't be found in the lab, but will ask, 'What do we mean by "cause"?' 'What do we mean by "law of nature"?'

In all these examples philosophy arrives *after* the first-order activity is under way and looks at the nature and validity of the thinking and talking that's being done at that level.

Metaethics, like the above examples, arrives *after* the first-order moral thinking is well under way and examines *it*. Metaethics deals with questions such as: What do we mean by the word 'good'? And: 'Is there really a difference between right and wrong or are we just kidding ourselves?'

There are 2 major metaethical camps:

1 *cognitivism*
2 *non-cognitivism*.

Each of these in turn splits into sub-camps. **Cognitivism** splits into:

1 *transcendentalism*
2 *naturalism*
3 *non-naturalism* or *intuitionism*.

Non-cognitivism splits into:

1 *emotivism*
2 *prescriptivism*.

Cognitivism

The word 'cognitive' simply means 'capable of being known', and this links with perception, intuition, and reasoning as different ways of coming to know things. For example, I *know* I'm wearing a green T-shirt because I can *see* it (*perception*). I *know* that I exist and that 5 is bigger than 4 because this is *self-evident* (*intuition*). If I know that the maximum capacity of the human head is 500,000 hairs, and that there are at least 500,000 people in New York, then I also know that this implies that there must be at least two people in New York with exactly the same number of hairs on their head, because I can *validly deduce* this (*reasoning*). Cognitivism in ethics is the view that we can come to know *moral* truths in one or more of these ways.

Cognitivists hold that, when we use moral language involving such terms as 'good', 'bad', 'right', 'wrong', 'duty', and so on, we're talking about *real* properties out there independently of us. So moral judgements such as 'Murder is wrong' are *true statements* about *facts*, which can be *known*. And since it's not just a subjective matter of opinion whether kindness is good, or telling the truth is right, these moral *truths* are *objective*. The bottom line is that we *discover* moral truth because it's already out there independently of us. So cognitivists agree there are knowable moral facts; where they disagree, and split into rival sub-camps, is with regard to *what kind* of facts these are, and *how* we come to know them.

Transcendentalists think moral values such as goodness and justice exist in some absolute supernatural sense beyond the physical universe, either as properties of God's eternal will, or in their own right as necessary eternal truths. They're knowable either via a divine revelation or through a determined exercise of abstract reasoning, and certainly not through the exercise of any natural means such as sense perception.

The naturalists, on the other hand, think moral values such as goodness are identical to, or deducible from, natural properties such as pleasure, and that we can know this via our five senses. Natural properties are those that belong to things in the normal physical world of everyday life. For example, greenness is a property of grass; sweetness is a property of sugar; tiredness can be a property of the body; and boredom can be a property of a mind. These are all knowable in relatively straightforward ways.

The non-naturalists, as their name suggests, think moral values aren't the same as natural qualities and can't be derived from them. Moral values stand alone out there on their own two feet. We get to know about their existence, not via the five senses, but by a specialized faculty of *intuition* that's geared to zooming in on non-natural moral properties.

Non-cognitivism

Non-cognitivism is the opposite of cognitivism and is closely related to the more personal, subjective areas of life such as emotions and feelings. So all you have to do to get non-cognitivism is simply deny everything cognitivists say. There aren't any moral facts or truths; goodness isn't a real property objectively out there; there's nothing to know, and moral judgements don't state facts, they merely *express* or *evoke emotions* (emotivism) or *recommend or prescribe actions* (prescriptivism). Morality isn't discovered as an objective fact, like gravity, but rather is *our invention*, a bit like etiquette. It's created by our *subjective* emotional and pragmatic responses to the world around us. For example, emotivists would say that the sentence 'Murder is wrong' is like saying, 'Murder! Yuk!!' This is neither true nor false. Prescriptivists would say that the sentence 'Murder is wrong' is like saying, 'Don't murder!' Yet again, this is neither true nor false.

The reason neither of these is true or false is that neither states any facts. They aren't statements, but are instead, respectively, an exclamation and an imperative. To make this clearer, try asking yourself these questions.

- Is it *true* that, Murder! Yuk!!?
- Is it *true* that, Don't murder!?

The reason these questions don't make sense is that exclamations and imperatives don't even set out to be true or false, so it's beside the point to ask this of them. That's why non-cognitivism thinks morals can't be true or false – because moral judgements, although they look like *statements*, are really a type of *exclamation* (emotivism) or *command* (prescriptivism).

Throughout this section we'll look at the twists and turns of the debates between cognitivism and non-cognitivism and the five rival theories that make them up. We'll follow the basic pattern of firstly explaining a theory, secondly looking at arguments for it, and thirdly considering the arguments against. Let's look at cognitivism first.

8   Cognitivism

Ethical transcendentalism: Plato

Plato (427–347 BC), world famous pupil of Socrates, was born in Athens into an aristocratic family, well connected politically. Some sources say his real name was Aristocles and that 'Plato' was a nickname he got in reference to his broad shoulders, and there's a suggestion he might have been a wrestler in his youth – a happy speculation I hope is true: I harbour a splendid image of Plato drop-kicking an opponent. He loved and admired Socrates, and the latter's execution in 399 BC had a profound effect on the young Plato, who was present at his trial. Plato was one of the philosophical groupies who followed Socrates about. Disgusted with the corruption of an Athenian democracy that was responsible for the death of his beloved mentor, he rejected a career in politics. After Socrates died Plato travelled around for a bit but finally came back to Athens in 387 BC and opened what many regard as the first 'university'. He called it 'The Academy' and the name stuck. It lasted an amazing 900 years before being shut down. Plato's brilliant dialogues made Socrates world famous and his killers infamous, so I suppose in the end he got his revenge, and then some.

Key Text: *The Republic* (*c.* 375 BC)

There are two basic kinds of ethical transcendentalism: religious and philosophical. One example of the religious kind is divine command theory, because it locates moral value in the will of a God who *transcends* or exists beyond the space–time universe. It's a cognitivist theory because it holds that God's will can be known via God's revealing his will in scriptures and through the church. However, since this position has already been considered in an earlier chapter, it will not figure further here.

Of the philosophical versions, including that of Kant, the most famous is Plato's, and so his theory will be the focus of the remainder of the chapter.

The theory of Forms

Plato is a moral cognitivist because he thinks judgements concerning things such as justice, courage, rightness, and goodness can be *true* by corresponding to the way these things are 'out there'. Actually it's a little more accurate to say '*up* there', because these ethical concepts *transcend* the everyday empirical world of changeable physical objects. They themselves exist in a state of perfection in a conceptual realm beyond the space–time universe. This realm *can be known*, but only by the pure reason of the mind itself – even purer and more abstract than pure mathematics – and not by gross and illusory sense perception involving the five senses. This sounds difficult to achieve, and it is, but the pay-off for the few who make it to the top of that intellectual Everest is that they discover *perfect* justice *does exist*, just not in *this* world. The same goes for perfect courage and perfect goodness. Plato calls these the Form of Courage, the Form of Justice, and the Form of the Good. Forms have several characteristics; they're absolutely perfect, eternal (outside time), immutable (unchanging), most real (they have *Being*, depending on nothing but themselves), and are the *only* objects of knowledge. They are everything this world is not. The world around us and in which we live is imperfect, temporal, changeable, tangible; it is a second-rate world of becoming, not being, a world of mere opinion and belief rather than knowledge, insofar as we make mistakes, are deluded, can't agree, get sick, and die.

There are many Forms besides the ethical ones in this perfect realm. It has the perfect version of every type of thing on earth. For example, there exists the eternally perfect Form of Triangle, the Form of Beauty, the Form of Man, the Form of Bed, and so on. But why did Plato think such a world exists, and how did he think we could know about it? Here are some arguments.

Arguments for the Forms

1 Argument from universals
A universal is a general term linking various individual things. For example, why do we use the universal 'table' to label such diverse objects as coffee tables, wooden tables, plastic tables, card tables, drop-leaf tables, and so on? Surely it's because they all have some *one thing* in common, namely they all share in tableness, for that's what *essentially* they are. So exactly *what* is *tableness*? This is to ask what is the Form of Table, and it must be with reference to this that we are able to identify each table we come across as being a table, because it to some extent participates in the Form of Table. But unlike ordinary physical tables, the concept or Form of Table can't be chopped up or

thrown in the fire and thus be destroyed or changed. The Form is not physical. It is perfect, and is the real meaning or definition of what it is to be a table, and if the Form didn't really exist the word 'table' would mean nothing. Since the word 'table' does mean something, it must refer to the Form of Table. The same will go for the Form of Beauty – as what all beautiful things have in common no matter what other differences they have – and the Form of the Good – as what all good things and actions have in common. For Plato, Beauty is definitely not in the eye of the beholder; neither is the Good, and the fact that we can use general terms meaningfully, *apart* from the things they bind together, as in the saying 'Youth is wasted on the young', shows that 'Youth' must mean the independently existing Form in which all young things participate.

2 Argument from knowledge, opinion, and ignorance

Plato understands these as different powers of the mind, capable of being distinguished on the basis of two things:

- their effects on the state of the mind
- their range of application, i.e. the kind of objects they cover – their target audience, as it were.

Firstly, anyone who claims to know x, and then finds that x isn't true, can't have known x in the first place. Plato argues that this must mean that knowledge is infallible, because what you know *must* be true. Its effect on the mind is a state of certainty, and its range of application must cover only objects that are *ultimately real*, because nothing less will guarantee the infallible and necessary truth needed for knowledge. Secondly, ignorance, being the opposite of knowledge, must be to do with what's not real, i.e. nothing at all. Its effects would be an empty state of mind having no thoughts at all. This leaves opinion, which seems to lie between knowledge and ignorance, because it's sometimes true and sometimes false. If it can be false, then it's fallible, and therefore it's neither the same, nor as good, as knowledge, which is infallible. But since one can have opinions about *things*, these things must already exist and not be sheer nothing, so opinion is better than ignorance and worse than knowledge. Its range of application will lie somewhere between the realms of being (ultimate reality) and nothingness. This middle realm is best described as the world of 'becoming'. Its effect on the mind is one of fallibility and uncertainty. Opinion is iffy, applying to the everyday world of becoming and change from birth to growth to death, or from liquid (water) to solid (ice) to gas (steam), and so on for every physical object.

This is why knowledge can't apply to the space–time universe, because knowledge requires the *settled being* of what forever *is*: an unchanging world of objects that are eternally themselves – a nailed down world of static, perfect essences or Forms. But the ordinary world is in constant flux, and so opinion reigns here. This goes for everything except the Forms. Good things may change and become bad, or appear simultaneously good and bad from different perspectives. They're therefore not really and truly good, or perfectly good, so we can have only *opinions* about what's good in this world, not knowledge, which means knowledge of what is truly good must require knowledge of the Form of the Good, which never changes.

3 Argument from grading

Some apples are better than others, being juicier, bigger, and shinier, but by what standard or criterion do we judge this? Plato argues that we need an absolute standard of perfection in place, and with reference to which we grade objects in this world, such as apples, and straight lines, and morally good actions. Well, then, aren't the better apples better because they more closely match the perfect apple – the Form of Apple? Aren't some lines straighter than others because we judge them to be closer to Absolute Straightness? Surely it's the perfect standard we have in mind when we try to draw straight lines, though none are ever truly straight. The same goes for moral judgement. No action is ever perfectly good, but we can judge some better than others, e.g. giving £100 to charity as opposed to 10p, because the former is closer to the Form of the Good, or perfect goodness. In this way the Forms act as perfect paradigms or patterns which justify our grading or evaluative moral judgements.

4 Argument from pointlessness

Socrates (469–399 BC) was born in Athens to a stonemason and a mid-wife. By all accounts he was plug ugly, but he could hold his liquor and had a great personality – charismatic, humorous, loyal, brave, and sharp as a razor. He is one of philosophy's all-time greats, writing nothing yet influencing everyone through his star pupil Plato, whose dialogues have Socrates as their main character. He has a strong claim to be the founder of moral philosophy, seemingly being the first to ask questions such as 'What is courage?' and 'What is justice?' He himself didn't know the answers to these questions, so he wandered the streets of Athens questioning the great and the good who claimed that they did. Invariably the conversations would end with the revelation that the know-it-alls were really the don't-know-it-at-alls, which was a very enjoyable and educational experience for the group of young twenty-somethings who witnessed these demolition jobs, which were tantamount to a philosophical mugging. This did not endear Socrates to those with some political clout, and in 399 BC they got their revenge. He was tried on charges of introducing new gods and corrupting the young, found guilty, and sentenced to death by drinking hemlock. He could have escaped but chose to stay and face the music, arguing that as a loyal citizen he should be prepared to take the bad with the good. He was a true man of principle.

In *The Republic*, Plato has Socrates say this: 'The good, then, is the end of all endeavour, the object on which every heart is set' (505e), and again: '. . . if we are ignorant of it [the Form of the Good] the rest of our knowledge, however perfect, can be of no benefit to us, just as it's no use possessing *any-thing* if you can't get any good out of it' (505a). Everything aims to achieve the good itself, not what merely looks good, but what *is* good. But only the Form of the Good *is* good, because only the Forms have the *is* of *Being*. Now, it would be pointless getting to know the Forms if they weren't perfect, but perfection requires goodness, and goodness in turn can't be had without participating in the Form of the Good, so that means the Forms themselves must participate in it. That makes the Form of the Good more valuable than all the other Forms, as a sort of Form of Forms, because it gives them their goodness and reality. Therefore, in a real sense, the Form of the Good can be said to give the universe its point, and provides the meaning for everything we do.

Assessment

1 Discussion of the argument from universals

This argument doesn't work because it fallaciously assumes that, in order for a universal term to have meaning, it must refer to some*thing*, i.e. pick out or denote some *existing thing*, and if not a physical thing, then an abstract thing, i.e. a Form. An example should help illustrate the mistake. Let's take the universal term 'scruff', as in 'He threw him out by the scruff of the neck.' What do we mean by 'scruff'? Everybody seemingly has one, and it's always for some reason at the back of the neck, never at the front. What do all the scruffs of the neck have in common? It must be, according to the argument from universals, the Form of Scruff, i.e. the perfect Scruff, but what could this possibly be? It can't be part of the neck itself, because you can't be thrown out by the scruff of the neck if you're naked; and it can't be a particular part of your clothing either, because fashion houses make collars, sleeves, pockets, hems, and even ruffs, but never scruffs. As can be seen from the above nonsense, it's absurd to engage in this wild goose chase for the essence of one's neck scruff in some perfect world of Forms. Surely its meaning is better understood as the part 'scruff' plays in the context of the usage of a language and the conventions of practical life. In other words, 'scruff' is meaningful without it having to pick out some *thing* (cf. 'knack' and 'sake'), which implies that terms such as beauty, justice, redness, and goodness don't need corresponding Forms in order to make sense.

2 Discussion of the argument from knowledge, opinion, and ignorance

There are two problems with this argument. One is that Plato mistakenly thinks you can only have knowledge of something that never changes, and so knowledge is not to be had in this ever-changing world. He's wrong because, despite constant change, knowledge is possible if tied to a *specific* time. For example, although a person's age constantly changes, this doesn't mean you can't know that they were born on, say, 1/6/1963. Despite all the changes that occur (e.g. well before this they didn't exist, and now they're no longer being born), still by linking one's judgement to a specific time it will always be true that they were born on this date, and if you had said this at any time before their birth it would still have been true. In other words, *knowledge and opinion* can be had about precisely the *same range of changeable objects*, not Forms, and can be distinguished instead with reference to their degree of evidential support. Presumably if you have a person's passport and birth certificate you can claim to know their date of birth, whereas if you just hear a rumour all you have is opinion, even if you're right.

The second problem is that Plato wrongly assumes that if something is true it must also be substantially real independently of human thought. But this is not so, for it's true that the Earth has an equator without having to conclude that the equator exists 'out there somewhere' in the independent Platonic sense. Along with lines of latitude and longitude, the equator is a useful conceptual and conventional 'fiction', and you would badly misunderstand its meaning if you went in search of it as if it were an independently existing object. This means we don't have to go to the so-called independently existing Forms to find truth and knowledge; we can have both right here by conventional agreement.

3 Discussion of argument from grading

Here are two counter-examples which show we don't need an absolute existing standard of perfection in order to grade things. Firstly, we're perfectly capable of judging 7 to be bigger than 6, and smaller than 1000, without having to have an absolute ultimate number in mind. In fact, numbers go on indefinitely, so an absolute is not needed. Secondly, it's clearly better if hospitals have smaller waiting lists, with reference to an ideal of no waiting list at all, but we can know this without having to believe that somewhere, in the abstract world of Forms, is the perfect Form of Non-Waiting which we're trying to approach.

4 Discussion of argument from pointlessness

Firstly, in answer to this argument it should be pointed out that the universe might just *be* pointless. There's no guarantee it's not. Secondly, whatever point life has may be underwritten, not by the Form of the Good, but by investing our energies in projects we deem worthwhile in terms of *this*-worldly causes, based either on what human nature *happens* to favour or on what we simply *decide* to value. *We* can give it point.

Further criticisms

Since Plato's moral cognitivism rests ultimately on a transcendent Form of the Good being real and knowable, any argument which undermines the Forms, either in general or individually, will indirectly further undermine the Form of the Good and with it his metaethical position. With this in mind, we'll consider some objections.

According to Plato, all small things are small because they participate in the Form of Small, which of course is absolutely small, being the perfect kind of smallness. But if so, then they participate either in part of the Form or in the whole of it, there being no third alternative. However, if in part, then they'd be smaller than absolutely small, which is logically impossible, and if wholly, then they'd be absolutely small along with the Form, because they'd have everything the Form had, and this is also impossible, since only the Form can have this.

Another contradiction is generated by the Form of Time, because if all times (past, present, and future) are times in virtue of participating in the Form of Time, then it must be perfect time. But how can it be perfect time if, as a Form, it is also eternal like all the rest, and therefore outside time? This would make it perfectly temporal and perfectly atemporal, which is self-contradictory.

Furthermore, if all murders are murders because they share in the Form of Murder, there must exist the perfect murder as a Form, but how can this be, for that would mean, being eternal and non-physical, that the perfect murder exists prior to anybody ever being killed? The perfect murder exists without a murderer, and that's no murder at all, never mind the perfect one.

Things quickly get out of hand when we begin to pull Forms out of the air like rabbits from a hat. Plato himself was worried about this possibility, envisaging Forms of Mud, and Hair. But we don't have to stop there. There must be the Form of Pimple which explains what all pimples have in common, and any new type of invention or activity will have its very own eternal Form in which it participates, e.g. the Form of DVD, or the Form of Download.

Besides, Forms don't really explain things at all. Is it really enlightening to be told that the reason a joke is funny is that it participates in the Form of the Funny? If not, then neither is it enlightening to be told that people are good to the extent they participate in the Form of the Good. This is just a dressed-up tautology.

The theory of Forms leads to an infinite regress, which is bad news for any theory. We must credit Plato himself for spotting this problem. It's called the 'third man argument' and it goes as follows.

Man number 1 and man number 2 are both men, explained by the fact that they have manhood in common. Having manhood in common is another way of saying that they participate in the Form of Man, considered as a *universal* property of all men. But now the problem is to explain how the Form of Man, now considered in its other guise as a *specific instance* of the Perfect Man, man number 3 (the third man), has manhood in common with man number 1 and man number 2. To explain this, it looks like we need a Super Form of Man, participation in which grants manhood to the two men and the Form of Man. But then what explains the sharing of manhood between the Super Form of Man, the Form of Man, and the two men? It must be the Super-Duper Form of Man, and so it goes on forever, in a vicious infinite regress that explains nothing.

Finally, there are two problems with the Form of the Good itself. Firstly, only an elite few can get to know what it is, because knowing the Form is extremely difficult and comes only after a long, arduous education which weeds out the less intelligent and dedicated people. This knowledge is so rare that even Socrates and Plato didn't possess it, which doesn't give the rest of us much chance. Plato's moral cognitivism can therefore be fairly dubbed elitist, having the corollary that most people's major moral decision will be simply to obey those who know what goodness itself is, following moral orders from the ethical experts. This means the responsibility for their actions is largely shuffled off, with the buck passing to their moral superiors. But surely ethics, if it's about anything, is about taking responsibility for your *own* actions, which means Plato's theory is wrong to deny this.

Secondly and lastly, even if you did at last succeed in knowing the Form of the Good, it seems totally useless in helping you to lead a good life or do good deeds, because it's just too abstract and empty of proper content, being too far removed from normal everyday life. To illustrate this, here's an imaginary

Socratic dialogue on the Form of Victory and its useless application to ordinary life. (In honour of 'The Euthyphro' dialogue I call this 'The Capello'.)

Socrates: Hello Fabio, where are you going?
Fabio Capello (England Manager): I'm off to the match to make sure England are victorious.
Socrates: Ah! So if you're looking for victory you must know what it is.
Capello: Of course. It's when we beat Germany 5–1.
Socrates: No, that's not what I mean. That's just an *example* of victory. What I want to know is what is victory *itself*?
Capello: Victory is scoring more goals than your opponent.
Socrates: But that won't work, because sometimes you can be victorious by drawing nil–nil at home and one all away, and that's not more goals.
Capello: But in cases like that, away goals count double, so you still win.
Socrates: So would you say that victory is winning against your opponent?
Capello: Yes Socrates, that's it. Victory is winning.

Let's assume that this is indeed the essence of victory – that the Form of Victory is Winning. Will knowing this help in actually achieving victory on the pitch? Imagine the following team talk just before a big match using only the knowledge of the Form of Victory.

England Manager: Okay lads. The key to victory is to know what it is you're after, and to be totally determined to achieve it. So what are we after? Victory of course! But what is that? I'll tell you: it is winning. This is the essence of victory, so now that you know what the Form of Victory is, you can go out there with confidence, knowing you're bound to win.

One can imagine the bemused faces of the England footballers as they troop out without any *specific* tactics or game plan, armed only with the abstract and useless Form of Victory. Determined to win – but *how*? Clearly, what's needed is specific and detailed knowledge of a host of *contingent particulars*, such as the strengths and weaknesses of various players in the opposing team and in one's own team. Who marks whom? Do we play defensively and attack on the break, or go for all-out attack, or a mixture? Do we hit the long ball up the middle or play a short passing game? This kind of knowledge does not come from armchair reasoning about a world of abstract Forms beyond the universe, but from a wealth of very down-to-earth experiences of actually playing football. The last thing the players need is bland abstractions about how good it is to win.

It seems the same would apply to the Form of the Good. Simply knowing this, if that's even possible, won't be of any help in our dealings with others in the everyday world of normal life. The Form of the Good is too empty of content and too far removed to do any good, and therefore seems irrelevant to the moral life lived amongst flesh and blood individuals, not bloodless abstractions. It's therefore fair to conclude, contrary to what Plato believed, that virtue is not knowledge, at least not knowledge in the transcendent sense of privileged access to another world of ultimate reality. If there is to be *practical* and *workable* moral knowledge of virtue, right, wrong, duty, and goodness, then it can't be transcendent; rather, it should be *immanent* to this world. That is, it must be in some way *natural.*

Naturalism

Naturalism is the view that moral terms such as 'good' and 'right' can either (a) be *defined* in terms of *natural* properties in the world or (b) be logically *deduced* from *natural* properties. But what counts as a natural property? Basically any physical or psychological feature of the world which is straight-forwardly accessible to us would count as a natural property, for example, colours, sounds, tastes, and smells – the greenness of grass, the sweetness of sugar and so on – psychological properties such as anger, boredom, pleasure, and more general physiological features such as health. Most forms of naturalism try to tie morality in to one or more psychological or physiological properties because these are most relevant to us and our well-being.

Naturalistic theories disagree over which natural property goodness should be defined as or deduced from. Included amongst these theories are utilitarianism and virtue ethics. For example, hedonistic utilitarianism holds that 'good' can be defined as (means the same as/is identical to) pleasure (a natural feature of sentient beings). To call something 'good' is to *mean* that it *is* pleasurable or causes pleasure, and of course 'bad' means the opposite, i.e. pain, or pain-inducing, another natural quality. Put simply, for hedonistic utilitarianism, 'good' = pleasure.

Other types of utilitarianism, while still naturalistic, may prefer the option of trying to *deduce* moral obligations and values from natural properties instead of trying to *define* them as being identical. For example, a utilitarian might use the following argument:

P1: Giving to charity *is* productive of increased happiness.
Conclusion: Therefore, we *ought* to give to charity.

What's happening here is that a *naturalistic* premise (the reason it's naturalistic is that it's a normal physical event in the everyday world that my five senses can tell me about) is being used to *deduce* or *infer* a *moral obligation* in the conclusion. In short, naturalism is the view that morality, with its values of goodness and kindness and its duties such as keeping promises, is completely dependent on natural features of the physical universe, and can be read off from these either by being identical to them (by definition) or by being derivable from them (by logical deduction).

Other naturalistic theories exhibit a similar pattern of analysis. A further example is virtue ethics, which holds that 'good' can be defined as 'what makes human beings flourish'. Here's an example of how they would deduce moral values (oughts) from natural facts (is's):

P1: Standing up to a bully *is* courageous.
Conclusion: Therefore, we *ought* to stand up to bullies.

Other types of naturalistic theory define 'good' differently. Evolutionary ethics, for example, is naturalistic because it defines 'good' as 'more evolved' or 'whatever feature improves your survival chances'. Cultural relativism is naturalistic because it defines 'good' as meaning 'whatever your culture, or society, or tribe *says* is good'.

So, if moral terms can be successfully equated with natural properties or facts, or can be derived from them, it would follow that the methods of discovering moral truths will be equally natural and empirical, e.g. via psychology, physiology, etc.

All naturalistic theories agree that ethics is reducible to some empirical or natural feature of life. Where they differ is regarding which natural feature morality is to be identified with.

Arguments for naturalism

1 Argument from our moral feelings

This argument appeals to our deep-rooted sense of outrage, intense resentment, and anger when we're the victims of injustice. These feelings are so strong that the only plausible way to explain them would seem to be that they're responses to *real, objective* wrongdoing that's *out there in the world.* When we hear of wanton cruelty, murder, and genocide, it's hard to accept that the intensity of our outrage and disgust is just a matter of subjective taste, like preferring tea to coffee. Many other moral feelings support this: feelings such as profound shame and guilt when we're caught doing something wrong; sleepless nights wrestling with our conscience; or anxious private deliberations we conduct with ourselves, agonizing over the right thing to do.

Surely this can't be all a big fake, which it would be if the non-cognitivists are right.

2 *Argument from moral* reasoning

Naturalism can account for our experience of having moral debates with one another in which we use *reasoning* to resolve the dispute. We're always appealing to natural facts in order to win the argument and show that our side has the *truth*. We appeal to things such as the natural consequences of an action as *evidence* that it should or shouldn't be done. For example, we might *argue* that it's wrong to give someone weed-killer to drink, for the very good *reason* that it will kill them. Or we might appeal to natural human needs such as food as a *reason* for feeding the hungry. If natural facts are being used in moral arguments, then surely moral values such as good and right are closely related to them either by **definition** *or* by **deduction**.

3 Argument from moral language

Moral language is objectivistic in the way we use it. It comes across as very different from subjective, personal judgements such as 'Coffee – mmm' or 'What a movie!', which don't claim objective truth with which others must agree. Moral judgements, on the other hand, are made in such a way as seemingly to *state facts* which are claimed to apply to *everyone*. There's a lot more objective weight behind 'Promises must be kept' than 'Promises – oooh!' These statements are far closer to fact-stating discourse than to exclamations or commands as the non-cognitivists would have it. For example, 'Pleasure is good' is very like 'Bananas are yellow', and since the latter clearly states a natural fact, surely the former does too. We also tend to say things such as 'It's *true* that lying is wrong' or 'It's a *fact* that kindness is good', and we use such sentences as 'I *know* that I ought to repay that money'. This points to morality being *factual*, because you couldn't *know* it if it wasn't *true*.

4 *Argument from* popularity *and* plausibility

Regarding popularity, it's clear that the vast majority of the human race throughout most of history have believed that morality was to do with objective natural facts in the world. Although this isn't a proof, still it's *unlikely* that they're *all* wrong, so the odds are heavily in favour of naturalism.

Regarding plausibility, goodness is so closely tied up with many natural features that you hardly even need to argue that they're good. A quick list could include pleasure, health, freedom, friendship, and so on. Don't the non-cognitivists have their work cut out trying to argue that these things aren't *really* good, but that we merely react positively to them? The naturalists will reply that surely the reason we do react positively to them is that we *recognize* they *are* good.

5 Argument from the appalling alternative

The alternative – that there are no moral facts, it's all an illusion, and we're fooling ourselves that there's a real difference between right and wrong – is too horrible to contemplate. If it's all in our minds, doesn't this mean that, in the real world, 'might is right'? What can we say to the likes of Hitler if it's all just a subjective matter of opinion? Couldn't he just tell us to mind our own business and stop interfering in other people's affairs? It would be like telling someone that it's wrong for *them* to eat Sugar Puffs because *we prefer* Cornflakes. And so the nightmare begins, since anyone whose *taste* ran to stealing, lying, cheating, and killing would be *morally free* to do so, since no action would be more justified than any other.

However, despite the seeming strength of these five arguments, at the turn of the twentieth century the English philosopher G. E. Moore (1873–1958) expressed deep dissatisfaction with the case for naturalism, and argued influentially for an alternative cognitive theory in which moral values were neither transcendent nor natural, but were instead *non*-natural – i.e. were objectively real, but existed as values in their own right, standing on their own two feet as it were, and not being reducible to natural facts or qualities. He targeted in particular the naturalists' argument from moral reasoning (argument 2 above).

Moore's arguments against naturalism

Moore was a non-naturalist, and in 1903 in his important book *Principia Ethica* he put non-naturalism on the map with what seemed like two devastating arguments against naturalism. The first and most important one was called 'the open question argument'. The second did not have an official title, but I shall call it 'the argument from moral motivation'. The power of these arguments was such that they killed off naturalism as a viable theory for about eighty years.

The two planks on which naturalism in particular rested were:

a) the ability to define moral terms such as 'good' into natural terms
b) the ability to deduce moral conclusions (oughts) from natural premises (is's) used as reasons for being moral.

Each of these formed part of its argument from moral reasoning (see p. 194). The open question argument hit (a), and the moral motivation argument hit (b).

The open question argument – What this argument tries to prove is that **any** attempt to define moral terms, e.g. 'good', as meaning the same thing as a natural property – *any* natural property – is doomed to fail as a result of committing what Moore famously dubbed **the naturalistic fallacy**. This is the supposed fallacy of trying to define non-natural terms into natural terms. The best way to explain how the open question argument works is to take an example of a naturalistic definition and apply the argument to it.

Naturalistic definition: **'good' = 'pleasure'**.

If 'good' is defined as 'pleasure', then 'good' means 'pleasure' and is therefore the same thing as pleasure. Now, the crucial point is that to ask 'Is pleasure really good?' is to ask an *open* question, i.e. a *significant* question whose answer could go *either way*, maybe 'yes', maybe 'no'. But the reason the naturalist definition is wrong is that it turns such obviously significant open questions into insignificant, pointless, closed questions. Here's why.

If 'good' = 'pleasure', then we should be able to substitute the word 'pleasure' for the word 'good' without any change in the meaning. So let's try this using our open question and see what happens. The significant open question 'Is pleasure really good?' becomes the pointless closed question 'Is pleasure really pleasure?' It's silly asking this, because the answer is so obviously 'Yes.' Moore concluded that 'good' couldn't possibly be defined as 'pleasure' *or any other natural property*, because the same argument applies no matter what natural property is used. If 'good' really did mean the same as 'pleasure', we should *still* have ended up with an open question when we substituted 'pleasure' for 'good' in the question, and since we didn't, it doesn't, so naturalism is wrong. It's wrong because this will happen with *every* definition the naturalists try, so naturalism must be given up as a dead loss, as it can't avoid the **naturalistic fallacy**.

The argument from moral motivation – This argument highlights another problem for all types of naturalism, namely that, if they insist on defining moral terms as natural properties, people thereby lose any motivating reason to be moral, and this blocks the derivation of moral 'oughts' from factual 'is's'. An example should help explain this. Naturalists will want to say something like 'You **ought** to produce pleasure, *because* it **is** good.' This uses the fact that pleasure is good (by naturalistic definition) as a *reason* for producing it. But if we again substitute 'pleasure' for 'good', this motivating reason disappears into the silly repetitive tautology 'You **ought** to produce pleasure, because it **is** pleasure.' This says nothing. Everything is what it is; it could hardly be anything else. The fact that a thing is what it is does not make it a reason for doing it, otherwise we should be cruel, because cruelty is cruelty. But this is absurd, so naturalism is wrong. This can be generalized to *any* naturalistic definition of 'good' used as a motivating reason to act morally.

Take naturalistic feature x. If we define x as good, then in reply to my sceptical query 'Why ought I to do x?' the naturalist can't respond 'Because x is good', because this just means 'x is x', and this is no reason at all to do x. You might just as well do y instead, because y is as much y as x is x.

It was these arguments that left the field clear for non-naturalism, which I shall briefly explain below before looking at some positive arguments in its favour.

Non-naturalism

Explanation of non-naturalism (intuitionism)

Basic moral terms such as 'good' and 'right' get their meaning by *referring to* or picking out special non-natural properties or qualities of things and actions. Goodness and rightness denote *unique* properties *in themselves*. They are **not reducible to or definable in terms of natural properties**. In fact, they are *not definable at all*. Moore said, 'If I am asked "What is good?" my answer is that good is good and that is the end of the matter. Or if I'm asked "How is good to be defined?" my answer is that it cannot be defined and that is all I have to say about it' (*Principia Ethica*, p. 6).

So moral qualities exist independently of us and are part of the objective reality of the universe, but they are not detectable via the five senses or any apparatus known to science because they're not part of the natural, empirical world subject to the laws of nature. The question now arises, how on earth do we manage to detect these mysterious moral qualities that seem to hover out there in the physical universe but which are not themselves physical? How do we *know* about them? The answer given by the non-naturalists is **intuition**, hence their alternative title 'intuitionists'. So what is intuition?

It's a kind of moral 'sight', except we don't literally use our eyes. It's like a sixth sense whose unique job is to zero in on moral qualities and make us aware of right and wrong, good and bad. It's different from our other five senses in that there are no moral 'vibes' out there analogous to light waves or sound waves which our eyes and ears can tune in to; and there's *no physical* moral *sensory organ* which intuition uses. Instead, it's a sort of *mental moral* radar. Intuitionists like to compare it to the way we simply just 'see' that 2 + 2 = 4, or that a triangle just *has to have* three sides. These truths are *self-evident*, and intuitionists think that *basic moral truths are also self-evidently true*. That it's true that murder is wrong is as certain as 2 + 2 = 4; we just 'see' that it's true, by intuition. The contention of intuitionists is that anyone who thinks carefully enough about a moral issue will know what to do on the basis of this unique kind of intuitive 'perception'. This is not to be confused with things such as inspired guesses, so-called women's intuition, gut feelings, or hunches.

So, non-naturalism is cognitivist because we can *know* moral *truths*; *realist* or *objectivist* because moral properties are out there in the real world independently of us; intuitionist because of our method of knowing these truths; and non-naturalist because the moral properties we come across aren't natural in any way. Moral judgements are factual statements that tell us about moral properties in the world, and they're true if what they say corresponds with these properties. In relation to naturalism you could say that, of the five arguments in its defence, non-naturalists would support argument 1 (the argument from our moral feelings), argument 3 (the argument from moral language), and argument 5 (the argument from the appalling alternative), because these arguments merely give reasons for *objectivism* and *cognitivism* which non-naturalists share with the naturalists; but they attack argument 2 (the argument from moral reasoning) and argument 4. (the argument from popularity and plausibility), which support naturalism *specifically*, because they think the open question argument refutes them.

No matter how popular or plausible such naturalistic definitions might appear, the open question argument seems to defeat them. Whether it really succeeds we shall see later.

Moore's arguments for non-naturalism

First of all, it's important to note a background assumption of Moore's (this assumption will be challenged later on). He assumes that words get their meaning by *referring to things in the world* (e.g. the word 'cat' has meaning because it refers to, or picks out, real cats in the world, and the word 'yellow' has meaning because it picks out or refers to the simple property of yellowness belonging to such things as custard).

Moore's task is to prove two things:

- **that moral values such as goodness are non-natural things**
- **that we know about these via a 'sixth' sense called intuition.**

He has one argument for each of these points.

Argument 1
The first argument supports the intuitionist view that moral values are non-natural things or properties.

P1: There are only three possibilities regarding the meaning of 'good'.
   a) 'Good' means/refers to a natural thing or property.
   b) 'Good' means/refers to a non-natural thing or property.
   c) 'Good' means/refers to nothing at all.
P2: The *open question argument* rules out option (a).
P3: The *argument from moral feelings* and the *argument from moral language* rule out option (c).
Conclusion: Therefore, that leaves option (b), so non-naturalism wins by default.

Premise 1 starts the argument off with a simple statement to the effect that, when it comes to looking at the meanings of words, the word 'good', like any other word, might work in three different ways.

   a) It might refer to something physical, just as the word 'chair' does.
   b) It might refer to something non-physical, just as the word 'beauty' or 'soul' does.
   c) It might refer to nothing at all, like the word 'fairy' does.

Regarding the claim made in premise 2, why does Moore think that the open question argument rules out option (a)? Well, as you'll recall, the open question argument says that 'good' *can't* be defined in terms of *any natural* properties. *All* attempts fail; for example, let's try 'good' = 'more evolved'. This definition won't work because, if these meant the same thing, it wouldn't make sense to ask 'Is what is more evolved good?', because it would be like asking 'Is what is more evolved more evolved?', which is a *closed* question whose answer has got to be 'yes'. But it *does* make sense to ask whether what is more evolved is good (the answer could be 'yes', or 'no', which makes it an *open* question), so 'good' and 'more evolved' *can't* mean the same thing; and this is why premise 2 claims that the open question argument rules out option (a) – precisely because option (a) claims that 'good' *can* and *does* mean the same thing as a *natural* property.

As for premise 3, the reason Moore thinks this is true is that our moral feelings are so strong they *must* be about something *real*, and this belief is also supported by our moral language being so utterly objective-sounding that it's just *got* to be about *real* things rather than *imaginary* ones. So Moore thinks premise 3 is right in ruling out option (c) because option (c) states that 'good' doesn't refer to anything real at all – that it has only imaginary content, like the word 'fairy'.

Since option (b) is the only option left, as it's the last man standing, it's child's play for Moore to conclude that option (b) must be true. But option

(b) is merely an outright statement of the non-naturalist position, so Moore has now proved to his satisfaction that non-naturalism is true.

Argument 2

Argument two supports the non-naturalist view that non-natural moral properties are known by a '*sixth*' sense called *intuition*.

> P1: Moral properties are *non-natural*
> (see the conclusion of argument 1).
> P2: We *know* these moral properties
> (see argument from *moral feelings* and from *moral language*).
> P3: Since they are *non*-natural there is no way we can know them by any *normal natural* method such as our five senses.
> Conclusion:Therefore, it's got to be by some *non*-natural 'sixth' sense which is specifically tuned in to moral 'frequencies'.
> This is what we call **intuition**.

These crucial arguments constitute Moore's case for non-naturalism, so if they fall, so does it. They will therefore be assessed in detail when we consider the case for and against non-cognitivism in the next chapter.

9　Non-cognitivism

There are two non-cognitivist theories, namely *emotivism* and *prescriptivism*, each with its very own distinctive features. However, for now we'll just concentrate on what they have *in common* as non-cognitivist theories. Later on we'll look at each separately to see how they differ. Non-cognitivism holds the following:

- Moral terms such as 'good' do *not* refer to transcendental, natural or non-natural properties 'out there'. They refer to nothing in the world or out of it.
- So morality is *not objective* and does not have a foothold in any kind of independent reality. We do *not discover* right and wrong.
- Instead we *invent/create/decide* what's right and wrong.
- There are *no moral facts or truths*.
- *Moral judgements are not statements about facts.*
- Instead moral judgements have *dynamic* meaning that *moves to action* either by *expressing emotion* or by *prescribing* action.
- Morality is *not* a form of *knowledge*. The reason for this is that to know x is to know x is true, but if there are no moral truths there can be no knowledge of them. In other words, it doesn't make sense to say that you know what is right, wrong, good, etc.

In the first section we'll look at the arguments that non-cognitivism uses to attack cognitivism in both its **naturalistic and intuitionist** forms (transcendentalism having already been disposed of).

Non-cognitivist arguments against cognitivism

This section will be subdivided into three parts:

- the case against *cognitivism in general*
- the case against *naturalism* in particular
- the case against *non-naturalism* in particular.

The case against cognitivism in general

1 The argument from moral relativity

The amazing variety of moral opinions down through history between different cultures, and even between individuals within the same culture, is strong evidence for the non-cognitivist view that there's no objective moral truth – that there are no moral facts, whether natural or non-natural – for if there were, surely there'd be much more agreement than there is. Here are some examples of significant moral differences:

> Eskimos allow their elderly to die by starvation . . . The Spartans of ancient Greece and the Dobu of New Guinea believe that stealing is morally right . . . Many cultures, past and present, have practised or still practise infanticide. A tribe in East Africa once threw deformed infants to the hippopotamus . . . Some cultures permit homosexual behaviour, whereas others condemn it. Some cultures, including Muslim societies, practise polygamy . . . Anthropologist Ruth Benedict describes a tribe in Melanesia that views cooperation and kindness as vices, and anthropologist Colin Turnbull has documented that the Ik in northern Uganda have no sense of duty toward their children or parents. There are societies that make it a duty to kill their aging parents (sometimes by strangling) . . . In parts of Northern Africa many girls undergo female circumcision, cutting out their external genitalia. (Pojman, *Ethics*, p. 26)

Contrast this moral mayhem with the settled scene in maths and the physical sciences, where there's widespread agreement across the world. Why? Because this is *real* knowledge, unlike morals.

2 Argument from no agreed methods of testing *moral claims*

In areas of proper knowledge such as science there's such a thing as scientific method. This incorporates accepted standards of observation, measurement of data, and experimentation in order to verify hypotheses, while in maths we have the deductive method of proof, starting from such agreed self-evident axioms as 'parallel lines never meet', and then deducing conclusions such as Pythagoras's theorem.

But there seems to be no agreed standards or methods of acquiring so-called moral knowledge, and none looks in sight. There's no accepted moral deductive system as in maths, no rigorous proofs that can't be doubted, no moral labs, no standard methods of measuring good and bad. The closest any moralist has come is Bentham with his hedonic calculus, but this is pathetically inadequate compared with scientific measuring devices, and in any case it has been rejected by all the other moralists, even utilitarians.

Here are some of the methods on offer amongst cognitivists.

- Divine command theory: find out God's will.
- Utilitarianism: calculate the consequences.
- Kantianism: universalize your maxims.
- Virtue ethics: follow the mean between the extremes.
- Intuitionism: follow your intuition.
- Plato: get to know the Form of the Good.

Cognitivists can't agree on any of these methods; they fight amongst themselves, which confirms that they don't know what they claim to know. And *why* are there no accepted methods of discovering moral truths? Because *there are no moral truths to discover*. There's *nothing out there* to be measured and cognised, so non-cognitivism must be correct.

The case against **naturalism** in particular

1 The open question argument
Non-cognitivists accept Moore's *open question argument* against naturalism's attempt to define moral terms naturalistically.

2 The argument from moral motivation
Non-cognitivists also accept Moore's other argument, the one from *moral motivation*, which points out that natural moral facts (is's) obtained by *defining moral terms naturalistically* cannot be validly used to infer moral obligations (oughts). You can't get an ought from an is; you can't get values from facts, which means that the naturalists are wrong in thinking that reducing morals to natural facts will give us motivating reasons to be good.

3 Appeal to Hume's Law
According to David Hume (1711–1776; Scottish philosopher), '*you can't deduce values (oughts) from facts (is's)*'. Here is Hume's famous statement of this law:

> In every system of morality, which I have hitherto met with, I have always remark'd, that the author proceeds for some time in the ordinary way of reasoning, and establishes the being of a God, or makes observations concerning human affairs; when of a sudden I am surpriz'd to find, that instead of the usual copulations of propositions, *is*, and *is not*, I meet with no proposition that is not connected with an *ought*, or *ought not*. This change is imperceptible; but is, however, of the last consequence. For as this *ought*, or *ought not*, expresses some new relation or affirmation, 'tis necessary that it shou'd be observ'd and explain'd; and at the same time that a reason should be given, for what seems altogether inconceivable, how this new relation can be a deduction from

> others, which are entirely different from it. (*A Treatise of Human Nature*, p. 469)

Notice how strongly Hume asserts this logical rule or law. He thinks it 'altogether inconceivable' how the new relation of ought can be deduced from is's, which are 'entirely different from it'; and this applies 'in every system of morality' he has ever come across. If Hume is right, and there is an impenetrable logical barrier separating facts and values, such that it's impossible to reason from the way things *are* to the way they *ought* to be, then it appears naturalism is doomed. But doesn't this just repeat the same 'moral motivation' argument in point 2 above? No. The difference is that Hume's law closes the door on *any* derivation of value from *any* natural fact, *whether or not it has been used to define a moral term such as 'good'*. This needs explaining. Suppose naturalists try to avoid Moore's moral motivation argument by trying to deduce 'oughts' from 'is's' without first defining the 'is's' in moral terms such as 'good'; in other words, they use *bare*, natural facts to deduce 'oughts'. This is where Hume's Law comes in. For example, take the following naturalistic arguments from 'is' to 'ought':

> P1: This person *is* starving.
> Conclusion: Therefore, you *ought* to feed him.

> P1: She *is* your mum.
> Conclusion: Therefore, you *ought* to respect her.

According to Hume's Law, these arguments are invalid – as indeed is any such argument. This means that the conclusion does not follow from the premise, i.e. the 'ought' can't be got from the 'is', because the 'ought' is a completely new term which is not found in any of the premises, and it is logically illegitimate to jump across the gap, no matter how many 'is's' you have in the premises. (You can't turn a rabbit into a greyhound no matter how many rabbits you use.) What this means is that you can't prove that there is a moral obligation, an 'ought', to feed the starving by simply pointing out the natural fact (the 'is') that people are starving, for it's quite consistent to accept that a person is starving without being forced to agree that you have to do anything about it, e.g. feed them.

Hume's Law says that naturalism, being the attempt to do this sort of thing, must fail as a matter of iron logic. The only way you could derive these 'ought' conclusions is to add an 'ought' premise, e.g:

> P1: This person *is* starving.
> P2: You *ought* to feed the starving.
> Conclusion: Therefore, you *ought* to feed him.

This argument works, but the problem is that it is no longer naturalism because, on account of the 'ought' in premise 2, it goes from 'ought' to 'ought', not 'is' to 'ought'. If naturalism is ever to become a viable theory, it needs to refute or find some other way round the blockage that Hume's Law sets up, seemingly prohibiting the move from 'is' to 'ought'.

4 Appeal to Hume's thought experiment

I can hardly do any better than again quote Hume:

> Take any action allow'd to be vicious: Wilful murder, for instance. Examine it in all lights, and see if you can find that matter of fact, or real existence, which you call vice. In whichever way you take it, you find only certain passions, motives, volitions and thoughts. There is no other matter of fact in the case. The vice entirely escapes you, as long as you consider the object. You will never find it, till you turn your reflexion into your own breast, and find a sentiment of disapprobation, which arises in you, towards this action . . . It lies in yourself, not in the object. So that when you pronounce any action or character to be vicious, you mean nothing, but that from the constitution of your nature you have a feeling or sentiment of blame from the contemplation of it. (*A Treatise of Human Nature*, p. 468)

Basically, what Hume is saying is that the wrongness/badness/evil, or whatever you want to call it, is not outside in the world, but inside us, as our emotional response of disgust. He is appealing to each of us to try this out for ourselves and see that what he says is true. Another way of putting this is to ask yourself whether a forensics team, no matter how meticulous, could ever come across the quality of wrongness at the crime scene in the same way they'd come across finger prints, blood samples, DNA, etc. The answer is clearly, 'No'; you can dust for fingerprints but not for badness. So naturalism must be wrong.

*The case against **non-naturalism** in particular*

Non-cognitivism uses a battery of *six arguments* to attack the non-naturalist position that Moore supported by his two arguments (which we looked at earlier). The first five attack Moore's first argument, while the sixth attacks his second. If both are destroyed, the non-naturalist position must be given up. The following pages will be devoted to an assessment of how these six arguments impact on non-naturalism and the two arguments supporting it:

1 **Error theory** of moral **language** and moral **feelings**
2 **Argument from queerness**

3 Ockham's Razor
4 Argument from moral motivation
5 Argument against the referential theory of meaning
6 Argument against intuition

Moore's **argument 1** is set out below for ease of reference.

> P1: There are only three possibilities regarding the meaning of 'good'.
>   a) 'Good' means/refers to a natural thing or property.
>   b) 'Good' means/refers to a non-natural thing or property.
>   c) 'Good' means/refers to nothing at all.
> P2: The *open question argument* rules out option (a).
> P3: The *argument from moral feelings* and the *argument from moral language* rule out option (c).
> Conclusion: Therefore, that leaves option (b), so non-naturalism wins by default.

The non-cognitivists accept premise 1 and also premise 2 (remember they agree with the open question argument). So the non-cognitivists agree with Moore that option (a), i.e. naturalism, is impossible. Premise 3 is the one that really comes under attack from the non-cognitivists' first argument, because it attacks the argument from moral language, which is part of premise 3.

1 *The error theory* versus *premise 3*

The error theory, as applied to the objectivity of moral language, insists that this is one big mistake. Our whole moral language, including terms such as 'good', 'right', 'duty', 'bad', 'evil', 'virtue', and so on, is systematically mistaken in this respect because the objective reference of its terms is bogus.

What does this mean? It means that, according to the error theory, the way we use moral terms, and the grammatical rules for constructing moral sentences, makes them *look like* genuine statements, and has, over many years, given us the *illusion* that they were about real values and ideals that exist in the world independently of us when, in fact, they do no such thing. The **error** is in believing this verbal illusion, for there are no objective values, despite our language telling us that there are. How did this happen? The non-cognitivists owe us an explanation. Why are they suspicious of our moral language being used as evidence to support non-naturalism? Why might it be tainted?

Their explanation is that Christianity, a religion advocating a cognitivist, objectivist ethic, namely divine command theory, has had such an enormous cultural influence on Western society over the past two thousand years and that, because of this tremendous pressure on our ways of thinking and expressing ourselves, our moral language has been infected by the erroneous objective virus that Christianity has injected into it.

If this explanation is along the right lines, it means that Moore's argument becomes a *vicious circle* (a kind of logical fallacy), because it ends up arguing that we should believe that morals are objective – i.e. it rules out option (c) – and the reason it gives for this is that our moral language has objective meaning. But *the fact that our **moral** language has **objective** meaning was in turn brought about by our believing for two thousand years that **morals** are **objective**.*

The circularity of this reasoning will be clearer when set out more formally as follows:

> P1: Moral objectivity is true (a Christian belief for 2000 years).
>
> P2: This caused moral language to sound objective (owing to profound Christian influence on culture).
>
> P3: Moral language sounding objective is evidence that moral objectivity is true.
>
> Conclusion: Therefore, moral objectivity is true.

This argument is useless; it ends at the same point it begins, going round in a circle, because premise 1 supports premise 2 and premise 2 supports the conclusion, which is really premise 1 all over again.

The error theory also affects the argument from moral *feelings*, because it insists that it is an error to infer that, if you feel *intensely* about something, then it *must* have an *objective* cause in *fact*. There are many counter-examples to this, such as feelings of shame and disgust at failing to keep to your diet; pride in your football team and hatred of the opposition; love for your stamp collection. But going on a diet, supporting a football team, and starting a stamp collection are all matters of *decision*, yet they can evoke strong feelings. The point is that, although justice and human rights are moral issues we feel deeply about, they too may be matters of decision. The intense feelings of a martyr are no proof that God really exists. This too could be a big error, just like believing in objective moral values simply because people feel strongly enough to die for moral causes such as human rights.

So, on the strength of the error theory argument, we can refute premise 3, which now means that option (c), namely that 'good' refers to nothing at all, is ruled back in as a *possibility*, and Moore's conclusion that non-naturalism, i.e. option (b), wins by default does not follow. Of course, option (b) is still a *possibility*, which means non-naturalism is still in the game. That means non-cognitivism needs *more* arguments to kill off option (b) so as to leave option (c), i.e. non-cognitivism, as the winner by default.

The arguments from *queerness, Okham's Razor,* and *moral motivation* (see list on pp. 205–6) are all intended to target option (b) and eliminate it from the running. If this works, non-naturalism will be dead, and it's just a matter of mopping up Moore's argument 2 on intuition. Here's a reminder of option (b):

Option (b) of premise 1 of Moore's argument 1 states that 'good' means/refers to a non-natural thing or property.

2 The argument from *queerness* versus morals as non-natural fact

These moral entities or qualities certainly seem weird or queer. The intuition-ists don't tell us much about them save to say that they are what they are. They can't say more because, of course, according to them they're indefinable, so they can't be further explained. They seem to hover in a ghostly fashion among the physical qualities of the natural world, colours, actions, people, motives, and so on, attaching themselves here and there to acts such as killing, helping others, and telling the truth, a bit like postage stamps stuck on letters.

Why acts such as these and not acts such as mowing the lawn, or buying a newspaper? The non-naturalist can't reply that it's *because* the former acts actually harm and help people, whereas the latter have no positive or negative effect on others, because that would be deriving an 'ought' from an 'is' – a moral value from a natural fact – and Moore argued that this was impossible.

This randomness is queer. It's also very like saying that a wine is cheeky, and meaning that the cheekiness is literally in the wine but can't be detected by a chemist because it's a non-natural property, or saying that a rabbit was cute (a value judgement), and meaning the cuteness was 'out there', existing as a non-natural quality of the rabbit in addition to its fur, ears, and so on, but not being detectable by any of our five senses or any scientific instruments. The argument from queerness appeals to this intrinsic implausibility as a reason to reject this non-naturalist account of moral values. They sit there awkwardly on top of the physical world, seemingly unrelated to it in any understandable way.

3 *Ockham's Razor* versus morals as superfluous non-natural fact

Ockham's Razor (attributed to the fourteenth-century logician William of Ockham) is a principle of rational economy, widely used in philosophy and science. It states: *'Never multiply entities more than you have to.'* Or, alterna-tively: *'When two explanations explain equally well, pick the simpler one.'* The non-cognitivists contend that they can explain moral language and moral feelings *just as well if not better* than the non-naturalists, and their explanation is *cheaper,* because it doesn't need the added extras of non-natural moral qual-ities lurking around. According to non-cognitivists, there are no such things; they are surplus to requirements.

Look at it this way: if you go shopping for a TV, and you see two equally good ones that do all the same things, but one's cheaper than the other, you'd be stupid to buy the dearer one; it wouldn't be rational. Well, this is all Ockham's Razor says you should do when you go 'shopping' for explanatory theories: get the cheaper or simpler one if it does all the same things as the dearer one. The non-cognitivist argument using **Ockham's Razor** goes like this:

P1: Our moral theory explains morals just as well as that of the non-naturalists.

P2: But our theory is simpler (there's no *extra* level of moral reality).

P3: Ockham's Razor says: 'Go for the simplest theory.'

Conclusion: Therefore, reject non-naturalism (option b), and pick us.

4 Argument from **moral motivation** *versus morals as non-natural*

What are the non-cognitivists doing using Moore's own moral motivation argument against *him*?! This is the very argument he used against the naturalists, along with the open question argument. Well, their point is that Moore is equally vulnerable to this argument, because it shows that it's *impossible* for *any fact on its own, **including non-natural facts***, to motivate us to action. Moore didn't realize this when he used it to attack the naturalists, because he thought it applied only to any *natural* fact. It was its *naturalness* that stopped any fact from being a motivating reason to act. Moore was wrong. It's their very *factualness*, no matter whether they be natural or non-natural moral facts, that stops them being motivating reasons to action. To explain what the non-cognitivists are getting at here, we need to take a little detour through the *belief–desire* explanation of human action.

This is a very plausible theory of human motivation, and it explains human actions as the result of a combination of beliefs and desires. Beliefs on their own aren't sufficient to move people to act; they need a desire too. *Beliefs are to do with facts alone.* For example, suppose I believe that it's raining. This is a *fact* about the world, but this on its own won't motivate me to put up my umbrella unless I also *desire* to stay dry. Beliefs are just us taking note of the way the world is. What we *do* about that depends on *desires*, and they come from *within*.

The next step is to realize that, when you desire one thing rather than another, this means that you *value* that thing more highly than the other, so it seems that values are generated (created?) by internal psychological states of desire and therefore cannot be objective. Values motivate precisely because they aren't facts in the world, even non-natural facts in the world, but are subjectively created via the desires within us. If we had no desires or preferences there'd be no values. This time, let's try an example of a non-natural moral fact. Suppose I, as a non-naturalist, *believe* that kindness is good, because I *believe that* kindness has a non-natural *factual* good quality attached to it. Why on earth should this *belief,* which merely *registers a fact,* lead me to be kind? The *fact* that kindness is good in this sense will mean nothing to me unless I also *desire* to be kind, *prefer* kindness to meanness, *care* about showing kindness to others.

What this shows is that, even if Moore were right about good being a non-natural property, it wouldn't have the slightest motivating power to cause people to be good, because you need a motivating *desire* to move you to be good. But the only thing the *fact-that-good-is-a-non-natural-property* can supply you with is the *belief* that it is so, and this is not sufficient to make you *do* anything. That's why the argument from **moral motivation** works against Moore and non-naturalism. It's the final reason why option (b), non-naturalism, should be rejected; so option (c), non-cognitivism, is the winner.

Although the non-cognitivists will be happy that they've won, *assuming* their arguments are sound, they still have a problem with the way option (c) is worded. Here's a reminder of what it actually says:

Option (c): 'Good' means/refers to nothing at all.

The problem is that the non-cognitivists want to be able to say that 'good' has **meaning** even though it **refers to nothing** at all in the world, but the wording of option (c) doesn't allow them to say this because it conflates meaning with reference – i.e. it holds that to *mean* is to *refer*. This entails that if a word doesn't refer to anything then it can't mean anything – i.e. it's meaningless. Now, since the non-cognitivists don't want to be stuck with a theory that says that moral language is meaningless garbage, they need an argument that proves that meaning is not the same as reference – in other words, that a word can have meaning and yet refer to nothing. They need to prove that the *referential theory of meaning* is wrong.

5 Argument against the referential theory of meaning

The referential theory of meaning is the important background assumption that Moore makes in his discussions about what 'good' means. This theory is easily disposed of because, as a *universal* theory of meaning, all that's needed to refute it is at least *one* counter-example of a word that obviously is meaningful yet refers to nothing, and there are lots of these. Here are some examples: 'as', 'and', 'so', 'but', 'if', 'not'.

None of these words picks out or refers to things in the world – there are no *ands* out there to which the word 'and' refers: its meaning derives from the job it does in the workings of the sentence itself. It might be replied that none of these are nouns, so the criticism is unfair, because the theory covers only nouns as having meaning by referring to things. However, there are other counter-examples of nouns that have meaning without referring to or picking out an existing thing – for example, the noun 'sake', as in 'Do it for my sake'. Sakes aren't *things*, so the word 'sake' can't refer to these, yet the word has meaning. Therefore, the referential theory of meaning is wrong.

The collapse of the referential theory allows the non-cognitivists to say that moral terms such as 'good' can have meaning despite not referring to anything in the world, thus avoiding the devastating criticism that their theory implies that words such as 'justice', 'goodness', 'right', and 'wrong' are just meaningless empty sounds. Where the non-cognitivists disagree is whether this meaning is emotive or prescriptive. It's now time to examine the non-cognitivist case against Moore's *argument 2* and its support for intuition. (For convenience, Moore's argument 2 – originally on p. 200 – is set out again below.) This argument supports the non-naturalist view that non-natural moral properties are known by a '*sixth*' sense called *intuition*.

Argument 2

> P1: Moral properties are *non-natural* (see the conclusion of argument 1).
> P2: We *know* these moral properties (see Moore's argument from *moral feelings* and from *moral language*).
> P3: Since they are *non*-natural there is no way we can know them by any *normal* natural method such as our five senses.
> Conclusion: Therefore, it's got to be by some *non*-natural 'sixth' sense which is specifically tuned in to moral 'frequencies'.
> This is what we call *intuition*.

6 Argument against intuition versus *Moore's argument 2*

In fact Moore's *argument 2* is *already* ruined before we even get to the argument against intuition, because the truth of its first premise relies on his *argument one*, and that has been refuted by the first five arguments above. Premise 2 of Moore's *argument 2* relies on the arguments from moral language and moral feeling, which have also been undermined by the error theory argument, and likewise fails. And premise 3 disintegrates because it depends on premise 1, which has already been destroyed. However, for completeness sake we'll go ahead and outline the non-cognitivist *argument against intuition* as it applies to Moore's *argument 2*. It's composed of five sub-arguments.

1 *Argument from* **queerness** *(again)* – Our so-called faculty of moral intuition seems as weird or queer as the non-natural qualities it's supposed to detect. Just

how do we perform this trick of tuning in to the moral wavelength? No one seems to know, including the non-naturalists. No physical organ is devoted to this weird sixth sense; there's no known way of testing its accuracy. All of this counts against its plausibility, so we probably don't have such a thing.

2 *Argument from **unreason*** – Our moral intuition is supposed to pick up *self-evident* moral truths, and our intuition simply *sees* their self-evidence; no further argument is needed or is available to us as to *why* we believe in our particular moral values. The problem with this is that, when we meet someone with contrary moral intuitions there's nothing left to reason about in order to try and persuade them that they're wrong – that their intuitions are faulty. Of course, their intuitions will be telling them exactly the same story about *us*. All that's left to do is shout at each other. But since we think reason should be able to resolve even our most basic moral differences, the fact that intuitionism doesn't allow this means it must be wrong.

3 *Argument from **subjective certainty*** – There doesn't seem to be any reliable way of distinguishing between our moral intuition that murder is wrong, and simply *subjectively feeling absolutely certain* that it's wrong. This is a big problem, because our subjective feelings of certainty can and have led us astray on so many occasions. Religious fanatics, political extremists, cranky scientists all feel with absolute certainty that they're right; *they* can *see* it – it's the rest of the world that's blind. Moral intuition is supposed to deliver self-evident truths, not cranky, fanatical, and dogmatic opinions. But if we can't tell the difference between intuition and feelings of subjective certainty, then intuitionists are wrong to claim that intuition is a way of knowing moral truths.

4 *Argument from **social prejudice*** – A similar problem arises if we can't tell the difference between moral intuition and the certainties we might accept via social conditioning, brainwashing, or indoctrination. Children are sponges that simply soak up everything their society teaches them is true, including all sorts of prejudices, wacky theories, myths, and half-baked ideas. By the time they're adults they'll have accumulated a whole army of 'intuitions' trustingly culled from their parents, teachers, church, friends, and community. What the argument from social prejudice boils down to is that, if you can't tell the difference between proper moral inuition leading to moral truth and the sort of deep-seated, socially instilled prejudices mentioned above, then intuition is not the route to moral truth.

5 *Ockham's Razor (again)*–Just as we asked why we should bother with an extra layer of non-natural moral values existing in addition to the physical

world, so we can ask why we should bother with an extra sixth faculty of non-natural moral intuition to detect these weirdos. If we can devise a theory of morals, such as non-cognitivism that explains things just as well as non-naturalism but is more economical in that it doesn't require these added extras, then Ockham's Razor bids us do the rational thing and go for the simpler theory. So expensive non-naturalism should be rejected.

With the collapse of both of Moore's arguments for non-naturalism, and the earlier demise of naturalism and transcendentalism, it seems that the cognitivist position is intellectually bankrupt, and that the road is clear for some version of non-cognitivism. We'll turn now to the two versions on offer to see what they have to say for themselves and what can be said against them. As you'll see, they don't have an easy time of it either.

Emotivism

As non-naturalism was reaching its sell-by date in the 1930s, a brand new commodity, emotivism, was beginning to be displayed on the shelves. Its two salesmen were the American philosopher C. L. Stevenson (1908–1979) and the British philosopher A. J. Ayer (1910–1989).

Emotivism, as put forward by both Ayer and Stevenson, holds that moral language does not state facts, and so isn't informative, but instead possesses *emotive* or *expressive meaning*. Its job is not to *refer* to moral qualities in the world, but to *express* the speaker's emotions/attitudes and/or *evoke* the emotions/attitudes of the listener. Saying 'Courage is good' is like saying 'Three cheers for courage!' or 'Hooray for courage!', and saying 'Rape is wrong' is like saying 'Rape, yuk!' or 'Boo to rape!' These are neither true nor false because they *don't state any facts*; they simply *express* the *emotive* reaction of the speaker and are intended to *evoke* a similar response in the listener. For this reason emotivism has become known as the *boo/hooray* theory, and is **not to be confused with** *simple subjectivism*.

Simple subjectivism holds that moral judgements, such as 'Kindness is good', *state* the speaker's emotions, and should be analysed as meaning 'I am in favour of (or I like) kindness'. It might seem that the difference between *expressing* an emotion and *stating* that you have an emotion is too trivial to bother about, but actually the difference is crucial. Why is this? Because, by analysing moral judgements as fact-stating assertions about one's likes and dislikes, *simple subjectivism* is classified as a *cognitivist* theory, since these statements can be true or false and consequently can be known, e.g. by the speaker. In fact, it is a form of *naturalism*, because it defines words such as 'good' in terms of *natural psychological facts* about the speaker's emotional state of mind. By mixing up emotivism with simple subjectivism, you'd be confusing a non-cognitivist theory with a cognitivist one.

In contrast to this, emotivism has it that saying 'Kindness is good' means 'Hooray for kindness!', and this is not stating anything, either true or false. It doesn't make sense to ask 'Is "Hooray for kindness" true?' or to state, 'I know that hooray for kindness', because the phrase 'Hooray for . . .' isn't a statement of any sort, it's purely expressive. Moral language is simply a way for the speaker to let off steam about issues they care about, and to work on the emotions of their listener to change them or reinforce them. The is–ought gap is the gap between facts and feelings; is's state facts, and oughts express one's feelings in reaction to is's. Emotivism can be compared to matters of taste. For example, suppose I enjoy a cup of tea, and I say, 'This tea is good', an emotivist would say that this meant 'Hooray for this tea!' or 'This tea . . . mmm lovely!' On the one hand there are the objective facts about the tea, where it was made, how old it is, how much of it there is, its chemical constituency, and so on. On the other hand there are my subjective emotional reactions to drinking it, expressed via 'oohs' and 'ahhs', or 'yuks' and 'ughs'.

According to emotivism, morals are just like this; on the one hand there are the objective facts (is's) about abortion, for example, facts such as the physical and mental condition of the mother and foetus, the law of the land, the drugs that are available, the skill of the doctors, etc., and on the other hand there are the various emotional reactions of people to the abortion, expressed in moral language (the oughts). The only *reasoning* that can be done concerning *ethical* issues is to do with the *empirical facts* of the case. But once any differences here are resolved, if there is *still* a difference in *moral* judgement – in other words, if people react differently in attitude and on an emotional level – there's *no more reasoning to be done,* because this area, i.e. morality, is to do with emotions and feelings, not facts and evidence. 'Abortion is good' = 'Hooray for abortion'. This is neither evidence nor fact.

Possible strengths of emotivism

1 Emotivism *avoids the naturalistic fallacy* (if there is one, more on this later).
2 It *acknowledges the is–ought gap* (if there is one, more on this later).
3 It *can account for moral motivation,* unlike cognitivism, because, as you'll recall, desires are what move us to action, not beliefs, and desires are a kind of feeling or emotion leading to a choice of action in response. Of course, emotivism is tailor-made to incorporate this into its theory, since it holds moral value judgements to be expressions of emotions that will motivate.
4 There are *no queer entities* out there in the form of non-natural properties.

5 Emotivism is *simpler than non-naturalism* because moral values aren't *things*.

6 It can *easily account for the amazing variety of moral values* around the world in terms of differences in subjective moral taste, attitude, and emotion, on a par with the differences of taste in food, fashion, hairstyle, and so on.

7 It can also *easily account for the common experience we all have that moral disputes never seem to get anywhere,* that basic moral differences seem impossible to reconcile. Its explanation is simply that reasoning does not apply here because there's no arguing about taste, and morality is a matter of taste. Just as I'll never get you to like Cornflakes instead of Sugar Puffs, given your feeling of disgust at the very thought of Cornflakes, no matter how many yummy noises I make when I eat my Cornflakes, so it's equally unlikely that I'll change the views of a racist no matter how vehement my moral language, for all I'm saying is 'Racism, yuk!!'

8 *Moral disputes are often highly charged;* people thump the table, get hot under the collar, shout. Here, again, *emotivism is excellent at capturing this kind of experience* in its theory. If morality is all about expressing emotions and evoking emotions in others, then it's no wonder people get het up about things such as abortion.

There's no doubt emotivism was a breath of fresh air after the complacent certainties of smug intuitionism, but it itself ran into some severe criticisms, which caused it to be superseded by its close relative, prescriptivism. We'll now look at seven arguments against emotivism.

Arguments against emotivism

1 Not all moral words are strongly or even mildly emotive. Take 'good', for example, as in 'Honesty is good'. Do you feel your pulses racing when you read this? Do you need a sedative to calm yourself down? Hardly, yet if this is supposed to work on your emotions, as the emotivists claim, it does a very poor job. The coolness with which we react indicates that this is closer to a statement of fact than an emotive outburst.

2 Emotivism doesn't capture moral language uniquely because lots of other types of discourse besides morality use emotive language; examples include advertising, politics, religion, and football. Yet it's supposed to be telling us just what is *distinctive* of moral language. Since it doesn't do this, it is incomplete as a theory.

3 When we're on our own trying to work out the right thing to do, it seems absurd for the emotivist to insist that all we're really doing is giving vent to our feelings rather than trying to discover some matter of fact, which is

what we think we're doing. Are our private moral 'reasonings' really pep talks in disguise, in which we go to work on ourselves in order to drum up the emotional enthusiasm to act? Surely the emotivists are wrong to think we're so deceived.

4 Emotivism can't properly analyse the situation where someone comes to you for moral *advice*. Clearly what they're looking for is some *reasoned guidance*, not some piece of *psychological manipulation* to which you subject them via the emotive power of your moral rhetoric. But, according to emotivism, all you can offer them is the chance to be *pressurized* into toeing your moral line. This seems an unsatisfactory analysis of what's going on.

5 Ultimately, emotivism reduces all moral debate to propaganda. It doesn't really matter whether you use valid or invalid arguments to influence your opponents, since there are no moral facts, no objectivity, and no truth or falsehood. It doesn't matter how, as long as you win. This might seem like an unfair criticism, because it's so extreme and portrays emotivists as highly cynical concerning the whole moral enterprise, but here's a notorious quote from Stevenson which lends plausibility to this criticism: '*Any* statement about *any* fact which *any* speaker considers likely to alter attitudes may be adduced as a reason for or against an ethical judgment' (*Ethics and Language*, p. 114).

6 An American philosopher called Brand Blanshard (1892–1987) has used a poignant example of a rabbit caught in a painful hunter's trap to highlight some absurd implications of emotivism (see Sterba, *Ethics*, p. 33–8). What we want to say, what common sense tells us, is that the rabbit's pain is bad *independently* of whether anyone sees it or not. The *rabbit's painful state is itself bad*, no matter how anyone happens to *feel* about it. But it seems that, according to emotivism, if no one comes by to witness the animal's distress and react emotionally to it, then its pain is neither good nor bad, since these words only express emotions and nobody is having any at the moment. Only when someone appears on the scene, and is morally upset at the sight and calls it bad, does the rabbit's pain become bad. What's even more absurd, this badness lasts only as long as we feel bad about it.

Let's say we take a pill and suddenly feel upbeat about the rabbit's pain; then the pain will magically become morally good because we feel good about it – that's all that calling it 'good' means, after all. Even if we are *mistaken* in thinking that the rabbit is in pain and we feel bad about it, this makes *no difference* to the morality of the situation. It's still equally bad if we feel the same way, because badness is only in the emotional expression. Doesn't the rabbit and its pain get a say in all this? No. The rabbit's dislike of its pain doesn't count, because rabbits aren't capable of morality and so can't make moral value judgements about the badness of the pain. No matter what agonies the hunter puts the rabbit through, this will not count as immoral until someone comes along and calls it bad or wrong. If emotivism implies these absurdities, then something has gone wrong with the theory.

7 Worse still, the most vicious crimes would become good if our feelings changed in favour of them, for this is all morality consists of. The nightmare painted by the naturalists in their fifth argument hoves into view. This is the appalling alternative that *anything goes*, as long as you *feel* good about it, or have a positive *attitude*, it's morally right for you, because for something to be morally right is merely for someone to feel an emotional pull towards doing it. But this leads straight to moral terror. Moral value becomes completely relative to each individual and how they happen to feel.

Emotivism had its heyday from the late 1930s until the 1950s, when the pressure of such counter-arguments began to lead some philosophers to look for an improvement. This led to R. M. Hare (1919–2002; professor of philosophy at Oxford 1966–1983) devising a new non-cognitivist theory called **prescriptivism**.

Prescriptivism

First I will briefly summarize *seven features* of prescriptivism that distinguish it from its cousin emotivism, and then explain these in more detail, along with their advantages, which enabled prescriptivism to deal with most of the problems that plagued the emotivists. According to prescriptivism:

1 The meaning of moral language is *prescriptive* (this is the obvious one), not emotive; that's to say, it functions more like a *command* or a *recommendation* to perform certain actions, rather than expressing emotions.
2 Moral judgements must be *universalizable*, for this is part of their prescriptive meaning. In emotivism this is *not* a requirement.
3 Universalizability brings in an important element of *consistency* in one's principles and actions, and this introduces *rationality* to moral discussion. In contrast to this, emotivism allows your emotions to blow hot one minute and cold the next, so consistency is not needed.
4 Moral principles are *decided* rather than *had* or *undergone* as a result of an emotional reaction.
5 Moral principles are *action-guiding*. This means that you're *logically bound* to obey the moral principles that you sincerely prescribe to yourself. This is another *consistency* requirement that emotivism doesn't have on account of the volatility of emotions.

6 Moral language is used to give *reasoned **advice*** to others, rather than merely to *influence* them psychologically, as emotivism holds.

7 Moral principles are *overriding*, i.e. they trump all other competing considerations when it comes to deciding what to do. No matter if morals clash with economics, religion, etiquette, or aesthetics, morals should always win. However, emotivism is silent about this, so presumably you're allowed to keep your money rather than give it to Oxfam if you feel more emotionally attached to *it* than to the starving.

Prescriptivism's seven features explained

1 Prescriptive meaning

Prescriptive meaning includes recommending, urging, advising, and commanding either yourself or others. Moral language works a bit like a doctor's prescription to take two tablets four times a day, except you're the doctor and you're prescribing things such as generosity, telling the truth, and fairness, instead of pills. Here are some examples of how prescriptivists would analyse moral judgements.

- Murder is wrong = Don't murder!
- I ought to tell the truth = Let me tell the truth!
- Kindness is good = Be kind! *or* I recommend kindness!
- Courage is a virtue = Try to become courageous!

2 Universalizability

This is where moral prescriptions differ from ordinary everyday commands. For example, if I order you to shut the door on a particular occasion, this does not commit me to giving you the same order on another relevantly similar occasion. I might, this time, decide instead to put up with the draught from the open door, or wear a scarf, or move to the other end of the room. But when it comes to moral prescriptions, the universalizability requirement, which is part of their *meaning*, does not allow this sort of variation on pain of inconsistency.

This is very reminiscent of Kant. If I think that doing x is right in situation y, then it must be right for *anyone* to do x in *any* situation that is *relevantly similar* to y, and this goes for *me too*. To prescribe one rule for myself and another for others in the same situation is to be inconsistent and irrational. So if I judge that it's wrong for people to avoid paying their bus fare in situation y, I can't go ahead and *not* pay *my* bus fare when I'm in situation y because, by saying that it's wrong, I have, in effect, issued a universal moral command, 'Nobody is to avoid paying bus fares in situation y!', and this includes me. If I don't pay it, I'm inconsistent and can be *argued* with and proved wrong.

Hare has developed a sort of imperative logic that demonstrates this, e.g.:

P1: All people in situation y should pay their fare.
P2: I'm a person and I'm in situation y.
Conclusion: Therefore, I should pay my fare.

If I reject the conclusion by not paying, while accepting the premises, then I'm guilty of a self-contradiction.

3 Rationality

To be guilty of self-contradiction is to be inconsistent. Inconsistency is a form of irrationality, as we've seen in the section on universalizability. It is this very concept that has enabled prescriptivism to *introduce rational debating procedures into the confines of moral discussion.* Points 4, 5, and 6 below extend reason's role in ethics, unlike emotivism, where reasoning is confined to *factual issues outside* of morality.

4 Deciding our principles

Again, the prescriptivist idea that we choose or decide our moral principles, in a similar way to the doctor deciding what tablets to prescribe, brings reason into the very formation of our ethics, in contrast to the emotivists, who hold that, in a sense, we *undergo* our moral judgements as we undergo our emotions, such as the instinctive disgust we would feel at biting into a sandwich and finding a beetle in it. But in contrast to this, to be able to *decide* our moral principles restores our *control* of the moral situation, and with it comes more *freedom* and *responsibility* for the values we've chosen by prescribing them to ourselves and others. In emotivism, to the (possibly significant) extent that we can't control our emotions, we won't be in control of our morality. Instead, our emotions *deliver* it to us.

Regarding prescriptivism, it's also worth noting that, because of the fact–value gap, we're not forced by the natural facts to decide any particular set of moral rules or prescriptions. The gap is so strict that it stops any fact reaching across to the value side and dictating our morals to us. In this respect, logically we're completely free to choose what our moral principles will be.

5 Action-guiding

However, once we've chosen/prescribed our moral principles, we're *logically bound* by the rules of *consistency* to obey these prescriptions. They are, after all, the commands we give ourselves. This is what Hare means by saying that our prescriptions are *action-guiding*. So if someone says that stealing is wrong, and you catch them stealing, you can accuse them of inconsistency. The only way they can refute this accusation is to claim that their original avowal of that moral principle was insincere, or that they had since changed their mind about the principle and now think that stealing is permissible. So here again reason plays a role in moral discourse.

6 *Advice, not influence*

If someone comes to you for some moral advice, prescriptivism allows you to give it without any psychological manipulation, unlike emotivism. For example, having discussed the principles with which they're struggling, you could point out possible inconsistencies between them, or test their rationality by universalizing them to see if they can be coherently prescribed to everyone, and you could recommend some other viable principle instead. All this may help your friend see the problem more clearly while leaving the final decision entirely to them, without you in any way *going to work on their emotions in order to get a result*. In fact, prescriptivism allows the possibility of your giving advice without the least expectation of its being heeded.

7 *Moral principles are* **overriding**

In any battle between doing the right thing and doing the polite thing, the pleasant thing, the cost-effective thing, the done thing, the artistic thing, even the cool thing, the *right* thing should *always* win. The moral 'ought' beats everything else; it overrides them. Morality constitutes our most important, fundamental prescriptions for humanity and how it should live. Emotivism, on the other hand, does not hold that morality is overriding, because it says nothing about the moral emotions being the most important or strongest among all the possible emotions we could feel about things such as art, etiquette, money, and so on.

Assessing **prescriptivism**

Advantages *over emotivism*

Firstly, it's worth pointing out that prescriptivism shares all the strengths of emotivism. It avoids the naturalistic fallacy, and avoids the is–ought gap, by distinguishing facts from prescriptions (oughts). It can account for moral motivation, not via emotion, but via the close logical tie between one's prescriptive moral principles and actually acting in accordance with these. This is the *action-guiding* element. There are still no queer value entities in the outside world, so prescriptivism is still simpler than non-naturalism because moral value is *decided in here*, not discovered out there.

This prescriptivist emphasis on moral judgements being the result of basic *choices/decisions* of moral value can also easily account for the amazing variety of moral systems around the world and the difficulty we find in resolving moral disputes; it's simply because people differ a lot subjectively as individuals, so it stands to reason they'll choose different moral principles that reflect their different priorities. And the reason why it's so hard to resolve moral disputes is that:

i) Morality is *overriding*, so each system of morality will see itself as unbeatable, and better than other so-called moral options.

ii) *Moral principles can float free of objective facts* because there's no logical tie between facts and value *choices*, so appealing to the facts won't necessarily do the trick when in a moral dispute. For example, when it comes to abortion, two doctors could agree on *all* the medical facts to do with the case, yet *still disagree* about what ought to be done, morally speaking, because they've each *decided* to adopt different moral principles.

iii) At the *most fundamental level*, where *basic* moral principles are *decided*, **reason** cannot force the issue between rival moral views, because reason only enters the moral arena once the principles *have **already been** decided*. Reason's job is to make sure that, *whatever set you choose*, the principles don't clash with each other, that each one is consistently universalizable, and that each person acts consistently in accordance with their chosen principles. The *actual choosing of the principles in the first place* is, strictly speaking, *not a matter for reason* because of point ii) above. The facts don't *dictate* our choice of moral prescription.

As for the eighth strength of emotivism, although prescriptivism analyses the *meaning* of moral judgements as prescriptive, not emotive, there's no reason why it can't allow feelings to enter *psychologically* into the decision-making process when it comes to choosing our moral values, and in this way it too can account for the common experience of people getting angry and thumping the table when it comes to arguing about morality.

So far, emotivism and prescriptivism are on a par. Where prescriptivism really comes into its own and appears superior is the way it copes much better with most of the seven criticisms aimed at emotivism (see pp. 215–17). Let's see how it deals with the first five.

1 The problem of moral words such as 'good' not being especially emotively bracing doesn't apply to prescriptivism, since it denies that moral words are essentially emotive.

2 The problem of not capturing the *uniquely* emotive nature of moral language doesn't apply for the same reason as given in point 1 above.

3 Prescriptivism can side-step problem 3 because it can interpret private moral anxiety, not as our attempt to work on ourselves emotionally, but as a rational concern to be morally consistent.

4 The problem of giving *reasoned* moral advice is avoided, because, unlike emotivism, prescriptivism permits advice without manipulation.

5 Universalizability replaces the moral propaganda of emotivism with rational consistency, and this fits in much better with our understanding of what we're doing when we engage in moral language and debate, i.e. that we're engaging in a form of *rational* discourse.

However, despite these good points, prescriptivism has come under some severe pressure from the cognitivists. Their main arguments are outlined below.

Cognitivist arguments against **prescriptivism**

1 *The problem of prescriptive meaning beyond ethics* – Since *other areas of discourse besides ethics*, such as the law and etiquette, are *equally prescriptive* in meaning, prescriptivism fails adequately to explain the *distinctive* meaning of moral language.

2 *The problem of non-prescriptive meaning within ethics* – Prescriptivism doesn't even get moral language right because there are some areas of ethics that plainly aren't prescriptive. For example, if a soldier dives on a grenade to save others, I can have moral admiration for this level of self-sacrifice. I can call it an amazingly good act without this implying that I must choose or prescribe such behaviour for myself and others. It's precisely because what this soldier did was *above and beyond* the call of duty that I can morally commend his behaviour without prescribing it as a moral duty for everyone. Prescriptivism doesn't cover cases such as this, and so is *incomplete* as an account of the meaning of *all* moral language.

3 *The problem of non-universalizability within ethics* – This problem follows directly from number 2 above, for if universalizability is an essential part of prescriptive meaning, and prescriptive meaning doesn't apply to all areas of ethics (see the soldier example), then universalizability can't apply to all areas of ethics either. So prescriptivism is inadequate here too.

4 *The problem of the impossibility of moral failure* – The *overriding* and *action-guiding* features of our morally prescribed principles generate a very

peculiar paradox, namely, *it's logically impossible for anyone to fail to live up to their moral principles.* This doctrine follows from prescriptivism because, when you decide on a moral rule for yourself, in doing so, you are prescribing or commanding yourself to act according to that rule, and so it becomes *action-guiding.* You're also giving it priority over all other non-ethical rules – the *overridingness* bit. So, as long as you're sane, healthy, and free, nothing should stop you acting on it.

But isn't it a common experience in our everyday lives, as we struggle to keep to our principles, that our weakness of will, lack of spirit, fear, and lethargy often prevent us from doing the right thing? That even while doing wrong we know it's wrong, because it's against the very principles we chose to live by in the first place.

Guilt and depression can follow the awareness that we've let ourselves down by failing to live up to the standards we've set ourselves. St Paul's is a common experience to which we can all relate. In Romans 7:18–19 he says, 'I can will what is right but I cannot do it. For I do not do the good I want, but the evil I do not want is what I do.' Prescriptivists try to explain this away by surmising that the seeming failure was not really a failure, because either you weren't sincere about your principles in the first place or your very 'disobedience' proves that you have since picked new principles which the 'disobedient' act actually obeys, so success is guaranteed. So no one ever does what they think is wrong.

To the extent that our moral experience contradicts this paradoxical thesis, to that extent is prescriptivism unacceptable. Surely it's possible *in the very act* of bullying a weaker person, or making fun of a disabled person, to *acknowledge that it's wrong,* and even enjoy it precisely *because* you realize this. If this rings true, then prescriptivism rings false.

5 *The problem of the rabbit example* – Prescriptivism has a problem with this for the same reasons as emotivism does. For example, the prescriptivist has to say that the rabbit's pain is not bad until someone appears on the scene and *decides* or *prescribes* it as bad; and if that someone happened to prescribe a moral principle that entailed that the pain was good, then that would *make* it good. And if they keep changing their mind, the rabbit's pain will be bad, then good, then bad again, without any change at all in the intensity of the pain itself. This seems as crazy as trying to change the colour of your blue wallpaper to yellow *merely* by *deciding* to *call* it 'yellow'. If you agree, then prescriptivism must be wrong.

6 *The problem of moral anarchy* – Again, this is just as much a difficulty for prescriptivism as it was for emotivism because, if people's subjective decisions to prescribe their moral principles do not have to be logically tied to any

natural facts to do with human welfare, then they have complete freedom to choose any moral system that suits them, whatever the cost to humanity, and irrespective of what anyone else wants.

And so the naturalists' 'argument from the appalling alternative' returns to haunt us. Imagine trying to play a game of Monopoly with everyone making up the rules as they go along, and you'll get some idea of how chaotic and frightening life would be if the naturalists are right about the consequences of non-cognitivism. But are they right? Would it be as bad as they make out? I think the prescriptivists have *two plausible replies.*

i) The naturalists are scaremongering; it wouldn't be anywhere near as bad as the nightmare they envisage because, although they're correct about the *logical* independence of moral prescriptions from natural facts being a part of our theory, there's still a strong *psychological* dependence, such that our moral prescriptions tend to be in line with what we need to survive and to hold society together. It just so happens that most of us prefer similar things; millions of years of evolution have seen to that, and it stands to reason that our moral prescriptions will tend to reflect this. Think of it like this: although each Monopoly player *could* make up his own rules as he goes along, it would not be as enjoyable a game as one where they all agreed to prescribe the same rules. Their similar psychological desires to have an interesting, competitive, yet friendly game will lead them to avoid the anarchic self-assertion of their own rules. The naturalists' bogey-man of moral and social prescriptive chaos will never happen because we have just too much in common to let it.

ii) If this *is* a problem for us, then it is *equally* a problem for cognitivism, which lets us off the hook. Here's why they're in the same boat.

The intuitionists can't get anywhere with moral fanatics whose intuitions tell them that gassing Jews is self-evidently true, and therefore morally obligatory. This allows anyone to follow their intuitions, no matter how bizarre, because there's no known way to prove them wrong except by appealing to your own intuitions and telling them that theirs are corrupt. This is useless, because they'll just say the same about yours, and there's no independent way of settling such an impasse.

The naturalists have a serious problem concerning moral motivation, namely the bare natural facts by themselves won't be enough to move anyone to act morally well, and this also goes for moral values such as 'goodness' defined as natural facts, such as pleasure. So even if there *are* natural moral facts out there, this can't prevent the possibility of a world where *no one **gives a damn** about the natural moral facts,* because they *just don't care*, or can't be bothered, or prefer their own evil plans. The prescriptivists can scaremonger just as much as the cognitivists, so this results in a draw.

7 *The problem of silly prescriptions* – It seems that prescriptivism must allow the possibility of **any** crazy prescription as long as it's sincerely chosen and universalized. This is because of the is–ought gap, which allows moral prescriptions to be about *anything at all* without having to be accountable to the *facts concerning human welfare*. This results in morality, under prescriptivism, not having any *specifiable content*. Logically speaking, morality is all about prescribing principles or rules, but *what the rules are about* is up to you. For example, suppose someone were sincerely to prescribe running round a tree ten times every day as their moral principle; despite this being utterly pointless, it would have to be considered a proper moral principle on a prescriptivist basis.

What seems wrongheaded about this is that such behaviour is totally irrelevant to the vital issues concerning *how to treat others*, which we feel morality *has* to be about. If the naturalists are correct in believing that morality *must* have to do with *human well-being* in some form or other, and that any behaviour outside this area is morally neutral (e.g. closing the door three times every time you leave a room, or jumping up and down while shouting 'I'm a planet!'), then prescriptivism is wrong, for it entails that silly behaviour such as this can become a moral duty for anyone who decides to prescribe this for themselves and is prepared to live accordingly. The problem for prescriptivism is that it would say that these were weird moralities, whereas it seems much more plausible to say that they are not moralities *at all*. On this count, prescriptivism is therefore implausible.

Having looked at the cognitivist critique of prescriptivism in particular, we're now ready to deal with the *remaining cognitivist arguments against non-cognitivism in general*.

Cognitivist arguments against non-cognitivism

The three arguments listed below are aimed at *all versions* of non-cognitivism, whether of the emotivist or prescriptivist variety, with the intention of refuting them completely. If successful, the way will be open for the re-establishment of some form of cognitivism.

1 **The argument from moral progress**
2 **The charge of relativism**
3 **The argument from moral convergence**

The argument from moral progress

It seems clear that we have made much moral progress in the past few hundred years. For example, we now think that slavery, racism, and sexism are wrong, where before they were seen as good and proper. We think this is a *real* improvement, and not just that we have *simply changed our minds* about these things while remaining *no better* than our predecessors. But non-cognitivism appears to imply that there cannot be such a thing as real moral progress, because moral values aren't really out there. We can't know better than our ancestors because there's nothing to know; there are no moral facts or truths.

But cognitivists can easily account for our belief in moral progress, because they hold that moral values are real facts and that real progress consists in getting to know more of them.

Non-cognitivist reply

This criticism is misguided because we can agree that there is moral progress; it's just that we understand progress differently. True, there can't be progress if by 'progress' you mean 'greater knowledge of objective moral facts', because we don't believe there are any. However, if by 'progress' you mean 'greater coherence among people's moral principles, greater consistency in universalizing one's principles, etc.', then there is moral progress according to the prescriptivists.

It seems to me that the emotivists have more difficulty here because they don't allow reasoning within ethics at all, and so can't appeal to things such as coherence and consistency. It seems all they can say is that moral progress consists of greater knowledge of the empirical, non-moral facts that form the background to moral decisions and that need to be taken into account. But this is to admit that it's not *specifically morality* that progresses.

However, the prescriptivists aren't home and dry yet because, if their idea of moral progress is to be believed, then it could turn out that the most *coherent* and *consistently* applied outrageously barbaric set of principles would constitute the ultimate in moral progress. After all, they don't have to be tied to human welfare. Surely that can't be right.

The charge of relativism

This is the charge that since, according to the non-cognitivists, there's no objective truth about moral values (because it's all a matter of subjective feelings and decisions), this must mean that all the various moralities in the world are *equally viable*, and *none is truer than the others*. This relativistic doctrine means that nobody has the right to criticize anyone else just because they do things differently. This means that, as a non-cognitivist, you'd be powerless to criticize other cultures' ways of doing things, even if they are very nasty things according to *your* moral code, for as long as *their* moral code permits or encourages these activities (e.g. female circumcision, human sacrifice, infanticide, etc.) then these are *right for them*. There would be no grounds for criticism, no such thing as 'taking a stand' against such practices, for it would be just your emotions or prescriptions against theirs. You'd have as little right to interfere as you would to stop someone eating their Frosties, just because *you* happen to feel nausea at the mere thought of them.

Since there are many circumstances in which we believe we have the right to intervene to stop immoral practices in other cultures (e.g. imposing sanctions on the racist apartheid regime in South Africa), there's a sense in which we don't believe in relativism when it comes to really serious breaches of our moral code, even when they occur outside our culture, which shows that we don't think it's just *our* code; we think, instead, that it is *the* code.

Non-cognitivism is accused of relativism, which does not cater for these feelings and justifies standing idly by, with no moral authorization even from your own moral code to criticize, never mind put a stop to, moral atrocities that happen to be in accordance with the moral code of another culture.

Non-cognitivist response

i)   We've seen more than enough of the disastrous effects on other tribal cultures of the dogmatic, arrogant colonialism characteristic of cognitivism to be very wary of imposing our moral views on others. It could produce more harm than good. Look at the disaster of the war in Iraq as the latest attempt to impose Western values of democracy on others.

ii) In seriously nasty cases we don't have to remain silent because non-cognitivism, being expressivist or prescriptivist, allows us to express our feelings and attitudes about these vile practices and lean on these other nations. It also allows us to engage in *factual* debate with them if they base their morals on factual beliefs about the gods, or mistaken views about the nature of women, and so on.

iii) Relativism promotes tolerance. Dogmatic objectivism, a tendency of cognitivism, promotes intolerance. Since tolerance is better than intolerance, this supports non-cognitivism.

Cognitivist response

With regard to i), citing misguided and arrogant applications of cognitivism does not mean cognitivism itself is wrong. Wouldn't that be like rejecting medical science as a whole just because a rogue doctor such as Harold Shipman abused his position in order to kill hundreds of patients?

With regard to ii), there can be no rational engagement with other cultures on an emotional or prescriptive level, because the only reaction available to non-cognitivists is logically impotent rage or ineffective and factually irrelevant moral prescriptions aimed at the rival culture. And engaging in factual debate is pointless because, even if you win, since moral principles and emotions are believed by non-cognitivists to float free from the empirical facts, this would still allow the rival culture to maintain their obnoxious ethic, despite being proved factually wrong (about the gods, say), as long as they continue *simply* to *decide* that these are the moral principles for them.

Lastly, with regard to iii), cognitivists can claim that,

a) We too can be tolerant, because on many occasions this is the best response even when you know others are wrong. For example, a cognitivist might believe truly that abortions are sometimes wrong, and yet be tolerant of them because it would do more harm than good to ban them under the law. This would simply drive the whole practice underground, exposing women to unhygienic conditions with unqualified 'doctors'.

b) At least cognitivism claims that it's *true* that tolerance is better than intolerance. Non-cognitivism is inferior in this respect, for it holds no ethical judgement to be true, and therefore it can't be true (or false) that tolerance is better than intolerance.

c) Non-cognitivists have to be very careful when they talk about the value of tolerance, for, if they're arguing that we should *all* be tolerant, then they appear to be raising at least *one universal objective* moral value, namely tolerance, which applies to *everyone* across the board, yet this seems to contradict their belief that moral values are *merely relative* to each culture.

The argument from moral convergence

This is simply trying to point out that there is much greater moral consensus around the world, especially on the basic core values of ethics, than the non-cognitivists acknowledge in their argument from moral relativity. True, on a superficial level there appears to be an amazing amount of diversity, but most of this can be explained, firstly, with reference to variations in the accepted factual beliefs about the gods, human nature, etc., and, secondly, with reference to the large variety of geographical, climatic, and demographic environments to which the peoples of the world have to apply their ethics. The cognitivists argue that the *core* beliefs in ethics are largely *uniform* throughout the globe, and that it is *the variety of **circumstances*** that makes their *application* so varied.

For example, we share the same core value of the protection of innocent life that they had in the Wild West, yet back then a man could be hanged for stealing a horse, whereas we would be appalled at the thought of this happening in Britain today. But the difference is the superficial one of application to different circumstances of our *shared core value*, namely the wrongness of leaving someone to die. Stealing a horse in modern Britain is not tantamount to killing its owner, but in the endless plains of the Mid-West of America, to have your horse stolen, your only means of transport to civilization and safety, was almost equivalent to being killed. Hence the harsh penalty for the thief. But we can *understand* this because we share the underlying value this law is meant to uphold, i.e. the value of a human life. Other basic values and principles that seem to be universally held are moral injunctions against murder, theft, lying, incest, and unjustly punishing the innocent. It's on this basis that cognitivists argue that such deep-seated uniformity of core values indicates that moral values are objective to all.

Now that non-cognitivism seems to have been successfully disposed of, the question is 'Where do we go from here?' Perhaps a reconsideration of cognitivism is in order, but which version? Transcendentalism has collapsed under its own weight (see arguments against Plato and divine command theory), and non-naturalism has taken a severe battering from which it is unlikely to recover. That leaves naturalism: but we left it marooned on the wrong side of the is–ought gap, with the open question argument, like a sentinel, guarding the chasm and barring the route from natural facts to moral values. If only there was a way of disarming the sentinel and closing the gap.

10   The Case for a Contemporary Naturalism

I will give four arguments that modern naturalists have used in their recent fightback after eighty years in the philosophical wilderness.

1 The attack on the open question argument

The success of the attack on the open question argument is vital to the survival of naturalism, but fortunately **it does succeed**. The following is a version of the simple but strong refutation.

It is an open question, i.e. it is meaningful to ask, 'Is water really H_2O?' because until it was discovered that this was so it might have turned out not to be the case. And indeed, even though this has now been discovered, this is still an open question to those who don't know basic science. But *if the open question argument were valid, the fact that 'Is water really H_2O?' is a genuinely open question would force us to conclude that water was **not** the same thing as H_2O.* Why? Because, if *it were the same*, this fact would entitle us to substitute 'H_2O' for the word 'water', since they supposedly mean the same thing, thus turning our sensible open question above into the pointless closed question 'Is H_2O really H_2O?' In other words, it follows from the open question argument that *water cannot be the same as H_2O* because, if it were, 'Is water really H_2O?' would be a closed question, and since it's not, *they can't be the same thing*.

Now, we **KNOW** that water **IS** H_2O; it's a basic scientific truth. So, any argument that leads to the obvious falsehood that water can't be H_2O *must be unsound*. Therefore, **the open question argument is unsound**.

Why did Moore go so wrong with this argument and lead a whole generation of philosophers down the garden path with him? Because he and they were seduced by the *referential theory of meaning* which ties meaning to reference. This was Moore's faulty background assumption throughout his whole ethics. What led him astray was that when he thought he had proved that 'good' could not *mean the same* as/be *defined* as 'pleasure', he also thought that this also proved that 'good' could not *refer* to pleasure – i.e. *be the same thing* as pleasure. But it proves no such thing.

Another very simple example should help clarify what's going on. 'Is

Clark Kent really Superman?' is an open question, because to those around him this would be debatable, and the answer could go either way. However, you'd be wrong to conclude *from this* that, because the name 'Clark Kent' *does not mean* the same as the name 'Superman', Clark Kent *is not **actually*** Superman; in fact, *they're one and the same thing.* The *meaning* is *different* ('Clark Kent' = 'bumbling reporter', whereas 'Superman' = 'Man of Steel'), but the *reference* is the *same* – the bumbling reporter *is* the man of steel.

Once we reject the referential theory *we can separate the meaning of a word from its reference* and allow it to *mean something different* from what it *refers to* or *is.*

Water *is* H_2O but doesn't *mean* H_2O because people knew the meaning of the word 'water' thousands of years before we found out that its chemical composition was H_2O. 'Water' *refers* to H_2O but its *meaning goes way beyond that.* The only thing the open question argument shows is that moral terms don't *mean* the same as natural properties such as pleasure. But it does absolutely nothing to show that they can't *be* natural properties, i.e. *refer* to them, in the very same way that water can *be* H_2O without *meaning* H_2O. So it looks as if **there is no such thing as the naturalistic fallacy**, for this rested on the strength of the open question argument, and we now know that this is a failure.

But the now defunct 'naturalistic fallacy' was the only thing barring the door to naturalism for the past eighty years, and with this impediment gone the door is wide open for naturalism to come in from the cold and attempt some identifications of moral terms with natural properties. If they can get a consensus on one or more of these, they're back in business.

2 The closing of the is–ought gap: Searle's attempt to derive 'ought' from 'is'

In 1964 the American philosopher John Searle (b 1932) produced an argument which, I think, successfully demonstrated one way of closing the is–ought gap. He employed a five-step example which I have set out below.

1 Jones uttered the words, 'I hereby promise to pay you, Smith, five dollars.
2 Jones promised to pay Smith five dollars.
3 Jones placed himself under (undertook) an obligation to pay Smith five dollars.
4 Jones is under an obligation to pay Smith five dollars.
5 Jones ought to pay Smith five dollars.

As you can see, there is a clear 'ought' in stage 5, so where is the 'is' from which Searle must start? Well, even though the word 'is' does not appear in stage 1, this is nevertheless the fact from which Searle wants to derive the 'ought'. It can easily be changed around so as to incorporate a form of the verb 'to be', thus indicating its status as a fact, e.g. 'I promise to pay you, Smith, five dollars' **were** the words uttered by Jones.

The crucial move from 'is' to 'ought' takes place between stages 1 and 2. The rest, from 2 to 5, are all in the 'ought' camp, being various ways of saying that Jones is obliged, or ought, to pay Smith the five dollars. Why is stage 2 an 'ought' statement when 'ought' doesn't appear in it? Because it's buried in the word 'promise'. Part of the very meaning of the word 'promise' is that when you make one you ought to keep it. Now the reason Searle's attempt appears to work is that he makes use of a special kind of fact called an *institutional* fact. These are facts that are, in a sense, *made* facts by the way society runs itself. Given the fact that society has certain rules for organizing its institutions, 'oughts' should be derivable from the mere fact that one is a natural part of the institution.

Let's take a simple example from chess, a sort of leisure institution with its own rules of play that constitute its nature. So now I can easily derive an 'ought' from an 'is' as follows:

P1: I'm playing chess (fact).
P2: I'm playing the white pieces (fact).
P3: In a game of chess the person playing the white pieces is always the first to move (*institutional fact*, being an **actual** rule of chess).
Conclusion: Therefore, I *ought* to move first (obligation/ought).

Searle's example is trying to derive an 'ought' from an 'is' in the same way, except that Jones is playing the promising game instead of a game of chess. However, as with chess, it has its own rules, and one of them is that when you say (in the appropriate circumstances) 'I hereby promise . . . etc.', the very fact of uttering these words in these circumstances entails that you are under an obligation to keep your promise, i.e. entails an 'ought'. Compare the reasoning with the chess example:

P1: I'm playing the promising game (fact/is).
P2: I'm saying the words 'I hereby promise . . . etc.' (fact).
P3: In the promising game (institution), when someone sincerely utters the words 'I hereby promise . . .', then they must keep their promise (institutional fact).
Conclusion: Thus, I ought to keep my promise (obligation/ought).

If you agree that this looks plausible, then naturalism will work for at least this range of facts. Institutional facts bridge the is–ought gap. (See W. D. Hudson, *Modern Moral Philosophy*, pp. 266–76, for a much more detailed discussion of Searle's argument.)

3 Hudson and Foot's 'good father' counter-example to the is–ought gap

This argument is directed particularly at prescriptivism's understanding of the is–ought gap. Philippa Foot (British philosopher, b 1920) sets out to show as absurd the prescriptivist idea that moral values (oughts) can be chosen and prescribed without any logical connection to the facts (is's). To illustrate this, W. D. Hudson (*Modern Moral Philosophy*, p. 304) imagines a conversation between A and B, where A is a prescriptivist, which graphically demonstrates Foot's point:

> *A*: Smith is a good father.
> *B*: But he neglects his children.
> *A*: I know.
> *B*: Then why do you call him good?
> *A*: If I could choose, I would always choose [prescribe] for myself, or others, a father who neglects his children.
> *B*: Oh, I see.

This seems daft. The puzzle is why A should think neglect of children a good thing. Just to spell this out more clearly, A is actually saying that he is in favour of being neglected, which could include hunger, disease, filth, no holidays, no smiles, no presents, no time spent with your parents, no fun, no help with education, rotting teeth, loneliness. Is it really *logically* open for *anyone* to choose *any* facts as being good? Surely you'd have to be verging on insanity to actually *want* these things and to *recommend* them to others. What Foot is arguing for is a limit to the range of possible natural facts which can be classed as good. If she's right about there being such a limit then prescriptivism is wrong in setting no limits.

4 Foot's argument for deriving moral values from natural facts

Foot doesn't mean here just any old natural facts; she argues that there's a limited range of *natural facts*, to do with human psychology, society, and biology, that *make* certain states of affairs *factually/objectively good* for us and others bad for us (think of the things listed under 'neglect' above). And since any reasonable person would *want* (a psychological *fact*) the good rather than the bad, they *ought* to value the good rather than the bad.

Now, at the level of selfishness or self-interest, this is a mere prudential 'ought', not a moral ought, but insofar as people have natural feelings (sympathy, altruism, etc.) for others' pain and distress, and morality seems to be essentially to do with our treatment of others, then it follows that some *moral oughts* may be derived from, or entailed by:

a) the *empirical/natural facts* concerning what *helps* human beings to have a fulfilled life;
    AND
b) the *psychological facts* of our *natural* human fellow feelings in these matters, i.e. the *fact* that we *want* to help others.

Refuting psychological egoism allows us the *possibility* of b), i.e. the ability *genuinely* to want to *help others*, **full stop**. But virtue ethics delivers both a) and the *actuality* of b) by arguing that the practising of certain **natural** *psychological* characteristics, such as courage and sympathy (i.e. the virtues), functions **empirically** to make each of us a more flourishing specimen of our species [these are the is's], and that therefore we **ought** to want to cultivate these virtues if we are mentally healthy individuals, i.e. our instincts are intact. These virtues *are* good for us, so we *ought* to be good. This is moral goodness tied to human well-being by reason and logic.

Foot's case for a modern form of naturalistic ethic seems plausible and eminently sensible to me. Who could seriously argue against the claim that the following sorts of natural facts are objectively bad for us as a vulnerable species trying to make our way on earth – that people don't do so well under torture, when starving, or abused physically and mentally; or raped, insulted, humiliated, treated as a mere thing, a slave; or impoverished, hated, lied to, duped and manipulated, isolated, confined, imprisoned, disfigured, robbed? They also tend not to flourish when they're murdered.

Having reached the end of our metaethical journey I hope you agree with me that, rather than any of the other watering holes along the way, neo-naturalism is the best place to set up camp. But whether you agree or not, you may need to make a more informed decision, and to that end I've supplied some suggested further reading below.

Further Reading
Warnock, G. J. *Contemporary Moral Philosophy*. London: Macmillan, 1967.
Miller, Alexander, *An Introduction to Contemporary Metaethics*. Cambridge: Polity, 2003.

Postscript

Looking back to the preface, where I expressed the wish that by the end of the book you would be travelling philosophically twice as fast in your Ferrari as you did at the start, I fully expect you to be doing about 100 mph now, and ready to receive your first speeding ticket from society – a sign of how philosophy can make other people a bit nervous. But philosophy itself has taught the West that it's self-defeating to imprison and kill those who *think dangerously*, because it closes off new paths to new truths. So keep speeding; we owe it to Socrates – and ourselves.

Selected Bibliography

Aristotle, *Nicomachean Ethics*, trans. J. A. K. Thomson. London: Penguin, 2004.

Aristotle, *The Politics*. Harmondsworth: Penguin, 1981.

Ayer, A. J., *Language, Truth and Logic*. London: Gollancz, 1936.

Benn, Piers, *Ethics*. London: UCL Press, 1998.

Benson, John, *Environments, Ethics and Human Concern*. Oxford: Alden Press, 1999.

Bentham, Jeremy, *An Introduction to the Principles of Morals and Legislation*, ed. J. H. Burns and H. L. A. Hart. Oxford: Clarendon Press, 1996.

Blackburn, Simon, *Being Good*. Oxford: Oxford University Press, 2001.

Bowie, Robert A., *Ethical Studies*. Cheltenham: Nelson Thornes, 2001.

Capra, Fritjof, *The Turning Point*. London: Flamingo, 1983.

Copp, David, ed., *The Oxford Handbook of Ethical Theory*. Oxford: Oxford University Press, 2006.

Curry, Patrick, *Ecological Ethics*. Cambridge: Polity, 2006.

Darwall, Stephen, ed., *Virtue Ethics*. Oxford: Blackwell, 2003.

DeGrazia, David, *Animal Rights: A Very Short Introduction*. Oxford: Oxford University Press, 2002.

DesJardins, Joseph R., *Environmental Ethics: An Introduction to Environmental Philosophy*. 3rd edn, Belmont, CA: Wadsworth; London: Thomson Learning, 2001.

De Waal, Frans, *Primates and Philosophers*. Princeton, NJ: Princeton University Press, 2006.

Dobson, Andrew, *Green Political Thought*. 4th edn, London: Routledge, 2007.

Driver, Julia, *Ethics: The Fundamentals*. Oxford: Blackwell, 2007.

Flew, Antony, *Thinking about Thinking*. London: Fontana, 1975.

Garner, Robert, *Animal Ethics*. Cambridge: Polity, 2005.

Gensler, Harry J., *Ethics: A Contemporary Introduction*. London: Routledge, 1998.

Glover, Jonathan, *Causing Death and Saving Lives*. Harmondsworth: Penguin, 1977.

Gore, Al, *An Inconvenient Truth*. London: Bloomsbury, 2006.

Graham, Gordon, *Eight Theories of Ethics*. London: Routledge, 2004.

Hare, R. M., *Freedom and Reason*. Oxford: Clarendon Press, 1963.

Hare, R. M., *The Language of Morals*. Oxford: Clarendon Press, 1952.

Henson, Robert, *The Rough Guide to Climate Change*. London: Rough Guides, 2006.

Hinman, Lawrence M., *Ethics: A Puralistic Approach to Moral Theory*. 4th edn, Belmont, CA: Wadsworth; London: Thomson Learning, 2008.

Hudson, W. D., *Modern Moral Philosophy*. 2nd edn, London: Macmillan, 1983.

Hume, David, *A Treatise of Human Nature*, ed. L. A. Selby-Bigge. 2nd edn, rev. P. H. Nidditch, Oxford: Clarendon Press, 1978.

Hursthouse, Rosalind, *Beginning Lives.* Oxford: Blackwell, 1987.

Hursthouse, Rosalind, *Humans and other Animals.* Oxford: Alden Press, 1999.

Jones, Gerald, Cardinal, Daniel, and Hayward, Jeremy, *Moral Philosophy: A Guide to Ethical Theory.* London: Hodder Murray, 2006.

Kant, Immanuel, *Groundwork for the Metaphysics of Morals,* ed. Thomas E. Hill, Jr, and Arnulf Zweig. Oxford: Oxford University Press, 2003.

LaFollette, Hugh, ed., *Blackwell Guide to Ethical Theory.* Oxford: Blackwell, 2000.

Law, Stephen, *Philosophy.* London: Dorling Kindersley, 2007.

Leopold, Aldo, *A Sand County Almanac.* New York: Oxford University Press, 1949.

Levy, Neil, *Moral Relativism.* Oxford: Oneworld, 2002.

Mackie, J. L., *Ethics: Inventing Right and Wrong.* Harmondsworth: Penguin, 1977.

Mencius, *Mencius.* Harmondsworth: Penguin, 2004.

Midgley, Mary, *Animals and Why They Matter.* Harmondsworth: Penguin, 1983.

Mill, John Stuart, *Utilitarianism and On Liberty.* Oxford: Blackwell, 2002.

Miller, Alexander, *An Introduction to Contemporary Metaethics.* Cambridge: Polity, 2003.

Moore, G. E., *Principia Ethica.* Cambridge: Cambridge University Press, 1903.

Mulgan, Tim, *Understanding Utilitarianism.* Stocksfield, Northumberland: Acumen, 2007.

Nietzsche, Friedrich, *The Gay Science,* trans. Walter Kaufmann. New York: Vintage, 1974.

Nozick, Robert, *Anarchy, State and Utopia.* Oxford: Blackwell, 1974.

Palmer, Michael, *Moral Problems.* 2nd edn, Cambridge: Lutterworth Press, 2005.

Phelan, J. W., *Philosophy: Themes and Thinkers.* Cambridge: Cambridge University Press. 2005.

Plato, *The Republic.* 2nd edn, Harmondsworth: Penguin, 1974.

Pojman, Louis P., *Ethics: Discovering Right and Wrong.* 5th edn, Belmont, CA: Wadsworth; London: Thomson Learning, 2006.

Rachels, James, *The Elements of Moral Philosophy.* 5th edn, rev. Stuart Rachels, Boston and London: McGraw-Hill, 2007.

Rachels, James, ed., *Moral Problems: A Collection of Philosophical Essays.* 3rd edn, London: Harper & Row, 1979.

Regan, Tom, *The Case for Animal Rights.* Berkeley: University of California Press, 1983.

Rowlands, Mark, *Animal Rights: A Philosophical Defence.* Basingstoke: Macmillan, 1998.

Shafer-Landau, Russ, ed., *Ethical Theory.* Oxford: Blackwell, 2007.

Singer, Peter, *Animal Liberation.* 2nd edn, London: Pimlico, 1995.

Singer, Peter, ed., *Applied Ethics.* Oxford: Oxford University Press, 1986.

Singer, Peter, *Practical Ethics.* 2nd edn, Cambridge: Cambridge University Press, 1993.

Statman, Daniel, ed., *Virtue Ethics: A Critical Reader.* Edinburgh: Edinburgh University Press, 1997.

Sterba, James P., ed., *Ethics: The Big Questions.* Oxford: Blackwell, 1998.

Stevenson, C. L., *Ethics and Language.* New Haven, CT: Yale University Press, 1944.

Taylor, Paul, *Respect for Nature: A Theory of Environmental Ethics.* Princeton, NJ: Princeton University Press, 1986.

Tulloch, Gail, *Euthanasia: Choice and Death.* Edinburgh: Edinburgh University Press, 2007.

Warburton, Nigel, *Philosophy: The Basics.* 3rd edn, London: Routledge, 1999.

Warnock, G. J., *Contemporary Moral Philosophy.* London: Macmillan, 1967.

Index

Index

'auto-icon' 14–15
autonomy
  and morality 41
  respect for 34, 44, 89
Ayer, A. J. 213

beauty 170, 185
becoming 184, 185
Being 184, 187
  and character versus doing 55
beliefs
  and desires explanation of human action
    209–10
  and facts 209–10, 228
  see also intuitive beliefs
Benedict, Ruth 202
Bentham, Jeremy 14–15, 121, 202
Bentham's utilitarian theory 15–22, 156
  criticism of 16–22
  features 15–16
  Mill's modifications 23–4
Bible 49–50, 51–2, 83, 85, 95, 101, 114–15
biocentric egalitarianism
  assessment 159–62, 166–8, 176
  explanation of the practical part 162–8
  explanation of theory 157–62
biocentrism, environmental ethics 155,
    157–68, 177
biodiversity 170, 172–3
biology 159
Bland, Tony, the case of 80–1, 93
Blanshard, Brand 216
blastocyst, splitting the 104–5
bodies
  made up of parts that have functions 59
  relations to souls 104
Bohr, Niels 169
'boo/hooray' theory see emotivism

capital punishment 81
categorical imperative 24, 36–44, 54
  applied to abortion 105–8
  applied to euthanasia 88–91
  contradictions between two formulations
    107–8
  example 37–8
  first formulation (universal law) 36–43,
    65, 88–9

  and freeloading behaviour 46
  inflexibility of 35, 45, 47, 48
  moral authority of 41
  second formulation (formula of ends) 44,
    65, 89
  universalizability test 36–8, 45, 46–7, 218
  versus hypothetical imperatives 41–2, 45
causes
  and effects, genetic fallacy 68
  see also efficient causation
character, in virtue ethics 55, 61, 62, 63, 64,
    67, 91–2
chess 232
children, evidence of non-racism 141–2
choice
  euthanasia and 77, 86
  Euthyphro dilemma 51
  facts and values in 221
  of moral principles 217, 219, 221
  normativity as a framework for 112
  of talents 40
Christianity 49–50, 51–2, 81–5
  and animal rights 114–18, 136
  and the error theory of moral language
    206–7
circular arguments 160–2, 207
classical utilitarianism 14–15
cognitivism 180–1, 183–200
  arguments against non-cognitivism 225–9
  arguments against prescriptivism 222–5
  methods of acquiring moral knowledge
    202–3
  moral 184–92
  non-cognitivist arguments against 201–13
  see also intuitionism; naturalism; non-
    cognitivism; non-naturalism;
    transcendentalism
colonialism 227
coma cases 77, 86, 89–90
community, versus individual 56, 65
compassion 139, 143, 145, 148, 150
composition, fallacy of 31, 32–3, 68, 171
conception/nature, contradiction in 38–40
concepts 179, 184–5
conflict resolution, (human versus nature)
    principles of 164–8
Confucius 143
conscience 81, 115, 193

240